An Australian born in New Zealand, Pamela Stephenson is famous for her starring role in 'Not the Nine O'Clock News' and other tv and film work. She and Billy live and work in Los Angeles, where she now practises as a clinical psychologist.

BILLY

PAMELA STEPHENSON

HarperCollins*Entertainment*
An Imprint of HarperCollins*Publishers*

HarperCollins*Entertainment*
An imprint of HarperCollins*Publishers*
77–85 Fulham Palace Road,
Hammersmith, London W6 8JB

www.**fire**and**water**.com

Published by HarperCollins*Entertainment*
An imprint of HarperCollins*Publishers*

9

A catalogue record for this book
is available from the British Library

ISBN 0-00-711045-6

Set in Photina and Gill Sans

Printed and bound by
Griffin Press, Netley, Australia

To the Connolly and McLean families,
in the spirit of healing through understanding;
and to all families who are divided by religious differences,
or who struggle with poverty, abuse or addiction.

'He must have chaos within him,
who would give birth to a dancing star'

CONTENTS

ACKNOWLEDGEMENTS

Val Hudson had the insane idea in the first place, that I should go where Eleanor Roosevelt went ... creatively speaking that is ... and write about my own husband. I believe I have the edge, though, since FDR was dead when she penned his biography, which let him nicely off the hook from those irritating non sequitur questions at midnight and beyond. 'OK, Billy, you've now told me of three occasions when you first decided to become a comedian. I've got a book to finish, for heaven's sake: which is it?' Of course, the recipient of such unsexy pillow talk deserves to be wholeheartedly thanked for managing to keep his temper. And it was particularly good of him to live such an interesting life.

I consider myself extremely fortunate to have had publisher Val Hudson overseeing my efforts with remarkable care and enthusiasm. I am immensely grateful for her admirable taste, judgment, insight and, above all, her tremendous sensitivity to the material and its impact on the lives of those who are described in this book.

Monica Chakraverty also deserves my many thanks for her tireless and constructive editings in the face of tight deadlines, and her good-humoured willingness to hand-count the fucks, for reasons that will become clear when you read the introduction. I am also extremely grateful to Rachel Smyth for designing the book at even shorter notice, and, in fact, to everyone at HarperCollins for being so wonderfully supportive.

I have talked to very many people whose lives have intersected with Billy's, and without their time, and in some cases the willingness to risk a serious nutting, the book could have been paraphrased 'Lots of Untrue Stuff You've Read Before About Billy'. In particular, Florence Dickson, Mattie Murphy, James and Cara Connolly, Michael Connolly, Hughie and Neil McLean, Eddie Connolly, Michael Parkinson, Gerry Rafferty, Ralph McTell, Peter McDougall, Phil Coulter, June McQueen, Joe West and all the welding gang, the folkies, the boyhood pals, the old girlfriends, the rockers, the stars ... deserve my grateful thanks, as does Steve Brown, whose wisdom and intuition were essential. My main support crew have worked extremely hard to provide me with writing time, especially Jock Edwards, and I would like to thank all Candacraig staff, in particular Martine and Paul Hicks.

Several trusty pals read the manuscript, and I am most grateful to Steve Martin for his incisive comments, such as 'You might want to think about changing the title ... to "Kevin" or "George".' In addition, Tania and Eric Idle, Marsha and Robin Williams, as well as everyone on the Internet who cracked my password, respectively offering constructive advice, support and new ways to get tits like Britney Spears. Thanks, guys.

INTRODUCTION

Much has been written already about the chimerical joker known to the world as 'Billy Connolly'. That creature, however, is a fictional one, a Bill-o'-the-wisp that dances from tabloid to tome with relentless inaccuracy. Nothing unusual about that: everyone who comes to public attention is reflected in fragments, half-truths and downright lies since every observer projects his own fantasy upon the famous person in an illusory *folie à deux*.

In any case, when it comes to chronicling a person's life there is no such thing as absolute reality, even if the writer happens to be his wife and a 'shrink' to boot. I, for one, subscribe to the notion implied by the Heisenberg Principle, that nothing in the universe can ever be accurately observed because the act of observation always changes it. For every one life, there are a million observed realities, including several of the subject's. 'A stranger caught in a portrait of myself,' as Nabokov described the phenomenon, is commonly reflected back to a bemused interviewee.

'Who HE?' Billy will shout, slapping down the latest visual or written appraisal he considers is a dark imitation of his former self. In my paradigm, every person holds the reality of his own experience either in his mind's eye or just below the surface of consciousness, or even deeper in the unconscious mind; but in the latter level we are all strangers, even to ourselves, and the mysterious workings of our unfathomed parts are revealed only in our dreams.

Even within families, shared times are experienced differently, coloured by the age, family role or state of mind of each member. Small wonder, then, that some of Billy's relatives and friends have disparate impressions of the following events. For Billy, reading each chapter after completion has elicited the shock of self-confrontation, accompanied by frequent laughter, occasional fury and a few precious tears as he painfully re-experienced many traumatic events. Most rewardingly for the author, the process of drawing together the following occurrences and providing insights might well have been a catalyst for his further healing, although Billy will have none of that: 'Pish!' he cries. 'As my old granny Flora used to say, "The more you know, the less the better."'

Another gem of Flora's was: 'Never clothe your language in ragged attire.' Billy obviously missed the word 'never' because, purely in an attempt to please his dear old gran, he continues to say the 'f' word in every single sentence and double on Sundays. I actually wondered about Tourette's Syndrome when I first met him. People try to stop Billy's profanity, but that only encourages him. I myself have found great utility in those special collars for large pet dogs, with the remote control device that administers savage electric shocks to the neck of any beast that gets too close to the mark. Undetectable beneath his polka-dot shirt collar, it came in very handy recently when Billy gave a graduation address at our children's school. You know where this is leading ... try to guess the number of 'f' words in this book before you read it. Be creative: it's just like guessing the number of marbles in a jar so run a sweep, raise money for charity or decide who buys the next round. The answer can be found on page 290.

Billy's real story is an utterly triumphant one. Not a day has passed since I met him twenty years ago, without my shaking my head and marvelling at his miraculous survival of profound childhood trauma. His ability to sustain himself beyond those days is equally impressive, for once he was known to the world, another challenge presented itself: to survive the trauma of fame. Every person who comes to public attention experiences an alienation of self, the formation of a deeply unsettling chasm between his true inner self and his public persona. The danger lies not in the confusion of those two as is commonly thought, but in the widening gulf between them.

Fortunately, Billy's survival skills ever sustain him. When I first asked the essential, penetrating question of how he always managed to summon the resources to turn trauma into triumph, I was hoping for insight and a lucid explanation. What I got was: 'Well, I didn't come down the Clyde on a water biscuit.'

The following is an attempt at a sensible answer.

I

'JESUS IS DEAD, AND IT'S YOUR FAULT!'

Billy Connolly, King of Comedy, Master of Mirth, Chancellor of Chortling, as his children have been instructed to address him, is quivering in the wings of the spectacularly cavernous Hammersmith Apollo theatre.

'Pamela, what the hell am I going to say to these people?'

Horrified, I turn to face him. Oh God, here we go ... he's not bluffing. Now there are two of us heading for a full-blown fight-or-flight fit. Is it possible that this time, the first in history, he might actually freeze, forget, stammer, storm off stage or batter someone? I do not fancy witnessing his death by four thousand excitable Londoners. They begin to roar as his name is announced, clapping in unison and stamping their feet. It's the start of tonight's war, the one he always declares then dreads.

'You'll be OK ...'

I watch him arm himself mentally with an opening shot. As usual, he'll take no prisoners. I'm a white-knuckled wimp when the enemy's battle cry reaches its pitch ... then suddenly he's off. A blinding circle of light assaults him and I see his face change to a fighting calm. 'Scot of the Anarchic' is stepping out fearlessly into the front line. He might be gone for quite some time.

The bastard's done it again. Frightened me to death, and he's going to win after all. I peer out into the centre of the fray and

5

witness a beautiful armistice, achieved in the first few disarming sentences from his scowling, apologetic mouth. There is always such a peace for him out there in that spotlight, probably the only place he's truly happy. Each time, it seems he's given another chance, a chance he's driven endlessly to re-create; it's a chance to gain mastery, to triumph over – he can almost see their faces out there in the audience – Mamie, William, Mona, Rosie. I notice that tonight it is especially Rosie who must be slain as he launches into hilariously savage tales of algebra and abject humiliation.

He is strutting, striding, tilting at windmills. I'm thinking, how weird that he is so aroused, furious and vindictive, yet his face at times seems almost beatific. Swathed in disgustingly musty wing velvets, I peek out at the front row. As individuals, these are hardly soldiers: T-shirted people, they are settled in comfortably to be transported to places where petrol prices, the babysitter, the in-laws, are replaced by tyrants and tenement buildings, by little old ladies in fat, furry coats, and the ubiquitous, noisy farts. It will all end in tears and some very sore bellies. I can finally breathe. He is blessed; encircled most brightly not by forty thousand watts but by his own fiery, evangelical fuck-youness.

~

Ironically, Billy's very earliest memory is one of being terrified by a circle of light. Until he was three years old, he and his beloved sister Florence slept in a curtained-off alcove in the kitchen. One evening she aimed a mirror reflection onto the wall, allowing it to pirouette and chase him until he screamed for mercy.

He had been born right next to that alcove on the kitchen floor, all eleven pounds of him plopping out onto freezing linoleum. The rage that followed this unceremonious introduction to the world has never left him, although it was a serendipitous launching for a future enemy of the bourgeoisie. For eight months he nestled in a wooden drawer with not one Fisher-Price contraption in sight.

His family's living arrangements were similar to those of thousands of other inhabitants of Glasgow, a city that had come to be defined by row upon row of late-nineteenth-century apartment buildings known as 'the tenements'. These fine architectural soldiers had originally been created by Glasgow's Improvement Trust, as model housing for working-class families. But by the time the Connollys moved into half of the third floor of 65 Dover Street in Anderston, many of them had deteriorated into rotting slums that would need more than a spot of paint to 'take the bad look off them', as Billy would say.

The classically derived elevations in red or yellow sandstone were usually pleasant enough, but the interiors were thoroughly depressing. A dingy central staircase, stinking of cabbage and cat piss, spiralled upwards to the flats. Two or more poky apartments were squeezed into each floor, usually with just two rooms apiece, and a communal lavatory out on the landing. Some families were lumbered with the 'coffin end', or corner apartment, which was even smaller than the rest.

The buildings themselves butted right onto the street and were usually entered via an interior alleyway known as a close. The 'Wally' closes, as some were called, were beautifully tiled halfway up the wall, with a leafy motif running along the top. Such finery, however, ended abruptly at the threshold of a darker, often treacherous, tunnel known as the 'dunny' (short for dungeon), that dead-ended in an enclosed rear courtyard, itself a veritable assault-course of broken bicycles, flapping knickers, and reeking middens.

Considering it now through a haze of nostalgia, Billy says the Glasgow tenement is a New York brownstone without a fire escape. Some of the buildings certainly had grandeur and, like their New York counterparts, are now sought after by the well-to-do. Billy's first home was not one of those. The Dover Street flat had only two rooms: a kitchen-living room, with a niche where the children slept, and another room for their parents. The entire family bathed in the kitchen sink and there was no hot water at all. As an enduring legacy of his early cramped existence, Billy is now quite uncomfortable in large living spaces. He sighs over the phone to me from fabulous hotels all over the world: 'They've gone and upgraded me again. Bloody Presidential Suite this time.'

I let him off lightly, because I know it's a genuine problem for him. Others who achieve renown cannot wait to sprawl sideways on a California King four-poster with a big-screen TV in every corner and a whirlpool on the deck, but not Billy. He has never really liked our Los Angeles house because of its unfamiliar spaciousness, and prefers to hide out in his tiny study for hours on end, drinking gallons of tea and plunking on his banjo.

~

It is 5.30 a.m. in wintertime Glasgow, 2001. On my way to the airport for a transatlantic flight, I ask Jim the taxi driver to make a detour.

'You know Dover Street?' I inquire. 'It's around here somewhere.'

The fact that the Hilton Hotel is now in Anderston speaks to the gentrification of the place. We cruise along Finnieston Street, now home of a Citroën dealership, PC World and the golden arches. 'It's quite a decent area ...' Jim is eager to be informative. 'Not as rough as it used to be.'

Argyle Street is now split in two by the motorway. As we approach Singh's corner shop, on the ground floor of an original tenement building at one end of Dover Street, it becomes evident that all the houses on one side of the street have been pulled down. In their place is a small, grassy square that faces a fashionable business centre on the next parallel street. Several modern buildings have replaced tenements on the other side of Dover Street itself, pale-brick imitations of the sandstone originals.

I search around in the drizzle and I am relieved to find that No.3 and No.5 Dover Street are still standing. The grimy, four-storeyed blocks of flats are graced with white lace curtains that deter me from peering into the street-level apartments. While Jim smokes patiently in the cab, I stand in the silent street trying to evoke the past. It's easy to become fanciful in the early light, seeing the spectre of Billy's mother, fast-wheeling the rain-soaked pram around Singh's corner to get herself and the weans into the shelter of the close.

When I arrive in Los Angeles, I describe the scene to Billy. He is unmoved. 'Yeah, they pulled my first house down and I'm upset,' he jokes. 'Now where are they gonna put the plaque?'

~

As an infant, William Connolly junior was a blond, brown-eyed puddin' with a face that would 'get a piece at any windy', as they say in Glasgow if you look pitiful enough to score free sandwiches. He was a war baby, born on 24 November 1942, just as his father was preparing to leave for Burma.

At twenty-three years old, William Connolly senior had been conscripted into the Royal Air Force, a fate that interrupted his career as an optical instrument maker at Barr and Stroud's. He always considered himself very lucky to have been accepted as an apprentice at that firm. If he had not been dux of St Peter's School in Partick, he might have been one of the many jobless victims of the rampant anti-Irish feeling that existed all around Glasgow at the time.

His father, Jack, was an Irishman whose family members were among the seven million victims of the potato famine, grinding poverty and relentless discrimination, who had been emigrating from Ireland since the seventeenth century. Many had sailed to the United States and Canada, risking typhus and dysentery in the 'coffin ships' and New World quarantine camps, but Jack's Connemara-born family had sailed to Scotland and settled in Glasgow in the 1920s. It was probably the better choice. The average length of life for Irish refugees who reached the Americas was six years after landing. The American streets were not paved with gold after all, but rather Irish immigrants were expected to pave the streets themselves and to do so for very low wages.

Expectations of Scotland-bound Irish emigrants were not so fanciful, yet Glasgow society echoed the Yankees in being highly prejudiced against the Irish, due to religious, racial, cultural and economic differences. In Glasgow, there was also the fear that jobs would be lost to the incomers. In America, the 'Know Nothing' hate group murdered Irish immigrants and destroyed their property; in Glasgow there was a concerted effort to deny them jobs and lodgings. One of the most popular songs of the 1870s said it all:

'I am a decent Irishman and I come from Ballyfad
And I want a situation and I want it mighty bad.
A position I saw advertised is a thing for me, says I,
But the dirty spouting ended with "No Irish Need Apply".'

Similar exclusionary signs were out in force in Glasgow in the 1930s when Billy's father was looking for work, hung in places where jobs were available for Protestants only. The notice outside Barr and Stroud's was only a little less overt than usual. 'Apprentices wanted' it read, 'Boys' Brigade Welcome'. Being Catholic and half-Irish, William had not been a candidate for membership of the staunchly Protestant Boys' Brigade, an organization founded with evangelical zeal in the previous century by one William Smith who wished to promote health, constructive activity, and a moral soundness among Glaswegian youth.

Jack Connolly had married Jane McLuskey, a Glaswegian lass from a devoutly Catholic family, who bore him seven children, six of whom survived. William, born in 1919, was the youngest child after Charlie, John, James, Mona and Margaret; while a younger sister named Mary died of tuberculosis when she was only eight. William himself was a sickly child, spoiled by his mother and bossed by his oldest sister, Mona. He had problems with his eyes, and needed several pairs of chunky, brown-framed spectacles. He was passionate about football, and insisted on the supremacy of the Celtic team until the day he died. Even though he had been promising at school, children of the depression had little opportunity for further education, so he taught himself logarithms, and how to speak Italian and German.

William was a strict Catholic, but it is unlikely that his tortured aspect and taciturn nature were entirely due to religion. His father Jack may have passed on some of his formidable qualities to his son for he was the epitome of stoicism and pride, as illustrated by a family story that has been handed down from the 1920s. The tale is set just before the pubs closed one New Year's Eve, or Hogmanay as they call it in Scotland, 'the same as other people's Christmas, but without God to knacker the proceedings', as Billy puts it. Jack, who was extremely fond of a drink, bought a 'Hogmanay carry-out': a paper bag with a bottle of whisky and a few bottles of Guinness in it. On his way out of the pub, he made the mistake of putting his parcel on the beer-soaked floor. He strode home to see out the old year and welcome in the new with a skinful of Guinness, not realizing that the brown paper had become sodden and weak. A few streets from home, the bottom fell out of the bag and, to his horror, the contents smashed and spilled into the gutter. Jack returned home empty-handed and recounted the sad story to his wife.

'What in heaven's name did you do?' she asked, appalled. Quite apart from the personal embarrassment, Hogmanay is the most important of all Scottish celebrations and there would have been no time or spare cash to replace his loss. The man stared into the middle distance, chin in the air. 'Jack walked on,' he declared.

Jack was a slim, good-looking man with a handlebar moustache. He managed to support his wife and children by working as a labourer, a plater's helper in the shipyards. The job required great strength so, despite his thin frame, he must have been quite wiry. His son William was also svelte as a youth, but he eventually tumesced into a bloated man with the biggest neck in the world. Nowadays, Billy always complains, 'I don't want to wear a tie. I'll look like a man with a head transplant!' He got that look from his father.

At Barr and Stroud's in 1940, William had not been fully focused on his work. At twenty years old he had met a teenager called Mamie McLean, of the McLean of Duart clan from the isle of Mull, who returned to her mother's house every evening with hands covered in fine red dust from polishing the lenses of rangefinders. She was a handsome and volatile sixteen-year-old, with long, dark hair and a forthright expression. The only girl in the family, Mamie had developed a strong personality and a self-protective sense of humour. She had a fine ability to stand up for herself, although that may be an understatement; some say she was the type of woman who could start a fight in an empty house. She was fast on her feet, and would always streak out ahead of her brothers, Neil, John, Edward (Teddy) and Hugh, in their holiday seafront races. At the Protestant Kent Road School in Glasgow, Mamie had shown herself to be bright, but with a war on there was generally little emphasis on education, and so she went to work.

Wartime Glasgow was a sinister place to 'court a lassie'. As evening fell, a sickly, green light spread through the streets as people scurried to get home before the blackout. Bombers occasionally dumped their lethal loads on the city, the worst occasions being two nights of non-stop bombing on 13 and 14 March 1941, which were devastating for citizens from the industrial areas of the River Clyde. The 'Clydebank Blitz' left two-thirds of that town's population homeless, and killed or wounded thousands, but the only casualty in the McLean household was their pet canary, who perished when a land mine blew open the shutters. Mamie's father, Neil McLean, was an air-raid warden and, before a local air-raid shelter was built, everyone in the largely Irish Catholic neighbourhood would sprint to relative safety in the bottom floor of his tenement. Every time there was even a hint of a bang or whistle from the skies above, Mamie and her brothers would be deafened by exhortations from their fellow refugees. 'Mary, mother of God, Jesus and Joseph and all the saints!'

They were nearly drowned in holy water. This must have been particularly irksome for Neil, a Protestant whose own father had been a Boys' Brigade officer. A diminutive Highlander from the west of Scotland, Neil's father looked out of place in Glasgow, still wearing his navy, deep-sea cap with a shiny peak. He had even hung fish to dry on a small rope outside his city tenement window.

'Well, Mr McLean,' the Catholic corner boys would bait Neil, imitating his 'teuchter', or country, accent, 'did you find the Lord today?'

'I wasn't aware I'd lost him.'

The 'corner boys' were the casualties of the jobless depression years. With no money and nowhere to go, men would stand around in clumps at every intersection of the city, just blethering and shooting the breeze. Neil McLean, however, was never one to be idle. He had been a warehouseman for McFarren, Smith and Glass, but when he lost his job he spent his time cycling and running a football team. They were hard times for him and the family, but unlike many of his contemporaries, Neil kept his standards and avoided strong drink. They were able to eat because his wife, Flora, managed to make a living cleaning houses and offices. One of her employers was a Highland woman, a Mrs Morrison.

'And what does your husband do, Flora?' she asked one day.

'Well, Ma'am, he has no work.'

'Did he ever think of trying to get into the Corporation?'

'Och, no one gets into the Corporation today.'

'I'll speak to Mr McKinnon.'

In those days, every bus and tramcar of the Glasgow Transport Corporation had 'General Manager: L. McKinnon' written on its side. Out of the gloom of the depression, Lachie McKinnon found Neil a job as a conductor. He was eventually promoted to an inspector and was with the company for forty years until he retired.

Neil, or 'Big Neilly' as he became known, was a rigid man, a strict disciplinarian who frightened the life out of his subordinates and caused his children to wish he would take a drink from time to time. He stood straight, walked like a guardsman, and never left for work without a starched collar, black tie, and gleaming buttons. Despite all that, it was rumoured that he was secretly quite timid, 'a big fearty' as they say in Glasgow, and would send Flora to the door whenever he was called upon in his role as air-raid warden.

Flora was a robust soul who did not agree with him in all things. She went to Mass on Sundays and made clandestine arrangements for the children to be baptized as Catholics, although at Big Neilly's insistence they were formally raised as Protestants. Small wonder religion was never openly discussed at home, although Flora and her sisters had a few tricks up their sleeves. 'Now remember, Mamie, which hand do you shake with? ... The one you use to bless yourself.'

Flora loved to laugh and decorate herself with clothing and costume jewellery. She would get herself 'all done up like a kitchen bed', as they say in Glasgow – tenement alcove beds were always made up early and carefully, in case visitors arrived. When Flora went carousing with her girlfriends at a tea dance in town, she was definitely the best turned out cleaner in Glasgow. 'There's nae pockets in a shroud,' she would say.

Her husband was no fashion victim, but believed in the importance of having just one made-to-measure suit for special occasions. His was wrapped carefully in brown paper and placed inside a tin in the wardrobe. Fortunately, there were very few special occasions to attend, so Big Neilly had no idea how often his good suit was missing. Flora, who was kind-hearted to a fault, saved many a near-destitute family by allowing them to pawn it until their crisis was over. Thus was the measure of poverty.

Mamie was their second-born. The McLeans, all seven of them, lived at first in a top-floor tenement flat with one room and a kitchen. Later, they flitted to a flat that seemed like a castle after the old one, for it had two rooms. Mamie's brothers required a great deal of attention from their mother. Ted had two or three operations for 'the mastoid', John sat at home in disgrace because he played truant, and Hughie was weak with chronic bronchitis. When war broke out, Hughie, a sensitive nine-year-old, was sent to Dunoon to stay with an aunt. He was not treated kindly, and sorely missed his mother. It broke his heart to see her only on Sundays, for the short walk from the ferry to his aunt's house and back again.

Mamie was always up for an entertaining time. After Hughie returned to Glasgow, she occasionally took him to the Metropole Theatre. There was a flourishing music-hall tradition in Glasgow in those days, and the pair particularly enjoyed the performance of a tubby singer called Master Jo Peterson, a strange woman with a strong soprano voice who wore a choirboy's uniform.

It is hard to imagine exactly what Mamie saw in William. He took life far more seriously and is said to have 'made stubbornness a virtue'. Later in life, he was known for the extroverted bear-hugs he forced on fellow punters at the Dowanhill Bar in Partick, but in the forties William was a somewhat morose and secretive figure who spent much of his life under the thumb of his sister Mona.

At twenty-one he was 'an older man' to Mamie, who by contrast was talkative, histrionic, and was easily led into good times. As World War Two was just beginning, the pair would tramp to the York Café at the bottom of Hyndland Street. They ordered hot peas in vinegar followed by a 'McCallum', a vanilla ice-cream sundae with raspberry sauce and Empire biscuits (they had been called German biscuits before the war). William and Mamie would chat for hours about their newest co-worker at the factory, the price of a pair of nylons, and the doings of Adolf Hitler.

Perhaps William offered Mamie an escape of sorts. One might speculate that, in the light of all the demands placed on Flora by her sons, her work, her neighbours, and her undoubtedly high-maintenance husband, she had little time to focus on Mamie. Certainly Big Neilly was no warm and fuzzy papa, so William may have been the first person to show a special interest in her. Whatever it was that connected her to him, in the space of a year or so she went from school to work to pregnancy to marriage, in that order, and almost entirely missed her adolescence.

At least William made an honest woman of her. They were married on 25 November 1940 at St Patrick's Church in Anderston, a fine, red sandstone, nineteenth-century building in William Street. The Glaswegian Irish never gained political power like their New World counterparts, who eventually dominated American politics, but they were similarly galvanized to establish their own churches, schools, hospitals and orphanages. There is no mistaking St Patrick's Irish patronage, for in addition to its name, the interior boasts polished wooden pews adorned with carved shamrocks. The building is clearly visible from the lift lobbies high up in the Glasgow Hilton.

'See that church?' Billy always forgets he's pointed it out a million times. 'I was christened there.'

Florence was born exactly five months after Mamie's wedding day, on 25 April 1941. She, William and Mamie moved into the grubby apartment in Dover Street, and attempted to have a life together. It was a boring one for the seventeen-year-old, who was simply not ready for marriage, let alone motherhood. She tried to cope with the baby most of the day, expecting some amusement in the evening, but when William came home, he had a face like a wet Monday and buried himself in his newspaper. Her second pregnancy must have been as unwelcome as the first, but Billy arrived nineteen months after Florence.

Billy's current nickname, 'The Big Yin', does not refer to his birth weight, but it would have fitted. He was an absolutely enormous newborn: eleven pounds, four ounces, to be exact. Mamie endured her labour alone, first in the freezing alcove, then finally squatting on the kitchen floor, no doubt fully regretting the day she had first met the co-perpetrator of her agony, who was by now busy planning his own escape. William's engineering skills were demanded by the Royal Air Force, so he flew far away to tend the engines of Lancaster bombers in India, Burma and Africa. Like thousands of other wartime brides, Mamie wondered if he would ever return.

It was the tradition in those times for girls who had left the family house to visit their mothers on Sundays. As far as rationing would allow, Flora would cook a Sunday dinner of stew and dumplings, or leftovers and 'stovies', a dish made with potatoes and onions. All the family gathered then. Hughie would help Mamie get the pram up and down the stairs and he soothed the little ones while Mamie chatted. But, apart from Sundays, Mamie had little of the social contact she craved. She rarely heard from her husband. His sisters Margaret and Mona would look in from time to time, but Mamie hated their nosiness and attempts to take control. She thought they came more to criticize than to help. 'She's just a daft wee girl,' sneered Mona behind her back.

Overcrowding and poor maintenance always ensured that tenement life spilled out into the streets, the grimy domain of vendors and tramcars being an extension of the inhabitants' living space. Socially, the tenement was a vertical village, and everyone knew everyone. A neighbour, Mattie Murphy, who was about the same age as Mamie, sometimes watched the infants when Mamie left the flat to do her washing in 'the steamie', as Glaswegian public laundries were called. She claims Billy was 'a cheeky wee devil'. He was full of mischief and had no problem answering back. One teatime, Mattie was cutting up a sticky bun covered with pink icing when Billy spied the end piece that had the most icing. 'I want that fucking piece!' It was startling language for a three-year-old.

'You'll get none,' threatened Mattie.

'Then I'll touch you with my chookie.' The infant hard-man began to unbutton his flies but, after catching sight of Mattie's horrified face, he ran around and pinched her bottom instead. He got no iced bun that day.

It was not the only preview of Billy's renowned outrageousness. Mattie's daughter, Roseanne, was sitting on the pavement with some other children one day after an exhausting game of 'Peever', a variation of hopscotch that was played with a can of shoe polish. Billy came sauntering along the road and decided that he needed to pee. In those days, little boys would just unbutton their flies and urinate into the gutter but, while he was doing so, Billy caught sight of the adjacent group of girls and just couldn't resist turning sideways and spraying their backs. He was definitely a handful.

Mattie found Dover Street life in the 1940s more riveting than the music hall. A woman whose livelihood was prostitution resided on the ground floor of one of the buildings. The residents of Dover Street apparently conspired to help this woman rip off her customers by ganging up on the men after they had paid their shillings. 'Bugger off,' they would cry. 'You're giving the place a bad name!'

This conspiratorial behaviour, however, was sporadic. Quite often the temperamental sex-worker would go for an evening stroll in her underwear, challenging other women who lived in the street, whom she accused of gossiping about her, to come out and fight. It got to the point where residents would bring chairs out each night and sit waiting for the show to begin.

Tragically, Mattie lost her own son. He was home from school with a cold and, short of clean nightwear, his mother had insisted he put on his sister's nightgown to keep warm. When both parents were out, Mattie's boy leaned over too close to the fire and a spark sent his nightgown up in flames. His sister was powerless to save him. Before the boy was buried, the streetwalker amazed everyone by turning up and throwing herself on his boy-sized coffin in a great demonstration of wailing and sadness, shouting heavenward at the top of her voice, 'Why couldn't you have taken me instead of the wean? I'm bad! I'm bad!'

Billy and Florence played out on the street from a very early age. It was Mattie who searched high and low for them after they disappeared one evening. Their neighbour, Mr Cumberland, had come home from work, desperate to get to the pub. 'You'd better get those bloody kids in first,' said his long-suffering wife, who also liked a drink or six, which is a fact Billy omits when he tells a version of the story on stage.

Mr Cumberland had eight children, so, driven by his thirst, the wily man went out onto the street and got as many Cumberlands as he could find, then just made up the numbers with any other children he spied. Billy and Florence were scooped up with no questions asked and thrown into bed with the others. Later that night two Cumberlands were found roaming the street, which gave the search party a useful clue, and the exchange was eventually made.

If only Mattie had been asked to help out more in those first years, Billy and Florence might have had an easier time. Mamie was disintegrating, probably depressed and, unknown to her family, was abdicating responsibility for the children who were horribly neglected. Billy had pneumonia three times before he was four. Officers of the Royal Scottish Society for the Prevention of Cruelty to Children were called in when Mamie left them alone with an unguarded, blazing fire. At three years old, Florence was expected to care for Billy without an adult present. She was an anxious, often tearful child, with dark curls flopping over a high forehead and charming 'sonsie', or roundly appealing, face. She was always Billy's 'guardian angel' as he calls her now, but she sorely needed one of her own. One evening when she was alone looking after Billy, she fell into some hot ashes. She screamed for help, but no one came. She never received medical attention at the time and as a result she lost the sight of an eye.

One winter morning in 1945, three-year-old Billy woke up wanting his mother. Wearing only a tiny vest, he went toddling along the freezing hallway to her bedroom. He hesitated just inside the door to her darkened room, surprised to see a stranger sitting on his mother's bed. The man was brown-haired and bare-chested, and stared at Billy as he finished putting on a sock. As Billy tottered closer, the stranger shoved his bare foot up against his forehead and gently pushed him backwards until he was out in the hallway again, then closed the door with the same foot. It was Willie Adams, his mother's lover.

~

Billy and Florence were alone and frightened when their mother left. She just closed the door and never came back. Eventually there was a lot of wailing and shouting, and then they were cared for by nuns in a place of polished wooden benches, stained glass and whispering. There was disagreement in the two families about who should bring up the children. Flora wanted them, but William's sisters, Margaret and Mona, stepped in and took over. It was Mona who, responding to a neighbour's concern about the constant crying resounding throughout the tenement, had gone along to the flat with her brother James and found Florence and Billy crouching together in the alcove bed, freezing, hungry and pitifully unkempt. She and Margaret eventually took young Billy and Florence to live in the Stewartville Street tenement in Partick that they shared with James, who was recently back from the war.

The children never saw their mother again when they were growing up. She came once to see them when they were still very young, but the aunts chased her off like a whore. Later she turned up with one of her brothers, but again, she was refused entry. That's when Mamie punched Mona. Flattened her right in the doorway.

Margaret and Mona were an odd pair. Mona was born in 1908 and was thirteen years older than her flightier sister. Like all unmarried women getting on for forty in those days, Mona was terrified of being stigmatized as an 'old maid'; by contrast, Margaret had a twinkle in her eye and no shortage of dancing partners. Billy found both sisters rather forbidding at the outset, although they tried to be kind and welcoming.

Margaret still wore her Wrens' uniform, a stiff navy suit with brass buttons and a collar and tie. She'd had the time of her life when she was based in Portsmouth but, after the war, she settled down to life as a civil servant, writing up pension claims by coal miners who were suffering from pneumoconiosis, the black lung scourge. Margaret had wonderful red hair. Some evenings Billy and Florence would watch her flounce off to the dance hall in a cloud of '4711' toilet water, stylishly draped in kingfisher-blue taffeta.

Mona was a dour and dominant force in the household. She was a registered nurse, working at night in a crowded ward for patients with chest complaints such as pneumonia and tuberculosis. On occasion, she did some private nursing so there were syringes lying around the place and strange rubber hoses in a drawer. The children could never work out what they were for. Mona dyed her curly brown hair a bright blonde, and was definitely no fashion plate.

Billy thought his Uncle James, on the other hand, was very glamorous indeed. He had been caught in a booby trap in France when he was with the Cameron Highlanders, so he now had only two fingers on his left hand. He modelled standards of grooming and hygiene that had previously been missing from the children's lives, always polishing his shoes, ironing his shirts, and inspecting Billy's teeth for adequate brushing. Both children had needed delousing when they arrived at Stewartville Street. Standing up naked in the sink, they were scrubbed vigorously with scabies lotion, a cold, viscous substance that left a milky residue on their skin. Their hair was deloused in an agonizing process involving an ultra-fine comb and a newspaper placed on the floor so they could see the lice when they landed.

Billy was grateful for the new and unfamiliar air of brusque kindness all around him. The four-year-old slept in a cot in the aunts' bedroom, and felt happy to be tucked into a clean bed, even if he was chastised horribly for peeing in it with great frequency. He could not understand their problem with that; in the past he'd always done it with impunity. Many things changed in the children's lives. They were given new clothing, sent to them from New York by their Uncle Charlie, William's elder brother, who had emigrated to America. Florence was over the moon with her new sticky-outy dress of pale lavender watersilk, while Billy became the proud owner of a pair of beige overalls. Nowadays, Billy has a pathological aversion to beige apparel, and especially attacks the wearers of beige cardigans, but back then he thought he was the kipper's knickers.

Consistency became part of the children's lives for the very first time. Every morning, right after their porridge, the children would be given a delicious spoonful of sickly-sweet molasses, followed by a vomit-making dollop of cod-liver oil. Billy begged to be given the oil first. 'Why, oh why,' he wondered, 'can't I have the nice stuff last to take away the nasty taste?' But he was always given the molasses first.

His aunts were not the only ones who believed the hard way was the best way, and that safety resided in suffering. Billy says that many a Glaswegian has cast his troubled eyes on a brilliant, sunshine day and muttered, 'Och, we'll pay for this!'

Every evening after supper, Uncle James knelt down beside his kitchen alcove bed to say his prayers. The notion of communicating with an unseen entity was new to Billy, but he happily went along to

Mass and quite enjoyed watching the whole colourful spectacle and singing loudly along with the congregation.

Then, as now, he enjoyed the pageant of life swirling around him, and the bustle of Stewartville Street was particularly appealing. Most days he played with marbles and little tin cars in the gutter outside his close. It was a perfect vantage point from which to study the activities of the milkman, the coalman, the ragman and the chimney sweeps. If he played his cards right, he could be heaved high up onto the horse-drawn cart of one of those workers for a 'wee hurl' to the top of the street.

One day, while Florence played 'chases' and 'hide-and-seek' with other neighbourhood children, Billy began drawing on the pavement with a piece of chalk. He was soon apprehended by an angry policeman who tried to march him indoors. The officer was barely inside the close when he was stopped short by old Mrs Magee, a tiny Belfast woman, who gave him a terrible time: 'Away and catch a murderer, you big pain in the arse! Leave the child alone!'

There was an evangelical establishment in the street at number twelve, called Abingdon Hall. It's still there today, a red-painted gospel hall run by the Christian Brethren that boasts regular social events such as 'Ladies Leisure Hour' and 'Missionary Meeting'. Back then, Protestant children could attend meetings of a youth club called 'Band of Hope'. Billy and Florence began to find creative ways to sneak in for the exotic experience of a slide show of the Holy Land, a cup of tea and a bun. Billy decided that the appeal of the Protestant faith was the absence of kneeling. Never one to shy away from a good sing-song, he joined in with the best of them:

'There's a fountain flowing deep and wide
Hallelujah!'

When their visits to that Protestant stronghold were discovered, Florence got the blame and was given a terrible row by Mona:

'You're the oldest! You should have known better!' It was as if they'd sneaked into a peep-show.

By now, Billy was becoming aware of the stigma that was attached to his assigned faith. One day he was with a little pal, happily shooting marbles into a drain, when he heard an upstairs window being hurriedly thrust open. Her grandfather leaned out, pipe in hand: 'Marie Grant! What have I told you about playing with Catholics!'

After a few months of living with the aunts, Billy began settling into their routine. He wondered where his mother had gone, but no one seemed willing to discuss that with him. He overheard adults around him gossiping about her in scathing terms, which further confused and saddened him.

Although Mamie had been banned from the house, her mother Flora visited the children from time to time and brought them sweeties and chocolate. There had been no sweets for them during the war so anything sugary was quite a treat. Grandma wore a fur coat, dangly earrings and lots of perfume, and looked exactly like a Christmas tree. The aunts disapproved, but Billy thought the sun shone out of her behind.

She was fond of boxing, and would sneak them pictures of her idol Joe Louis and talk about all sorts of interesting things. She always knew when Billy was talking rubbish. 'Your head's full of dabbities,' she would cluck – a dabbity was one of those cheap transfers children licked then stuck on their arms. Flora became known for her trenchant sayings. She had left school at thirteen to go to work, but always had a ready answer for anyone who tried to outsmart her. 'Well, if we were all wise, there'd be no room for fools!' she'd jibe, or, 'Perhaps I didn't go to school, but I met the scholars coming out.'

All too soon, Uncle James had a bride-to-be. Her name was Aunt Peggy, and she was delightful, fresh off the boat from Ireland. She was entirely comfortable with her country ways and resisted changing them her whole life. Billy was fascinated by her style of speaking. She addressed everybody as 'pal' and referred to boys as 'gossoons'. The newlyweds eventually moved to the nearby district of Whiteinch and were sorely missed by the children.

Someone must have told Billy that his father would be coming home soon, because every time an aeroplane went by he would gallop to the window and ask if it were he. Everyone knew it wouldn't be long, as over a million men had been demobbed and returned to their homes after D-Day had lured the citizens of Britain into the streets for dancing and endless celebratory parties in 1945. It was a time of great rejoicing when William finally walked in the door in March 1946. Billy hid under the table and watched huge, black Oxfords and stocky, navy trouser legs enter the room and march towards him. A vaguely familiar head topped with an air-force 'chip poke' hat (the shape of the paper packets in which chips were sold in Glasgow) appeared under the table. It scrutinized him for a few seconds, and then a meaty hand proffered a shiny gift to coax him out. It was a wonderful toy yacht, with its hull painted green below the waterline and red above. Billy loved that boat. It had real ropes that actually worked, and he sailed it many times on Bingham's Pond just off the Great Western Road.

It was odd having their father back. As was so often the case when men returned from the war, he was a stranger to his children and had been robbed of the chance to establish an early bond with them. William never spoke to Billy and Florence about their mother's departure. He simply settled into the Stewartville Street house, stashing his massive metal air-force trunk under the bed. His name and service numbers were painted on its side, along with the words: 'NOT WANTED ON VOYAGE'. That sign always troubled Billy. Why, he wondered, didn't they want my father on the voyage? What did they have against him that meant they wouldn't let him go with the rest of the men? Florence and Billy used to heave out the trunk and inspect its mysterious contents. They thought it was brilliant.

They found bits of engineering equipment, their father's wire air-force spectacles, and photos of him in India standing around with five other men, all in outlandish leopard coats, grinning and posing for the picture.

On Sundays, William occasionally took the children to the Barrowland market, known to all Glaswegians as 'The Barras'. It is a bustling place for street vending, which used to be as much a market of human variety as of inanimate goods. Billy and Florence were amazed to see grown men eating fire and selling devilish cure-alls.

Billy was astounded to see men allowing themselves to be chained inside sacks, and women throwing knives at them until they miraculously escaped. Mr Waugh, a circus 'strong man', actually bent six-inch nails with his teeth before Billy's very eyes.

'Stop Barking!' boomed John Bull, a balding man in a double-breasted suit who stood in Gibson Street hawking his Lung and Chest Elixir. 'Asthma! Bronchitis! Whooping Cough! Croup! Difficulty breathing and all chest troubles! Absolutely safe for all ages!'

Billy eagerly sought out 'The Snakeman', known as Chief Abadu from Nigeria, who claimed his snake oil cured everything from hair loss to a stuffy nose. He acted out crude impersonations of a woman gripping her chest in pain or all blocked up with catarrh, offering to rub samples on selected folk's hands. To Billy's disappointment, no child ever got a whiff.

'He was way ahead of his time,' observes Billy, who is currently fascinated by the 'faith-healing' evangelists who use similar, charisma-reliant methods to sell God and health on the born-again Christian television channel in California. 'Look at those pricks,' Billy winces, 'they must think people zip up at the back.'

One of the best parts of any Sunday outing was the journey, for they took the tramcar. Glasgow had an excellent system of tramcars, known in the dialect as 'the caurs'. They had a peculiar electric smell, and shook from side to side so many passengers

turned green after a very short while, but everybody loved them.
Conductors, who were usually female, collected the fares on board:
'Come on, get aff!' they would shout, rudely shoving people. 'Move
up! move up!'

These cheeky women were both the scourge and the sweethearts
of Glasgow, and they were immortalized in the music hall:

'Mary McDougal
From Auchenshuggle
The caur conductoress,
Fares please, fares please ...'

One conductor's smart-arse retort reverberated around the city:
'Does this tram stop at the Renfrew Ferry?'
'I hope so. It cannae swim.'

In 1947, Billy's Uncle Charlie came back from America to visit them
with his young son, Jack, in tow. Dolly, his daughter who had
Down's Syndrome, had stayed at home with her mother. Everybody
loved Charlie: he was the family love story. He had fallen for Nellie, a
charming Glaswegian lassie whose family emigrated to the United
States. Charlie saved up enough money to follow her to Far
Rockaway, Long Island, where they married and settled down in
that beach-side town. Far Rockaway is the closest point to Scotland
in the whole American continent and Charlie lived there his whole
life, never travelling further than Philadelphia.

Charlie was a hoot. Out of his grinning, 'smart-ass' mouth came
some great sassy American expressions, such as 'Hey buster, how'd
you like your eye done – black or blue?' He would sit in the tenement
window three floors up with one leg dangling. 'Hey guys, you
wanna drink?' He would squirt them with a water pistol.

Even Margaret and Mona loosened up when Charlie was around,
and they all went to the variety theatre together. Billy used to tell

people they were all going to America to live on his Uncle Charlie's ranch and they were going to get a car each.

There is a hefty, red sandstone Victorian apartment building in Stewartville Street that was originally St Peter's School for Boys. The sunken car park was once a playground full of youngsters careering pell-mell from corner to corner and Billy loved to sit with his legs dangling through the railings, watching them with envy. Sometimes he even caught some of the older students hurrying out at lunch-time, heading for a nearby shop where they could buy a single cigarette for a penny, and a slice of raw turnip for a half-penny. Billy thought they were gods. He simply could not wait to be a schoolboy, and imagined himself smoking cigarettes, eating turnips, and wearing fight-smart, studded boots that made sparks in the street. He soon got part of his wish, for the aunts decreed that it was time for both him and Florence to attend school.

Very young Catholic boys attended St Peter's Girls' School, and then moved on to the boys' school once they turned six. Billy's first teacher at kindergarten was Miss O'Halloran and, at five years old, he doted on her. In her classroom it was all Plasticine and lacing wool through holes in cards. Miss O'Halloran was amazed he could already write (Florence had taught him) and Billy was paraded round the school as a great example. He even went to Florence's class where to everyone's amazement he formed the letter 'J' on the board. But, despite his early star pupil status, Billy was terrified of the nuns, and was especially wary of Sister Philomena who had pictures of hell on her wall that looked like travel brochures. Billy assumed she'd been there.

When he moved up to the boys' school at six years old, there was a harshness he'd not experienced in kindergarten. In the main hallway there was a massive crucifix, a bleeding, life-sized Christ that thoroughly spooked him. Billy had not yet been fully indoctrinated into the faith, but once he was at the boys' school that occurred as swiftly and as subtly as a fishhook in the nostril: on his first day at the new school his teacher Miss Wilson informed him that Jesus was dead and that he, Billy, was personally responsible. And that wasn't the only bad news. From now on, he was to be addressed as 'Connolly' instead of 'Billy'.

Things were changing at home as well. William, who was probably traumatized by his wartime experiences, seemed remote and gruff to his children. He was generous as far as his means would allow and Florence and Billy looked forward to Fridays when he would come home from his job in a machine parts factory, bearing comic books, *Eagle* for Billy and *Girl* for Florence. But, although he could be quite flush with a full pay packet, he generally proved to be an inconsistent and absent parent.

As time went on and the children became less of a novelty, the aunts began to fully comprehend the sacrifices they would have to make in order to bring them up. It gradually dawned on Mona and Margaret that their single lives were now over, for dating and marriage would hitherto be difficult at best. Consequently, they began to sour, and the atmosphere at home changed drastically for the worse. There was a hymn at the time, a favourite of Billy's. It was called 'Star of the Sea':

'Dark night has come down on this heavenly world
And the banners of darkness are slowly unfurled.
Dark night has come down, dear mother and we
Look out for thy shining, sweet star of the sea.
Star of the sea, sweet star of the sea
Look out for thy shining, sweet star of the sea.'

And that's what he felt had happened. 'This is definitely different,' he thought to himself at six years old. 'God's dead, my first name's gone, and the whole fucking thing's my fault.'

2

'HE'S GOT CANDLES IN HIS LOAF!'

It is late fall in Philadelphia, 24 November 2000. An eclectic crowd is jammed into an arts-district theatre. Few people are still hugging their weatherproof outerwear, so under the seats are strewn woollen, nylon, or leather garments that have slid silently downwards as bodies began to relax and shake with hysteria.

Election time in the United States is a comedian's gift of a social climate. 'If you don't make up your mind about your president pretty quick, the country's going to revert to us British,' threatens the shaggy, non-voting Glaswegian with the radio microphone, 'and look at the choice you've got! Gore – what a big fucking Jessie he is ... and George W. Bush – God almighty!' A rant against politicians follows, and so do cheers and applause from this thoroughly fed-up bunch of voters. 'I've been saying all along: don't vote! It only encourages the bastards!'

The harangue eventually switches to introspection, and soon the theme is the march of time, probably inspired by the fact that this is the night of his fifty-eighth birthday. He bashfully announces this to the throng, which prompts a rowdy bunch on the right-hand side to instigate a swell, until the entire audience is singing happy birthday to Billy.

'Shut the fuck up!' he wails at them. 'Behave yourselves!' Every single detail of his highly embarrassing prostate exam has just been shared with all these strangers, yet the intimacy of a birthday celebration is making him very uncomfortable.

Later on, in the dressing room, there is a tiny cake from his promoter. Billy has just moaned to his audience that his birthday cake now holds nearly three boxes of candles, but the promoter's sponge-and-frosting round has only four snuff-resistant flames dancing above a chocolate greeting. As always, Billy is shattered, sweaty, and still in a fragile trance from the show. I shower him with kisses and praise for a brilliant performance, but he slumps glumly in the couch, staring fixedly at the cake.

~

He is transported to the circus in Glasgow more than fifty years ago. Among the most terrifying characters from his six-year-old experience were, ironically, clowns, and one of these scary, painted monsters is riding a unicycle while balancing a birthday cake on his shoulder. Unaccustomed to being celebrated for being alive, wee Billy has never seen a birthday cake before that moment. 'Look!' he cries, to the amusement of his sister and aunts. 'He's got candles in his loaf!'

Nowadays, I like to order an extravagant loaf of bread-shaped chocolate birthday cake with candles for Billy, which he always hugely enjoys, but back then, at St Peter's School for Boys, special treats were unheard of. Absolutely everything seemed threatening. A boy was to march in file and remember his arithmetic tables or else. The punishment for noncompliance involved several excruciatingly painful whacks with a tawse, an instrument of torture made in Lochgelly in Fife. It was a leather strap about a quarter of an inch thick, with one pointed end, and three tails at the other. The teacher's individual preference dictated which end Billy and the other boys would receive. Most liked to hold the three tails and wallop the culprit with the thick end. When a boy was considered a candidate for receiving this abuse, he was forced to hold one hand underneath the other, with arms outstretched. The tawse was supposed to find its target somewhere on the hand, but Billy noticed that teachers seemed to take great delight in hitting that very tender bit on his wrist, and making a nasty weal. Most of the boys, however, were quite keen on having battle scars.

Rosie McDonald, the worst teacher of the bunch, whom Billy describes as 'the sadist', would make her victim stand with hands, palms up, about an inch above her desk. When she wielded her tawse, the back of his hands would come crashing down painfully on top of pencils she'd placed underneath. That was her special treat in winter, when the chilly air made even youthful joints stiffer and more sensitive. Among her pupils, Rosie had favourites, but Billy was definitely not one of them. Scholastically, he did not seem to be grasping things nor keeping up with his homework, so Rosie assumed that he was lazy and stupid and punished him viciously.

Everyone who knows Billy today is aware of his considerable, albeit unusual, intelligence. However, he does not process information the same way that many others do. Psychologists currently ascribe diagnoses such as 'Attention Deficit Disorder' or 'Learning Disability' to such a way of thinking and, in the more enlightened educational environments, there is understanding and help for such children. In addition to having a learning difference, however, Billy is and was a poet and a dreamer, as well as a person suffering from past and present trauma, and these factors all conspired to make concentration and left-brain activity extremely challenging for him. Rosie thrashed him for many things that were unavoidable, considering his organic make-up: for looking out the window, for breaking a pencil, for scruffy writing or untidy paper, or for looking away when she was talking. He used to stand outside her classroom because he was too scared to go in. Eventually, someone would either push or pull him inside, and Rosie would start on him for his tardiness. 'Well look who's here! Well, well, well! Slept in, did you? Well, maybe we should wake you up.'

Once she got her favourites, James Boyd and Peter Langan, to run him up and down the classroom holding an arm each. The most humiliating part for Billy was seeing his play-piece, a little butter sandwich that he carried up his jersey, come jumping out in the process, and being trampled on by all.

Rosie was always furious and suspicious with the class. When she strapped people, she did it so violently that she invariably back-heeled her leg and kicked her desk at the same time, so eventually it featured a massive crater of cracked wood. Other teachers would pop into her classroom from time to time for various reasons and Billy would be amazed to see them occasionally having a laugh with her. 'They think she's normal,' he would marvel, 'a normal human being. Probably if you asked them what she was like, they'd even say she was nice, this horrible, terrifying beast.'

Billy still believes the bravest thing in his whole life was the day he decided to stop doing homework. Just never did it any more. The first morning after this epiphany, he awaited the inevitable with a new-found, insolent calm.

'Have you done your homework?' demanded Rosie.

'No.'

'Out here.'

Thwack! Thwack! Thwack!

'Sit down.'

The next day it was the same thing, and the next, and the next. Reflecting on it now, Billy recognizes that he probably wouldn't have been able to do Rosie's maths homework anyway, and was too intimidated to ask for help. In common with most people who have a learning disability, he is afraid of many tasks and procrastinates as a way of trying to deal with that fear.

Rosie was not the only tyrant in Billy's six-year-old life, for Mona had started taking her frustration out on Billy, and he was experiencing her, too, as a vicious bully. Mona was exactly like Rosie: suspicious, paranoid, and sadistic. She had started picking on him fairly soon after they had settled into Stewartville Street. At first it was verbal abuse. She called him a 'lazy good-for-nothing', pronounced that he would 'come to nothing', and that it was 'a sad day' when she met him.

She soon moved on to inflicting humiliation on Billy, her favourite method being grabbing him by the back of his neck and rubbing his soiled underpants in his face. She increased her repertoire to whacking his legs, hitting him with wet cloths, kicking him, and pounding him on the head with high-heeled shoes. She would usually wait until they were alone, then corner and thrash him four or five times a week for years on end.

Billy, however, had been in a few scraps in the school playground and had decided that a smack in the mouth wasn't all that painful. The more experience he had of physical pain, the more he felt he could tolerate it. 'What's the worst she could do to me?' he would ask himself. 'She could descend on me and beat the shit out of me ... but a couple of guys have done that to me already and it wasn't that bad ... I didn't die or anything.'

In fact, the more physical, emotional and verbal abuse he received, the more he expected it, eventually believing what they were telling him: that he was useless and worthless and stupid, a fear he keeps in a dark place even today. As a comedian whose brilliance now emanates largely from his extraordinarily accurate observation of humanity, he has gloriously defied Mona's favourite put-down: 'Your powers of observation are nil.' She was the only person Billy ever knew who said the word 'nil' when it wasn't about a football result.

Florence was sometimes physically present when Mona mercilessly scorned and beat her brother. She would stand there frozen and helpless, immobilized by fear and horror. The mind, however, has a marvellous capacity to escape when the body can't. Psychologists call it 'dissociation' and view it as a survival mechanism. Florence mentally flew to a far corner of the ceiling and watched the hideous abuse from 'safety'. 'I was there, but I wasn't there,' she explains now. 'I was outside, looking in.' It was very traumatic for her too, and very dangerous, for dissociation can leave an indelible mark on the psyche.

Billy, on the other hand, put his energy into trying to defend himself from Mona's blows by shielding his face and body with his arms. His adrenaline would surge and, although he was no match for her, at least he managed to avoid getting broken teeth. He remembers the blood from his nose dripping onto his feet. Billy is a survivor: in common with many traumatized children, he adopted a pretty good coping strategy. If you ask him about it now, he says, 'It sounds hellish, but it was quite bearable once you got your mind right. It doesn't kill you.' But his scars ran deeper than flesh wounds, especially those from the humiliating words that accompanied his beatings. Being too young to come up with a rational, adult explanation for it, he could only make sense of Mona's sadistic treatment by fully accepting what she said, that he was indeed a sub-standard child. 'I must deserve this,' he decided.

Mona's paranoia and suspiciousness were relentless, pathological and extremely alarming. An older boy at school gave Billy a small model boat that he had made in woodwork class.

'Where did you get that?' Mona asked him accusingly.

'A big boy gave it to me.'

'Don't tell lies. Why would anyone give you a boat for nothing? Come on! Tell me! Where did you really get it?'

There was no other answer, so she pounded him until he bled.

Margaret wasn't as manic a bully as Mona but she was on her side. She had been very beautiful when she was younger, a hair-dresser's model at Eddy Graham's. Eddy's shop smelled of rotten eggs, and Billy always wondered how she could sit through such a terrible smell. Billy admired Margaret's sense of style, but thought Mona looked an absolute mess most of the time. For a start, she never put her teeth in unless she went out. This wasn't all that unusual, for at that time in Glasgow there was a fashion for having no teeth. When National Health false teeth became available, people of all ages thought it was an excellent idea to replace their existing teeth with those new, shiny, perfect ones. Some would actually have their teeth taken out for their twenty-first birthday, as a pragmatic choice, since they were eventually going to fall out anyway.

Whenever the auburn roots of Mona's dyed blonde hair began to grow out, she would send Billy down to Boots to buy her peroxide.

'A bottle of peroxide, please, twenty volumes.'

He would carry home the little brown bottle and be swept in by a vision in slippers, a pale cardigan and a skirt and apron. Hoping to catch some young man's eye, Mona and Margaret both dolled themselves up whenever they ventured out. When nylons were in short supply, the sisters would get creative with Bisto, plastering the gravy all over their bare legs and wandering around the city stinking like a Sunday dinner.

On 8 May 1949, when Billy was six and a half, Mona mysteriously produced a baby son whom she named Michael. Her paramour was a local man who had no inclination to marry Mona; his identity remained a puzzle to his own son until adulthood. No one ever explained the situation to the growing Michael at all; as a matter of fact, he was presented to the world as a brother to Billy and Florence and nobody seemed to question it. In those postwar years, there were many similar situations and, curiously enough, the otherwise judgemental society seemed to tolerate it.

Today, having a famous 'brother' has hardly helped Michael to ward off speculation about his birth circumstances. At first he thoroughly resented those who drew attention to his situation. 'But I've learned to just shrug it off,' he says now, with questionable insistence. 'Whatever people say about me, Billy or the family ... I don't care.'

Michael's arrival at Stewartville Street was, in many ways, received as a great blessing to the Connollys. The group of uncomfortably related individuals that made up their family were able to focus their love and attention onto the tiny, innocent being who was unconnected to Mamie and provided biological mother-hood for Mona. He was an angelic baby, doted on by his mother. Billy was enchanted by him too and would heave him around in a 'circus-carry'. Even William could love him, without interference from the past; when he looked at his own children he saw Mamie, but that thorn was absent in his relationship with Michael.

'I think we were a normal family,' Michael maintains. 'I had a great childhood.' In contrast to the experience of Florence and Billy, Michael received plenty of positive attention, gifts and special treatment. Looking back now, Michael believes he was spoiled, but I think he just received what children rightfully deserve, a sense of being loved and appreciated.

Everything Michael did was magical to the adults in the household. 'Listen to him sing!' they would chime. 'Look at the way he eats!' As a toddler, Michael did have one interesting talent. There was a collection of 'seventy-eight' records in the flat and people would say to him, 'Fetch me the record of Mario Lanza singing "O Sole Mio"' and Michael could always select the correct one, even though he couldn't read.

Michael was unaware of his mother's treatment of Billy, for Mona was very secretive about it, and, understandably, he still finds it difficult to accept. Billy is convinced that his father also did not know about all the beating and neglect that was going on at home. William was absent most of the time, for he worked long hours at the Singer sewing-machine parts factory and was then out most evenings. Florence experienced William as a shadowy figure, coming and going with irregularity. 'He just thought home life was boring, I think, and pissed off,' is how Billy explains it now. 'Fuck knows where he was going ... I have no idea.'

When he wasn't working, William was usually off playing billiards and having a great time with his mates. This was fairly typical for men in those days. It was the job of women to raise children and, besides, who wouldn't have wanted to escape that household? William was a member of a club of men who'd been friends since childhood. The 'Partick Corner Boys' rented a room behind the cinema. On the bottom floor was the meeting room of a secret society called the 'Buffs', the Antediluvian Order of Buffaloes, and upstairs was William's club, which was always jam-packed with drinking men playing billiards. William would take the children up there after twelve o'clock Mass on a Sunday so Florence could practise on the piano. Billy would roll the balls around the billiard table and William would chat with his friends.

This relaxed atmosphere was a stark contrast to life at home. There, the normal misunderstandings of childhood were tolerated in Michael, but not in Billy or Florence. One day, Jesus had come into conversation at home and Billy referred to Jesus as having been a Catholic, which was his seven-year-old misunderstanding. Aunt Margaret corrected him. 'Jesus wasn't a Catholic, Jesus was a Jew.'

'Oh,' he said with innocent surprise, 'does that mean we're Jews?'

'Where did you come up with that one?' she sneered, and continued to ridicule him about that until he was in his teens. 'Does that mean we're Jewish?' she would mimic him.

Even Billy's friends who were much poorer seemed at least to have love in their houses. Frankie McBride had a mother and granddad who loved him; the McGregors down the road were a wild bunch, but their parents adored them and their house was fun. They were always shouting and laughing, and they were rejoiced in for things Billy and Florence were being pilloried for. Of an evening, the oldest girl would be going out with her boyfriend and her younger siblings would be teasing her:

'Your boyfriend's skelly [cross-eyed]!'

'No he's not!'

Their mother would intervene: 'He's a lovely boy. Don't you say that!'

Then the father would stir: 'He's a big bloody Jessie!'

'No he's not!'

In the Connolly household, the children daren't say 'boyfriend': there would have been an explosion. It would definitely have been unwise for Billy to have mentioned the kiss he got from pretty blonde Gracie McClintock. It happened in Plantation Park, known to Billy and his pals as 'Planting Park', in front of the Queen Mother maternity hospital. The Cleansing Department had a dump there where the boys would find all kinds of interesting rubbish, bits of bikes, old rags and even machine parts. One day, when he was foraging there, some friends called to him: 'Billy! Gracie's in the bushes! If you come down here, you can get a kiss!'

So Billy joined the line of five or six youngsters and eventually it was his turn to have a totally new experience. 'It was the nicest thing I remember from my childhood,' he says now. 'It was like a bird landing on my mouth. Nobody had ever kissed me before: adults, children, anyone. I used to hear boys at school complaining about their mothers kissing them, and I remember thinking, "That must be amazing! No one ever kisses me ..."'

As Billy sat in his school classroom, doing battle with Rosie, he could see the windows of his home across the street, and the prospect of returning there in the evening was far from appealing. He loved having school dinners because it meant he didn't have to go home. Mona couldn't cook to save her life, and Margaret was worse. Billy and Florence ate mostly fried foods and foul stews, and pudding would usually be a piece of dried-up cake smothered in Bird's Custard. Mona specialized in repulsive sprouts, and Billy was beaten in the face until he ate them. 'Billy tried Mother's patience,' reports Michael. 'She wanted things organized and she was loud about it. She would say, "It's Billy's turn to do the dishes" and he would say "No!" and run out.'

No doubt Billy was viewed as an ornery child. He is still disorganized and oppositional, the former being a wired-in state and the latter a coping style. Typical early difficulties for people with learning differences include tying shoes and telling the time. Billy could do neither of those things until he was around twelve years old, and he was absolutely pounded for it. Everybody tried to teach him to tie his shoes, but they all eventually lost patience. One fateful summer day, he was with his father on holiday in Rothesay. On the pier there was a clock next to a garish light display of a juggling giraffe. William was peering at it. 'Eh, Billy, what's the time on the clock over there?'

Billy began to reply, but never finished the sentence. 'The big hand is on the ...'

WHACK! 'That's not the time! What's the time?'

'I don't know.' Billy can still remember the very spot on the pavement.

'You don't know?' William exploded. 'What do you mean, you don't know? How old are you?'

William's remoteness and constant absence from home meant he knew little about his children. His role became pretty much reduced to that of 'Special Executioner', administering extra-harsh beatings for especially vile sins. 'Sometimes,' recollects Billy, 'when father hit me, I flew over the settee backwards, in a sitting position. It was fabulous. Just like real flying, except you didn't get a cup of tea or a safety belt or anything.'

Billy was aware that his father was thrilled with Florence's excellent scholastic progress, although William never once told her this. Billy himself was a great disappointment, since he did not seem bright, and was rotten at football. He dreamed of having a son like Billy's friend and hero, Vinny Maron – a football genius, even at eleven years old. When Billy and Vinny practised heading the ball against the wall, Billy barely managed to get to ten. Vinny, however, could do four hundred. Grown men would gather to watch him playing in the street. Eventually, Celtic Football Club tried to sign him up as a professional player, but he went away to become a priest and ended up drowning in a swimming accident during his time at Sacred Heart College in Spain.

There was a very insistent priesthood recruitment process at Billy's school. A stern man in a soutane would sweep into the classroom. 'Who *doesn't* want to become a priest?' So, of course, everyone had to want to be a priest and was required to sign a piece of paper verifying that fact.

Then the recruiter would try a new tack: 'Does anyone want to be a Pioneer?' This meant swearing off drink for life and, to prove it, a Pioneer wore a white enamel badge displaying a red sacred heart, with tiny gold rays emanating from it. You can still see Pioneer pins around Glasgow, sported by men in their sixties or so, who are very proud of them.

Therefore, at seven years old, Billy and his pals all swore off the drink as nasty bad stuff, even though Billy had peeked inside pubs and really looked forward to being a man and doing 'manly' things like getting pissed. The pub seemed to him like a fabulous place to be. A peculiarly appealing smell of sawdust, beer and smoke came wafting out of the door, and he could see all the men roaring and shouting and having a great time.

His local pub, the Hyndland Bar, was on a corner, and boasted one door in Fordyce Street, and the other in Hyndland Street. One of the coming-of-age challenges among Billy's peers was to avoid being apprehended while running deftly in through one door of this adults-only establishment, past all the customers, and out of the other door. It was considered very heroic to have achieved this several times.

Another great challenge was the terror of the cobbler's dunny, or dungeon. There was a cobbler's shop nearby, owned by an unfriendly little man with a moustache. This cobbler was always repairing his shoes, mouth full of nails, facing the window of the store so he could keep an eye on passers-by. Like all tenement dunnies, his was very dark, made so deliberately because these were places where lovers would go when they came home from the movies or dances. There were few cars for courting, or 'winching' as it's called in Glasgow. Johnny Beattie, another Glasgow comedian, says you can still see the mark of his Brylcreem on a dunny wall in Partickhill Road.

The goal for Billy and his seven-year-old pals was to run the gauntlet of this long, murky, subterranean corridor. It had offshoots where all sorts of weird and wild things dwelled – everybody knew that – things gruesome and dreadful, with terrible intent. At the end of the run there were stairs that curved sharply before eventually leading back to the close. Horrible murder and torture lay just around that bend, not to mention ghosts. If a boy had done the cobbler's dunny, and had made it uncaptured through the Hyndland Bar, he was a leader of men; he was Cochise, the heroic Apache chief from Billy's Saturday afternoon cowboy movies.

Billy was always gashed, scarred and full of stitches from his attempts at such glory. Once he got caught in the cobbler's dunny by the man himself, and was heaved into his house. 'You crowd of bastards, I'm fed up with you. I'm telling your father.' That was the moment when Cochise shit his pants.

～

'Now I'm gonna tell you all something that will probably prove very useful in your lives,' Billy announces to a Scottish crowd. 'I'm going to tell you what to do if you get caught masturbating ...' I had been sitting in the audience wondering when would be the most appropriate time to allow our three youngest children to come to see their father in concert. As I watch him play proficiently and enthusiastically with his caged penis in front of three thousand hysterical people, the words thirty years old flash into my mind.

'The opening line is all-important,' explains Billy. 'Say "Thank God you're here! I was just walking across the room, when the biggest hairy spider came crashing out from behind the sideboard there and shot up the leg of my trousers. The bugger was poised to sink its fangs into my poor willie ..."' The activity in question is, of course, a healthy one if privately or consensually performed; however, Billy's outrageous and frantic self-pleasuring pantomime, as well as that thing he does about having sex with sheep, were giving me substantial pause for thought.

~

Billy's battle with the morality of masturbation, indeed of sex in general, began when he started to go to confession. At first his confessed sins were pretty tame, such as telling a fib or stealing a biscuit, not enough to shift the padre's gaze from the football results. On Saturdays the *Glasgow Evening Times* sports edition was a pink paper, and was clearly visible through the grille. One evening, however, Billy scored heavily: 'I've had impure thoughts, Father.' His confessor had been checking to see how Partick Thistle was doing, but the nine-year-old's precocious words got his attention.

'Oh, and what were these thoughts?'

'I was thinking about women, naked women ... Father ... Frankie McBride's got a book with naked women in it.'

Frankie McBride was a little pal who lived around the corner from Billy.

'Oh dear. Oh dear. Three "Hail Marys" and count yourself a lucky boy. That could lead to terrible things. You know, son, these books aren't in themselves sinful, but what they're known as is "an occasion of sin". Do you know what an occasion of sin is?'

'No, Father.' Billy knew fine well.

'An occasion of sin is something or someone that leads you into sin.'

'Oh yes, Father.'

'You beware when you're around those books. There are many books like that. Any impure acts?'

'Yes, Father.'

'With yourself, or with another?'

'With myself, Father.'

'You should stop doing that immediately.'

'Yes, Father.'

He never told Billy he'd go blind: that was a school-playground tale. The school playground was an excellent place to obtain misinformation about sex, a new anti-Protestant joke or a drag on a scavenged cigarette-butt. There was entertainment there as well, in the form of regular executions. Mr Elliot used to chase chickens with an axe in the school's kitchen garden and he would chop off their heads right there in the playground.

Despite his doubts about the clergy, Billy longed to be an altar boy. He helped out in St Peter's Church, doing chores right next to the sacristy, where the priest emerged, and where the vestments and Communion wine were stored. Billy was fascinated with the vestments and was captivated by the gorgeous colours and embroidery. Priests would often come to school during the week and quiz the boys about the colour of the vestments, in order to check if they had been to Mass the previous Sunday. Billy was a regular Mass-goer at that point, but sometimes he couldn't remember the visual details and he would be beaten.

Billy never dared to steal the wine like some of his pals. The sacristy was full of surprises. Someone discovered that Communion came in a tin, and had even been brave enough to try some, but in those days Billy was shocked: 'That's Jesus,' he thought, 'you can't go eating Jesus, stealing him out of a tin.'

His bid to be an altar boy was thwarted when he and some other boys, who were all the same height, were chosen by a priest to help at Benediction. In that service, most of them would be lined up along the altar railings holding candles. The envied, glorious one, however, was the boy who stood up higher than everyone else with the golden thurible, proudly dangling the vessel so it puffed out incense at the end of every swing. Everyone wanted to be that exalted creature, so when Billy and his same-height friends filed into the sacristy and saw the thurible hanging there on its special hook, each and every one of them made a dive for it.

'I saw it first!'

'No you didn't!' There was a loud and furious scuffle that ended when the priest stormed in and grabbed them all by the jerseys.

'Out! Out! And don't you darken this door again!'

Billy continues to love incense, although the last time that sweet and heavy smoke drifted towards him was years ago at Bob Geldof's wedding, when the late Paula Yates glided down the aisle in a scarlet ball dress. It's really a good thing he doesn't go to church any more, because if he saw a thurible nowadays he might loudly interject, 'I don't like to spoil the party, but your handbag's on fire.'

Despite his early horror at the graphic gruesomeness of Catholic statues, Billy grew to like the ritualistic aspects of the religion and he was grateful for the safety and comfort it provided. He loved the hymns, and today laments that many of the old tunes have changed. 'Now the Catholic Church sounds like the fucking Bethany Hall,' he moans.

At school, he had religion every day, just before lunch. It included music taken from books of folk songs, which delighted Billy, and launched his interest in folk music. They used to sing 'Lilliburlero' (now the signature tune for Billy's favourite radio station, the BBC World Service) and 'The Lincolnshire Poacher', and 'Glorious Devon'. 'Heart of Oak' was a great favourite, too, and Billy would give strong voice to the rousing chorus:

'Steady boys, steady.
We'll fight and we'll conquer, again and again!'

With the exception of the folk singing, Billy was frustrated at the dullness of religious studies at school. What really piqued his interest was the stuff no one would cover, such as 'Did Jesus have brothers and sisters?' The teachers seemed to dodge such subjects, and were not open to questions. Billy certainly had a great deal of curiosity about many things. For example, on the back of his classroom jotter was a table of weights and measures. It was headed 'Avoirdupois', which he pronounced 'avoid dupoy', and he longed to know what it was all about, but no one even mentioned it. There were so many intriguing mysteries. He was madly interested in geisha girls but, when he asked a teacher what they were, he was beaten for 'being immoral'.

~

Billy's cousin John, a very thin boy, also attended St Peter's. Billy largely ignored him, since 'Skin', as they called him, was in a lower class, but reports of John's cleverness, elaborate practical jokes, and truant behaviour filtered through the school. John's mother was at her wits' end. She would watch her son being escorted into the classroom in the morning, but by the time she got home, John would already be sitting comfortably in their kitchen, warming his feet and drinking a mug of milk. Legend had it that when John's father had returned from the war, three-year-old John had darted out from behind the door and savagely kicked him, in protest for having returned to spoil the cosy life he had with his mother. Apparently, this Oedipal rage never left him. Billy's father advised his brother to take a very hard line with John. William's thinking on many subjects was very black-and-white.

After Michael's arrival, the living space at home had become even more cramped. Mona and Margaret shared one room, with Michael in a cot. In the other room, which was a living room by day, Billy shared a sofa-bed with his father. Late one night, when Billy was ten, he woke to find his father 'interfering' with him, as he puts it. Then, and for the next four or five years, his father's frequent sexual abuse was a mystery to him, like being in an accident. 'The most awful thing,' says Billy now, fully grasping the anatomy of shame, 'was that it was kind of pleasant, physically, you know. That's why nobody tells. I remember it happening a lot, not every night, but every night you were in a state thinking it was going to happen, that you'd be awakened by it. I would pray for the holidays. I couldn't wait for us to go to the seaside because then we had separate beds.'

It's hard to know exactly why William molested his own son. He had the appearance of being extremely religious and, since the Catholic Church was very strict about the sanctity of marriage, he saw no possibility of divorce from Mamie or remarriage at any point: however, that doesn't really explain why he chose this particular form of sexual expression. It wouldn't be the first time extreme sexual repression in an ostensibly religious person has led to 'unspeakable' acts. As Carl Jung explained, denial of our shadow side will often cause it to rise up against us. Perhaps William himself had been sexually abused in childhood, as is so often the case with perpetrators. In fact, historical accounts of that culture and time would suggest that, in those overcrowded conditions, incest was extremely common.

At any rate, Billy kept the dark secret locked away until the early eighties, when he and I were sitting in our car outside the Glasgow hospital the night his father died. 'That creep.' I cried with him, and not because his father, in his scheme of things, was about to meet his maker. It was William's hypocrisy that really got to both of us. He was always passing judgement on Billy for his 'sinfulness' and lack of conformity to the Catholic faith, while at the same time he was hurting him so profoundly ... in so many ways. Since that moment, Billy has found various ways to heal and make adult sense of all his early abuses, but back then, when there was little safety anywhere in his life, what saved him?

For one thing, he absolutely loved reading. Not his schoolbooks – he thought they were very dull, although the class would sometimes be read to on a Friday, and that was quite soothing. *White Fang* and adventure stories from Canada and the Yukon were popular. Billy often imagined himself donning a huge, woolly jacket and striding into the northern wildernesses to pan for gold, a perfect way to escape from Stewartville Street.

There was a comprehensive library system in Glasgow, and his local branch, a vast pseudo-classical building, was just across the tram-lines in Partick. It was wonderfully warm inside, and full of people of all ages, especially elderly folk. Every newspaper was there, mounted on a board with a special cord for turning the pages. Billy had worked through the infants' section years ago, steamed right through the boys' corner (*Just William*, Enid Blyton and all kinds of adventure stories), and when he became twelve he was finally able to swagger up the street with not one, but two books. That's when he discovered Tibet. Once he came across *Seven Years in Tibet* he was completely hooked, fascinated by its isolation from the rest of the world.

Billy devoured books that carried pictures and diagrams to help him spot different types of fighter aircraft by the colour and shape of the wings. He made models of some of them, and spotted a number of war planes that were still flying in the fifties, such as the Dakota, a massive transport plane, and a couple of fighter planes, the Gloster Meteor, which had tanks on its wings, and the two-tailed Vampire. In those days, all aeroplanes were very different and so were the cars. No one would ever mistake a Humber Hawk for a Standard Vanguard, or a Ford Prefect for an Austin Seven. Billy's favourite was the sporty Sunbeam Alpine, though he was thrilled when he spotted an Armstrong Siddeley, with its badge shaped like a sphinx, or a Triumph Mayflower, like a petite limousine.

Nowadays, Stewartville Street is accessible only to pedestrians, but at that time cars could drive in and park in the centre of his street. These beauties were never locked, so he would sneak inside to toot the horn and take in a deep whiff of leather seat. He thought all vehicles were wonderful things.

Another saving grace in Billy's life was his love of being a Wolf Cub. In his navy pullover, green cap with yellow piping, Wolf Cub badge and an orange-and-green 'neckie' with its leather woggle, Billy happily trotted to school after hours.

'Dyb dyb dyb dyb.'

Their tribal leader, Akela, also known as Mrs Lamont, a posh woman from up the road, would stand in the centre of the ring of Cubs.

'Akela, we'll do our best!'

'Dyb dyb dyb dyb ... Do your best.'

'We'll dob dob dob dob ... WOOF!'

Later on, when Billy graduated to becoming a Scout, he found the boys were divided into patrols that had animal names. He had fancied himself as a Cobra or a Buffalo and was embarrassed to be placed among the Peewits. However, being a Scout gave him a love of the outdoors that has never left him. Billy still jokes about the novelty of a country visit for Glasgow city children of the time: 'They take you to the countryside once a year. It's supposed to be good for you. The teachers say: "See that green stuff over there? Grass. See the brown things walking about on it? Cows. Don't break them and be back here in half an hour."'

Scouts had their own campground with a real totem pole at Auchengillan, near Loch Lomond, but Wolf Cubs went on day trips to nearby jamborees and threw themselves into the annual bob-a-job fund-raiser, doing jobs for neighbours for a shilling a time. Billy loved having the chance to visit strangers' houses and observe their lives. He was particularly curious about people who seemed to be different from him. The social differences in people and the rigidity of class divisions were just now becoming apparent to him. Not yet imbued with working-class pride, or fury at those born into more advantageous stations in life, he was intrigued by the variety in society and comfortably embraced people of all classes.

He had one great customer, a wonderful upper-class man in Byres Road. To his amazement, this gentleman wore a sports jacket, flannels and tie around the house, and warmly welcomed Billy whenever he appeared. 'Oh, is that you? Come in, sit down!'

Billy's task was to polish all his shoes, and he had an enormous collection, brown brogues with curved designs on them, and black Oxfords. All the polishes and brushes were laid out, and the two of them would sit on either side of the fire. Billy would go to work on his shoes, and the gentleman would tell him all about his early life in the Caribbean. Nowadays Billy has a ridiculously large collection of shoes and boots (73 pairs on my last count), several of which are brogues and Oxfords. Buying these shoes and keeping them shipshape has very pleasant associations, for the gentleman's kind and appreciative treatment of Billy was rare and very meaningful for him. 'Do you collect stamps?' the man would ask. 'Well, I've got some for you ... from Trinidad and Tobago!'

Billy's great affection for many 'upper-class' people seems to stem from the great kindness he received as a Wolf Cub. He has often been criticized for such friendships, as if he were somehow betraying his roots. As a 'classless' Australian, I have always been astounded by all that hoo-ha. Fortunately, Billy's attitude is a sensible one: 'What am I supposed to say? ... "I can't come to dinner with you because I'm working-class"? I'd look such a prick.'

Sometimes Billy's bob-a-job task would involve cleaning out the cellars of wealthy folk who lived at the top of the hill. As he sorted out tents and climbing boots, fishing rods and skis, he thought, 'God, it must be brilliant being a toff! You can just take off and do these amazing things all the time!'

When he wasn't being a Wolf Cub, Billy spent his spare time with a number of close pals who lived near his house. Mrs Magee's grandson Gerald lived on the ground floor of his tenement, and opposite him lived Robert Alexander. Ronnie and Billy Meikle were upstairs, along with Jimmy and Kay Whitelaw. Ian Meikle lived behind them in the next street and Billy could hear him through the wall, practising his pipe-band drums. Billy had a great time with this jolly gang of ruffians. They played rounders, kick-the-can, and an omni-directional form of cricket. They had chalk-drawn a set of wickets on the wall with 'LBW' (Leg Before Wicket) written above. Naturally, the wickets could never fall, but they invented an ingenious way to get a player out: they soaked the ball so it made a wet mark to show where it hit the wall.

Another game was a risky assault course, beginning at the Dumbarton Road fruit shop, and continuing fast around the corner into Hyndland Street, where the fishmonger and the remnant shops were practically side by side. The object of the game was to avoid being caught. It was one of Billy's favourites and its name describes the rules. It was called 'steal an orange, slap a fish, and spit on a remnant'.

Depressed and hopeless children often take heart-stopping risks, almost hoping that they won't survive. 'Jumping the dykes' was a shockingly dangerous game that involved leaping between air-raid shelters, walls and middens. The air-raid shelters were eight to ten feet high, but the biggest risk lay in leaping from shelter to shelter, which was easily a five-foot stretch. There were names for the various jumps: there was the Wee Sui (short for suicide), and the Big Sui. The Wee Sui was a jump from a tall air-raid shelter onto a small midden, but to achieve the Big Sui one had to run across one air-raid shelter, leap onto another, then run like hell in order to leap a huge gap onto the Wee Sui. Billy did the Big Sui when he was nine. Word went around the street whenever it was conquered, but many of these long-jump warriors went to hospital. I marvel that Billy only broke an ankle, for quite apart from the risks of skeletal damage, the middens themselves were ripe with bacteria and chemical poisons.

Cochise was not the only character on whom Billy modelled his suicidal heroism. In fifties movies, there was a whole line of desperately unrealistic white movie stars who portrayed Native American tribal chiefs. At both of the cinemas Billy attended, the Western and the Standard, the audiences were extremely rowdy and irreverent, and typically booed the cowboys and cheered the underdog 'Indians'. They identified with the Apaches partly because they were glamorous renegades who had the best horses, but there was probably a deeper reason. Their struggle against the cowboys may have struck a chord for Scottish people, resembling their own past battles and present fury with the English. At the Standard, the tune 'God Save the Queen' was once played at the end of each performance. When people ignored it and simply stampeded out to catch their buses, the playing of the National Anthem was moved to the middle of the film, in an attempt to enforce some measure of decorum. Scots have long objected to the pejorative lines once used in the Anthem:

'God grant, and with a mighty rush,
Rebellious Scots to crush'.

Not surprisingly, Billy has proposed the institution of a new National Anthem. The tune would be the theme from the long-running and popular BBC radio series, *The Archers*, while the words would go:

'Dum de dum de dum de dum
Dum de dum de dah dah
Dum de dum de dum de dum
Dum dee diddle de dum.'

Left: So that's where Billy got the dimple in his chin! His grandfather, Jack Connolly, with bride Jane McLuskey.

Below: Billy's parents' wedding day. Best man Barney McConville is on the right, and bridesmaid *(left)* has managed to upstage the bride.

Left: The man who gave Billy that 'head transplant' look. Billy's father, William, shows off Florence, his first-born.

Right: Defining the 'sonsie face'! One-year-old Yin *(foreground)* in pale blue and white, holding his sister's hand.

Below: A couple of gooseberries: Billy and Florence with Mona *(right)*, Margaret, and gentlemen friends Mick McGowan *(left)* and Mick Conway.

Above: The 'cheeky wee devil'. Billy at four, at Big Neilly's tenement in Stobcross Street.

Below: Off to school: Billy, Florence and tiny pal in Stewartville Street. Their tenement was to the right.

Below: His little guardian: Florence at six shields Billy in the 'Botanic' Gardens in Glasgow's West End. Taken by their father.

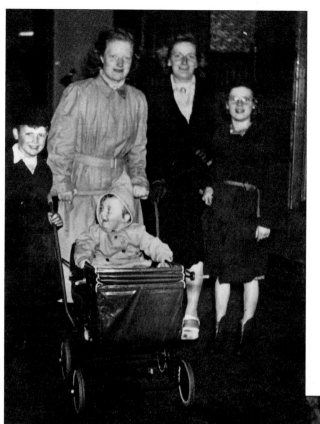

Left: Off to Mass in the drizzle. Mona and Florence beside Aunt Margaret wheeling Michael's pram, while Billy grins on the left.

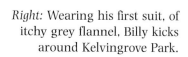

Right: Wearing his first suit, of itchy grey flannel, Billy kicks around Kelvingrove Park.

Above: The Partick gang in a bomb site they named 'Bumbee Park'... *Back row:* Gerald McGee, Frankie McBride, Tom Laurie, Billy. *Front row:* Johnny McBride, Michael, Tom Mackie.

Above: Billy, in his favourite T-shirt with racing cars on it, and his Aunt Mona on their family holidays in Rothesay, 1954.

Left: Florence at sixteen strolling down the promenade in Rothesay, known as 'the prom'.

Right: 'Ha ha!' says Billy, now a Doctor of Letters from Glasgow University.

W4758

The Corporation of Glasgow
Education Department

TELEPHONE:
GOVAN 1581

St. Gerard's Senior Secondary School,
Southcroft Street,
Glasgow, S.W.1

28-10-1958.

William Connolly

The above-mentioned boy attended this
school for 3 years, leaving June, 1958.
During his attendance here he was found
to be trustworthy and dependable. He
was a good attender and always punctual.

JOHN J. McKEE

Headmaster.

Below: St Gerard's school photograph. Spot the thirteen-year-old Billy (*second row from the front, second from the right*).

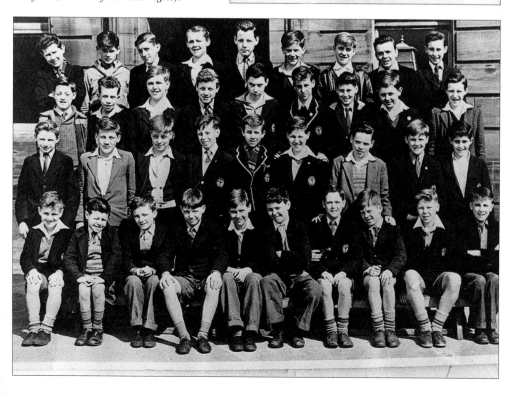

Left: Shipbuilding on the Clyde in Billy's apprentice days. Now only the cranes remain.

Below: 'Look at my wee skinny body!' Billy (*front in white T-shirt*) on a 'bucket' in Nigeria, being hoisted up from work on the oil rig, 1966.

Below: At a Queen's Park demonstration by the Upper Clyde Shipbuilders, when the company wanted to close down the yard. The workers themselves eventually took over the shipyard. Tam Harvey is on Billy's right. Cara calls this picture 'The Chosen One'.

Govan Initiative Ltd
- Business Development
- Physical Development
- Education & Training
- Marketing & Promotion

For further details on our range
of services contact:
The Director, Broomloan House
170 Edmiston Drive
Glasgow G51 2YS
Tel: 0141-427-6066

The Govan Press

A WEEKLY NEWSPAPER FOR

Govan, Kinning Park, Plantation, Ibrox, Cardonald, Mosspark, Pollok, Crookston, Hillington, Penilee, Bellahouston, Dumbreck, Linthouse, Drumoyne and Craigton.

ESTABLISHED 1879

Govan Initiative Ltd
Business and the Arts
...bringing the Arts to your area...

For further details contact:
Broomloan House
170 Edmiston Drive
Glasgow G51 2YS
Tel: 0141-427-6066

84TH YEAR-NO. 43   POSTAGE OF THIS PAPER IN UNITED KINGDOM, TWOPENCE HALFPENNY   DECEMBER, 6 1963   THREEPENCE

All Three Govan Teams
Beaten
-TOMORROW IS SCOTTISH CUP DAY

Govan's three main football teams -Rangers, St. Anthony's and Benburb - were all defeated in league games last Saturday. Rangers were trounced 3-0 by Hearts at Ibrox; St. Anthony's were beaten 5-2 by Yoker Athletic at Moore Park in Copland Road and Benburb went down by the odd goal in three to Vale of Leven at Alexandria.

Tomorrow is Scottish Cup day for the Juniors. St. Anthony's have Whitburn as their guests at Moore Park. This is the team that gave the Ants their walking ticket in the Scottish last season.

There is a touch of history in the Newtongrange Star versus Benburb game. Twenty-eight years ago Newtongrange Star were the guests of Benburb in a Scottish Junior Cup tie when they opened their present Tinto Park. Newtongrange won this tie with the only goal scored in the game.

When Benburb visit Newtongrange tomorrow they will play on the first football ground in Britain to have floodlights installed.

Yard Meeting Votes Yes

APRIL	M	T	W	T	F	S	S
						1	2
	3	4	5	6	7	8	9
	10	11	12	13	14	15	16
	17	18	19	20	21	22	23
	24	25	26	27	28	29	30

3

IN SEARCH OF A DUCK'S ARSE

There is a grown man in the bed beside me, crying in his sleep. I am woken by the pitiful child-like sounds emerging from his greying beard. His anguish seems to intensify, to the point where I can no longer tolerate it, and I decide to wake him. In his dream he was drowning, running out of breath as he swam underwater. He was trying desperately to get up to the surface, searching in vain to find air.

'Why the hell did you wake me? I didn't get to the good bit!' He's furious with me for interrupting this five-decades-old recurring nightmare too soon. What normally happens, he explains, is he discovers he can breathe underwater. Apparently it is exhilarating for him to rediscover, every time, that he does not need to die, for he has discovered a way to manipulate the physical world.

It is 4 a.m. but I lie there silently marvelling at the symbolism in his dream, for under traumatic, even life-threatening conditions, Billy did manage to survive where others would not have done. In childhood, that dream must have been a hopeful message from his unconscious mind that there were highly creative solutions to the horror of his daily life. In adulthood, he has certainly found them.

≈

After failing the eleven-plus exam the first time, Billy eventually scraped into St Gerard's, a secondary school that proved to be a far more comfortable environment for him, for he received better treatment by his teachers. His uniform was smart enough to impress his father: a green blazer, grey flannels, green tie and new shoes. To his horror, the aunts completed the outfit with a maroon canvas briefcase. No one else had one of those. The hottest book-carrying item was a gas-mask holder converted into a shoulder bag.

Billy's first maths teacher at St Gerard's was Mr McNab, who made a striking entrance in a blue serge suit, white shirt, claret-coloured tie, black shoes and a modern haircut. McNab eyed his new class as if they had just fallen off the Cleansing Department wagon and the boys knew from day one there was no kidding this man. His first move was absolutely excellent: he swaggered over to the metal wastepaper basket beside his desk and stamped his foot inside it. Without taking his eyes off the class, he back-heeled the basket so it slid across the room and crashed against the door to prop it open. 'You got your books? You'd better have.' Every book hit the desk.

Billy idolized him and was inspired to enjoy his subject. It was the same with Mr Costello who taught geography. Everyone remembered his lessons because he was so funny and nobody ever failed. Costello smoked in the classroom, although he was obviously a chest case, wheezing and coughing all the time. Other teachers would raid the toilets where boys were smoking and would sling the culprits into detention, but Costello would cruise in and ask for a light.

The school environment was filled with a refreshing cast of characters for Billy to observe and sometimes emulate. In the technical-drawing class, Mr Corrigan's stunted moustache earned him the nickname 'Hitler'. McGarrity who taught woodwork was nicknamed 'Faith, Hope and Charity'. Barney Hill taught English and would re-enact scenes from Shakespeare astonishingly badly, bringing the house down.

Campbell, another maths teacher, was not above thwacking people; however he had the thinnest belt in the school so no one minded. He called his belt 'Pythagoras' and the name was inscribed on the leather. There was a huge ruckus when 'Pythagoras' suddenly disappeared. Billy discovered later that it was his cousin John who stole it, cut it into bits, and put it back in the drawer ... a great act of derring-do, and a most symbolic act considering John's persisting Oedipal angst. Eventually, the great day came when Campbell got a new belt.

'I'd like to introduce you to my new best friend,' Campbell announced to the class. He brought 'Pythagoras 2' out of the drawer.

'OOOOOOH!' went the class.

'Who'd like to be first?'

All the hands shot up.

'OK, everybody out!'

So they all got it, one at a time, and relished it.

Billy still struggled with his academic work, but the atmosphere at St Gerard's was much more supportive and he managed to pass his tests. He still couldn't get a grip of arithmetic, so Florence tried to help him at home. Fractions and decimals were fine, but long-division was torture. Algebra lost him altogether. 'Why should I learn algebra?' he fumes at his audience these days. 'I've no intention of ever going there.'

Part of Billy's problem turned out to be lack of retention. He could understand a lesson perfectly, but an hour later he hadn't a clue. To this day, it's the same thing: he can read a book and enjoy it immensely, but afterwards he remembers remarkably little about it. 'I only ever needed to buy one book and read it every month,' he boasts.

By the time Billy was fourteen, the inner-city population had grown to the point where the Glasgow Corporation was alarmed by the level of overcrowding in the tenement houses, and began a programme of slum clearance. In some neighbourhoods, the dilapidated buildings were torn down altogether, but in Stewartville Street a proportion of the families were moved elsewhere in order to reduce the number of inhabitants in each building. Billy's family, along with hundreds of other tenement dwellers, was relocated ten miles away, in a housing estate in Drumchapel.

Within the cheaply built, two-storeyed house with a pebble-dash façade, the Connollys' new flat was more spacious and they were overjoyed to have a bathroom and separate kitchen for the very first time. Most importantly for Billy, he no longer had to share a bed with his father and, presumably due to the lack of opportunity, his sexual abuse came to an end. Mona continued to beat him, but Billy was getting bigger and it didn't seem to hurt him so much. Recognizing her physical disadvantage, she moved on to sly mind games, such as leaving accusatory notes for him in drawers and biscuit jars, and undermining his confidence with peers.

Drumchapel itself, known as 'The Drummy', was an ugly, litter-strewn wasteland. There was mud everywhere from the building sites and people had nowhere to congregate, not even a little café. Shops appeared after a couple of years, but until then everyone had to buy food from mobile grocers and butchers. Billy thought it was a dreadful, primitive way of life. Florence had some friends who had also moved to Drumchapel, so she was quite pleased about the move. Billy and Michael were less thrilled. There were no schools in Drumchapel so they were given travel passes to take the bus into Glasgow, but the buses back home were full of bevvy merchants with 'broken pay'. Traditionally, men were expected to hand their sealed wage envelopes straight to their wives without spending any of it. Since there were no pubs in Drumchapel, they would leave their work and head straight for the pub in town before heading for home drunk and thoroughly skint.

It was pleasant, though, to be right on the edge of the country-side. There was an extensive woodland near Drumchapel, the

Bluebell Woods with little burns, or streams, and fields with grazing cows. Children could roam around paddocks, swing from trees and chase rabbits. Billy caught a glimpse of a wild animal for the first time, and couldn't believe his eyes. Wild humans also abounded: 'rough' kids from Pilton Road would hang out in the woods, acting like Jesse James. They ambushed Billy a few times, so after a while he was scared to go there.

The Connollys, who now lived in Kinfauns Drive, looked down on the people living at right angles to them in Pilton Road, whom they considered ruffians because they were 'slum clearance people'. The Connollys had been moved out of a slum, too, but they felt there was an important difference: their building in Stewartville Street was not being torn down, rather it had just been emptied. They were really quite snobbish towards the Pilton Road folk, and disapproved of their lifestyle and lack of respect for their own property. There were paths trampled right through the middle of their gardens, since they weren't the kind of people who were delicate about daisies.

Billy loved lying in bed listening to the Pilton Road folk on a Friday night, when they all had riotous shindigs and ended up plastered and punch-happy; he and Florence would scream with laughter. The party always sounded jolly at the beginning. An accordion would be playing and the folk would be belting out 'On the Wild Side of Life' and 'Nobody's Child', but Billy and Florence never had to wait long for the ominous sound of breaking glass that heralded a 'handshaking', a fight to settle a grudge. The terminology of violence in Glasgow is wonderfully understated: a 'Glasgow kiss', for example, is a brutal head-butt, while a 'Glasgow grin' is a knife-slash across the face. The familiar sound effects would continue. Amidst cries, curses and the crash of breaking china, someone would shout, 'Stop the band,' and the accordion would whine down. Then, Biff! Boff! There'd be a general 'rammy' or free-for-all.

'Get tae fuck!' would punctuate the air, then the slamming of a door as if someone had been tossed out on his ear. The troublemaker could then be heard marching down the close:

'Shove yer party up yer arse!'

'And don't you come fucking back!'

Nowadays, Billy performs fragments of parties and sing-songs that originated in Pilton Road: Scotsmen have this great habit of singing about missing Scotland when they're still there:

(*Singing*)'When I'm far across the sea ...!'

'No you're not, you're in the living room.'

'Shut up, it's the only song your father knows.'

Every family in Drumchapel was given a minuscule piece of land for growing vegetables or flowers, so the Connollys had a garden for the first time. Billy was put in charge of growing potatoes, but he had no idea what to do with the curious seeded vegetables he was given, so he just dug a hole, threw them in and scattered some earth over the top. After waiting in vain for them to grow a few times, he finally got the hang of making furrows. He bought packets of flower seeds from Woolworth's and planted purpley-red primulas, Livingstone daisies and sickly-pink gladioli.

It was in Drumchapel that Billy developed his penchant for night-scented stock, the fragrant flower whose lovely perfume wafted into the house on summer evenings. When the weather was decent, Billy liked to cycle. Most of the children in Drumchapel had bikes or tricycles. Billy's father gave him a second-hand New Hudson bicycle, a beauty in metallic purple. He would cycle away along the Great Western Road towards Loch Lomond and, in clement weather, he would even ride to school.

The New Hudson was not really a racing bike, but Billy winged his own Tour de France, in toe clips and Reg Harris Fallowfield cycling shoes with a Union Jack on the tongue. His granny let him have Uncle Teddy's old woolly cycling jersey with the name of a local team, the 'Glenmarnock Wheelers', on the front. It was full of holes, but Billy loved it, imagining it made him look a bit like a real cyclist.

It was such a relief to be able to escape from home and visit his pals who lived in other towns. Billy McKinnel came from Bearsden, an up-market district in north-west Glasgow. It was absolute luxury to sit watching television on Mrs McKinnel's white-and-gold, floral sofa in its squeaky, plastic covering. The Glaswegian comedian Chic Murray, a hefty riot of a man with a tartan suit and a cloth cap, came on the box one day, telling a story about two men called 'Simmet' and 'Drawers' – 'simmet' means singlet in Scotland and, of course, 'drawers' are underpants. Chic's tale was all wordplay and absolutely the funniest thing Billy had ever heard. Mr and Mrs McKinnel were roaring along with the boys. In the story, the Drawers' son had just announced to his father that he wanted to go and live in America, and his father was admonishing him: 'Don't let the Drawers down!'

At that moment, Billy slid over the arm of the couch, for he lost all mastery over his body. He lay on the floor completely convulsed, and Billy says he knew right then, without a shadow of a doubt, that he would spend his life being a funny man. The only comedians he'd previously heard were radio stars like Ted Ray, who all had English accents. Chic Murray, and the variety theatre comic Jimmy Logan, had a profound effect on Billy because they spoke with Glaswegian accents and talked about things that were familiar to him.

≈

One afternoon in March 2001, spluttering laughter from a thousand mourners violates the sombre atmosphere of Glasgow Cathedral. Billy has stepped into the pulpit, nicely understated in a black suit, with bright orange Buddha beads and a diamanté scarf. 'I bet you never thought you'd see me here!' He smirks at the largely Protestant congregation.

BILLY

Billy glances down at Jimmy Logan's Saltire-draped coffin lying beneath him in the nave. 'I made him laugh one lunchtime,' he boasts. 'There was ham on the menu so I told him, "You've been doing it for years, so you might as well have a bit!"'

~

As a young teenager, Billy found himself drawn to following funeral processions and visiting graveyards. Thoughts of suicide were not uppermost in his mind, but he was intrigued, perhaps even obsessed, with some notions of death, especially tragedy, martyrdom, glory and the peacefulness of resting below the earth's surface. There was certainly something very appealing about a state in which he no longer had to do battle with Mona, Rosie and William. It was a dangerous time for Billy for, like all teenagers, the finality of death had not yet sunk in.

At seventeen, Florence was struggling too. She had boyfriends and tried to keep them a secret, for she was bearing the brunt of Mona's jealousy and frustration at the lack of romance and advancement in her own life. Terrified that her niece might become pregnant outside marriage, as she herself had done, Mona became more intrusive and paranoid than ever. One of her dirtiest tricks was trying to get Billy to follow Florence when she went out one evening. He complied as far as the end of Blackcraigs Avenue because he knew Mona could see him from the window. When he saw Florence enter a friend's house he waited for a while before returning with some story to mollify his aunt.

The more Mona sensed that Florence was slipping out of her grip, the more she verbally attacked her, frequently accusing her of 'getting above her station'. 'Who do you think you are? Who are you trying to kid?'

Fortunately, Florence had her own room by now, and she simply retreated there most of the time. She was enjoying considerable success at school and had already applied for teachers' training college. She knew the time would soon come when she would be out of the house altogether. She was lucky enough to have a small transistor radio, so she could drown out Mona's tirades by listening to Radio Luxembourg: 'And now, according to the time on my H. Samuel Ever-Right Watch, it's time for David Jacobs,' the announcer would boom.

~

Billy found a different way to escape. During his last year at school, he worked as a milk boy. He has that in common with his friend, hero and master of sibilance, Sean Connery. At the opening of the Edinburgh Film Festival a few years ago, someone asked the actor if he'd ever honoured them with his presence there before. Sean replied, 'Yeah. I used to deliver milk here.' Mark Knopfler, who eventually made his name in the rock band, Dire Straits, was on Billy's milk route, as were two rival football heroes: Bobby Evans, who was a Catholic Celtic player, and Willie Waddell, who played for the Protestant team, Rangers Football Club.

'Should I pee in Willie's milk?' wondered Billy.

Billy and his fellow frozen snotters made their deliveries from a little electric milk float. They ran back and forth to distribute the milk, while the float just kept gliding along the street. When snow lay on the ground, there were excellent high jinks to perform, for they could hang onto the back of it and ski. The boys rose at four in the morning to collect the milk at a farm, where they made tea to warm and waken themselves. Ever intent on tomfoolery, Billy liked to wait behind the cow for the raw milk lads to arrive, then whip the safety catch off an udder and zap them with milk. It took him ages to perfect this technique, but he eventually became an expert.

Psssht!

'You dough-heid you!'

BILLY

Billy loved playing practical jokes. His and every other Glasgow schoolboy's favourite shop was Tam Shepherd's Joke Shop, which sold the best stink bombs known to man, rich with sulphuric awfulness. It was considered a great wheeze to saunter in there and inquire, 'Hi Tam, how's tricks?'

A favourite prank the milk boys relished was leaving empties where someone would fall over them in the middle of the night. They would listen gleefully for the crashing and cursing that meant their wicked strategies had paid off. Unfortunately, the tables were turned on Billy one freezing morning, after another wee dobber threw a snowball at him. Billy ducked and ran, but he took a flier over a knee-high fence. He clattered down on top of his bottles, cutting his left index finger to the bone and slashing a tendon. His subsequent tendon transplant surgery meant that he was off school for months on end. When he returned, he was immediately belted on the injured hand for letting off stink bombs on a bus headed for the sports ground.

Billy's tendon transplant had far-reaching academic consequences. He left school with nothing except proof that he had been there and a couple of engineering certificates. His cousin John stayed on and eventually shone at university.

~

A crowd of Glaswegian schoolteachers is clustered around a microphone in the MacDonald Hotel, singing their own specially written version of 'Que Sera Sera'. The performance is for the benefit of Florence at her surprise sixtieth birthday party. I can't make out the words but their performance is accompanied by giggles and knowing winks.

Billy chats with his cousins, Carmel, Mark and Sean, who are Uncle James's grown-up children, while I whirl around the dance floor with John's brother Eddy. Florence looks happily bewildered.

Her grandchildren are tearing around the room chasing each other with a slimy silicone sausage. Later, as I sit with Mark, who is now a priest, discussing our shared passion for the Asian continent, I am distracted by a vision in scarlet crushed velvet. It is Billy, who has taken to the floor with his sister.

'Look at them ...' I murmur.

Father Mark smiles indulgently, unaware of my focus. 'They actually made it this far.'

~

Just before she turned eighteen, Florence was accepted into the teachers' training college at Notre Dame in Glasgow. She was over-joyed at the prospect of living on campus with her friends and away from Mona. Florence had made sense of her life by developing a strong Catholic faith, which continues to sustain her to this day. 'It's really worse than death,' she decided quite early on, 'living a hellish life. There has to be something beyond it, just for the fairness of the thing.'

When Billy visited her on campus, he noticed a distinct, positive change in her. She had grown away from the rest of the family and he was very happy for her. They still went on Sunday outings together with Michael and pals from school, first slurping down hot orange at an Italian café in the Dumbarton Road, then heading for either the Botanic Gardens or the Art Gallery. The city of Glasgow boasts some gorgeous buildings and the Kelvingrove Art Gallery is certainly one of them. Some say that, after it was erected, the architect who designed it committed suicide out of despair, for the building was built backwards by mistake; but Billy says that's just an urban legend.

Youngsters who visit the Art Gallery today are treated to a life-size *Star Wars* Imperial Storm Trooper replica carrying a 'blaster rifle' but, as a youngster, Michael was content with a slide in the vast atrium, where there were wonderfully slippery floors in black, white and gold patterned marble. If a boy landed on his backside during a slide, he could glance to the ceiling for a visual feast of turquoise-and-gold panels and gilt Tudor roses on a lush, red background. The names of famous composers were displayed on balconies above, and Billy learned their names long before he ever heard their music: Rossini, Wagner and Beethoven.

Billy loved the paintings upstairs. Salvador Dali's 'Christ of St John of the Cross' was there as well as French, Dutch, Flemish and British masterpieces. Billy always needed a cup of tea after drinking in so much art, so it was lucky there was also a tearoom. They would finish off by poring over model ships from every era, suits of armour for very short kings, and terrible triumphs of taxidermy. Best of all, it was free.

Just after Christmas in 1957, not long after rock and roll had been invented, they saw a teddy boy right there in the gallery, languishing by a pillar beneath the massive pipe organ. Billy was in heaven; he had never seen a real teddy boy before, only cartoons, yet there he was, with his long jacket, drainpipe trousers and fat suede shoes with crepe soles. This god also had a bop haircut with big 'sideys' and a 'DA' (a duck's arse) at the back, plus an earring. Billy had never seen a man with an earring before.

A week later, Mona was beating him up for something or other, and in the middle of it she suddenly accused him: 'I know what you want. I know exactly what you want. You want to be a teddy boy!' It was Billy's finest hour. 'Yes I do,' he defied her bravely. That was the moment for him. She laid into him again, but by then he was untouchable.

Florence was already getting the bop look, with back-combed hair, white lipstick and dark eyeliner. She wore white high heels and net petticoats she stiffened by dipping in sugar and water. Unable to buy clothes, Billy too tried to get the bop look with what he already owned. He had some old narrow trousers that he strutted about in, but one day he came home to find that Mona had ripped them apart.

Then, one magical evening, a girl who lived in the next close invited Billy to the Girl Guides' dance. When he arrived, couples were mostly dancing Scottish reels, but then one of the girls pulled out a Dansette record player and put on a seventy-eight record. It was 'Heartbreak Hotel'.

'Well, since my baby left me,
I found a new place to dwell.
It's down at the end of Lonely Street
at Heartbreak Hotel.'

Everyone started jiving, and Billy had never seen or heard anything like it in his life. Shocked at the power of it, he thought, 'That's for us! It's not for them, it's ours, it's *our* music!' It was really rock 'n' roll that saved him. From that moment, he never looked back.

4

OXYACETYLENE ANTICS

It is winter in Los Angeles, 2001, with temperatures at a low of 74°F and air quality at fair-to-awful. The landscape below our plate-glass kitchen wall is a typical Hollywood Hills scene: the lights of Universal Studios spread out before us, with only the hourly explosion and pyrotechnic display from the 'Waterworld' show interrupting the dull roar of the freeway. Billy is looking unusually smug as he approaches our kitchen dining table, carrying a steaming bowl of his own excellent macaroni cheese.

'One helping for Doctor Connolly,' he grins mysteriously as he spoons out the delicious pasta for me, then goes to serve himself, 'and one for the *other* Doctor Connolly.'

I glare at him suspiciously. 'If someone has gone and offered you an honorary doctorate, I'm going to puke.'

'Glasgow University. Doctor of Letters, no less. I'm to receive it in July. Wanna come?'

It had only taken me six sleep-deprived years to achieve my PhD in Psychology. 'Try to be nice,' I tell myself.

~

It is another remarkable and well-deserved milestone for a man who as a boy had been labelled 'stupid'. Billy left school at fifteen years old, along with many of his friends who were not considered candidates for higher education. His academic shortcomings had become more and more apparent to those who subscribed to the notion that intelligence is the ability to do maths and write essays that have a Beginning, a Middle and an End.

Billy certainly does have an extraordinary, creative intelligence but, early on, he did not have a key to his unique filing system. Now that key is miraculously found when he gets on stage. He has filed away an astonishing wealth of otherwise useless information that emerges only during his show. His kindred spirit, he says, is the actor Sir Michael Caine, who is given to ending his idiosyncratic trivia vignettes with the words, 'Not many people know that.' Billy adores Michael as a fellow potato-grower, thespian, and head-chatter merchant. 'He's the only man I know who thinks a bit like me,' he declares.

With school behind him, Billy had to decide on a career path and join the workforce. He had been drawn to engineering, although he told his science teacher, Bill Sheridan, that he aspired to be a comedian. 'Well, I saw you playing football at lunchtime,' said Mr Sheridan, 'and I think you've already achieved your ambition.'

Billy became a messenger boy in John Smith's bookstore, delivering books to readers all over Glasgow and beyond. In between deliveries he sat in a tiny space beside the dispatch desk, exactly at eye level to a range of Nevil Shute novels. 'Might as well give them a go,' thought Billy.

He began with *A Town Like Alice* and tore through every one, for he appreciated Shute's simple storytelling style. Next he found his way to the Robert Burns shelf, and laughed out loud at his poem *To a Louse*. Billy thoroughly connected to the national bard's outrageous and irreverent notion of writing a poem to a louse he spied crawling around the bonnet of a woman he saw in church. He has had a passion for Burns ever since.

Billy did not last long at John Smith's. He had been puzzled when he noticed some fellow employees throwing what seemed to be perfectly good books into the dustbin outside the back door. The men were operating a book-stealing scam, and Billy became one of the casualties of a purge that occurred when the thefts were discovered.

There was an opening at Bilsland's Bakery in Anderston, so Billy became a van boy, delivering bread and cakes to grocers as far away as Bathgate and Armadale on the road to Edinburgh. Later on he helped out on the run to Paisley, adjacent to Glasgow. The bakery is now some other business, but Billy says you can still see the square chimney tower displaying 'Bilsland's Bread' from certain rooms in the Hilton Hotel.

Billy thought the van drivers were hilarious patter merchants, always cracking jokes and making irreverent asides about the management. Tony Roper, who later became an actor and director, was a driver-in-training when Billy met him. He was a sharp-looking chap, with Tony Curtis hair, long bug-ladders (sideburns) and drainpipe trousers. He had shortened his brown bakery coat in order to complete the teddy-boy look.

The drivers and delivery boys got a very early start, first congregating in the bakery canteen to make themselves sandwiches with the fresh-baked bread, then swishing down tea from a jam jar at their first delivery stop. Billy was learning new and vital universal truths, such as the dangers of eating a fried egg sandwich while standing up; when he bit into it, the yolk would explode and fly down the sleeve of his Bilsland's jacket. Egg stain, he noted, is nature's Superglue.

The Bilsland's management issued cotton work coats to protect the delivery team from looking like giant floured cutlets when they returned home. At first these jackets were a faded hazelnut-brown but, shortly after Billy started in the job, there was a policy change that turned out to be a drastic mistake. Billy was among the few who were delighted when Bilsland's issued new green jackets with a yellow half-belt to replace the old brown ones. The management had failed to realize that the new uniforms represented a victory for the green-wearing Celtic supporters and there was uproar by employees who happened to be blue-wearing Rangers supporters. They insisted that, for the good of the company, there was still plenty of wear in the old brown coats, so they carried on wearing them.

Billy hankered after a job that involved travelling to exotic foreign parts. On his way to school, he had crossed the River Clyde every day on ferries run by Highland men. 'Mind your foots!' they would shout. Chugging across the Clyde, Billy had been able to observe welders at work in the shipyards, as well as ocean-going whisky ships that regularly crossed the Atlantic to the United States of America. Billy became desperate to go away to sea, to the interesting-sounding places where the ships had been registered ... Arabia and Shanghai, Baltimore and Tierra del Fuego. The steamers provided constant proof that there was a whole fascinating world out there, ready to be visited.

'I think I'll join the merchant navy,' he announced.

'You're off yer head ... they're all homosexuals in that outfit!' his father thundered, in a staggering display of denial and homophobia.

So Billy applied for a job where he thought no self-respecting gay man would ever be found, as a tradesman in the shipyards. 'I became a welder to escape the worst excesses of homosexuality,' he explains to people, with a large degree of truthfulness.

The various shipyards on the River Clyde provided the most employment in Glasgow at the time. The shipbuilding industry had grown massively since the first shipyard opened in Govan in 1840. When Billy was taken on as a welding apprentice in Stephen's Shipyard, the industry appeared to be a thriving, testosterone-driven domain. No one would have predicted then that its glory days were over and that, by 1980, the docks would be empty, with just a few rusty cranes rising out of vast riverside wastelands.

While lamenting the demise of Glasgow's shipyards, Billy appreciates one positive effect: 'Glasgow used to be a black city,' he says. 'It looked as though it had been drawn in ink. Now it's lost its industry, Glasgow looks like a watercolour. It's as though someone has learned to work the skylight.'

Billy remains unshakably nostalgic about the Clyde. 'The Clyde almost runs through my veins ... I touched it all my life.'

The schools along the Clyde fed the shipyards with employees. The neophyte entering them was in for a great cultural shock, for when the massive gates closed behind them, it was a very male society. At the end of the day, the horn would go 'whooo!' and thousands of 'bunnets' would run out, the lame workers first in case the able-bodied tradesmen ran over them. 'If you were just driving innocently by and saw that,' observes Billy, 'you'd say, "Fuck! Those shipyards are a bit rough, aren't they?"'

Before taking up his apprenticeship, Billy was required to work in other shipyard jobs until his sixteenth birthday, so he first helped out in the joiner's store, sorting out screws, hinges and other supplies. His supervisor, a tall, one-legged man in his fifties called Willie Bain, liked to entertain himself by putting the wind up his new assistants. He would complain loudly and pointedly about not being able to get the kinds of boys he wanted, and he had Billy quite terrified of running errands to the cellar.

'Mind them rats now! They're the size of collie dogs!' he would shout, adjusting his cloth cap. On Billy's first day, Willie took him to visit the glue-maker. It was important to be friendly with the man up at the glue pots because he might let a boy heat up his lunch pie on his stove. It was just before morning break when they stopped by the glue-maker's hut. 'Right Tam, we've got a new boy.'

'Aye, right,' said the glue man, wiping his hands on his messy overalls. He hurried over to peer closely at Billy's face for a few seconds. Billy was intrigued by the man's bunnet, stiff and greasy with the putrid stuff he created. Then the glue man stood back and squinted at him through half-shut eyes. 'Turn him round. Aye.' He surveyed his profile. 'Aye, turn him the other way. Turn him right round again. Aye ...' There was a short pause. 'Catholic!' he pronounced confidently. Apparently, the glue man had never been wrong.

Billy's first day as a full welding apprentice, the day he turned sixteen, was unbearable because of the noise. All around him, men were working with machinery that screeched and whined as it sliced through metal. The caulkers, whose job it was to make the ships watertight, were hammering with pneumatic tools that sounded like machine-guns fired at close quarters. The noise was so ear-splitting, Billy never thought he'd last the week but, within a few days, he had suffered permanent partial hearing loss, so it became quite bearable.

Every one of Billy's senses was assaulted. The searing light that showered out from welders' equipment nipped his eyes, while a putrid stench from the adjacent sewerage works wafted around his nostrils, overlaid with the sweet, sticky odour of HP sauce, jam or biscuits, depending on the cooking schedule at the nearby co-operative factory. Nowadays, Billy loves the Australian phrase, 'That smells like someone just puked in a gardenia patch' (it has to be said with the right accent). The expression takes him right back to the shipyards.

A group of sixteen-year-olds: Christopher Lewis, Hector Clydesdale, Ginger Brown, Joe West, George Picket and Billy all started their apprenticeship together in 1958. They were a lively collection of lads who were about to go through a great deal together, including puberty.

Christopher Lewis, known as Wee Lewie, was six inches smaller than the rest. Billy himself was only five feet tall and could get a child's fare on the bus until he was seventeen, so he was relieved to have Wee Lewie to look down on. Lewie was a dark, pointy-featured imp who was always the ringleader when it came to any kind of mischief. Hector was his physical opposite, a strong, sturdy lad from Maryhill. He was more mature than the others but was severely teased because his middle name was his mother's maiden name, which made him 'Hector Jolly Clydesdale'.

Ginger had the nicest red hair Billy had ever seen on a man. He was a very friendly soul, as was George, a lanky, die-hard Celtic fan. Billy already knew Joe since their first day at primary school. They had attended St Gerard's together, and Joe had even been at Bilsland's for a few weeks while he was saving up money to go to Lourdes. Joe was a handsome leader, very popular with the girls, and Billy emulated him in the way he smoked, dressed, and went dancing at the weekend. Joe, on the other hand, had always felt sorry for 'Wee Billy', as he called him. Sensing his shyness and sensitivity, he tried to protect him.

The expert-in-charge who taught them all to weld was Willie Hughes, a lovely, fat man with a moustache who resembled King Farouk of Egypt and was appropriately nicknamed. Farouk would never be seen without his soft hat because he was as bald as a baby's bum. He was a true shipyard man, born in Taransay Street, a road in Govan that had houses on one side and the shipyards on the other.

All the apprentices had expected to be conscripted into the army, but had missed it by eighteen months, when National Service was abolished. Billy was terribly disappointed; he had been looking forward to being in the forces like his father and flying off to see the world. He had noticed that his slightly older contemporaries who went to the army were men when they came back. They had only been abroad for a couple of years, but their voices were deeper and they had all sorts of clever tales to tell, of visiting exotic places and meeting fascinating people from other cultures.

The boys knew Farouk had fascinating war tales to tell and, when they were fed up with welding, they would seduce him with his own nostalgia. 'Were you ever in France?'

'Och, aye.' He would then launch into some hair-raising story in which his regiment served as cannon fodder for a beach landing.

Their welding school was about eight by twelve feet and each apprentice had a welding cubicle that was safely partitioned off from the harmful rays of his neighbour. The boys practised welding pieces of scrap metal together in every possible position: flat, curved, overhead and vertical. After being cloistered together there for a few months, the novices were finally allowed out to work with other tradesmen. Once in the main section they did the preparatory job of tacking, applying tiny temporary welds to hold a stretch of prefabricated ship section together until a journeyman came along to complete the work.

The apprentices were distinguishable from the fully-fledged welders by their jackets, which were brand-new, ivory-coloured rawhide. More experienced men's were rust-coloured and thoroughly worn. Everything the apprentices had was new-looking. Their tea cans were shiny, their steel toe-cap boots, known as 'steelies', were unscuffed and their jeans were pristine. Everybody else was in rags with the general ruftytuftyness of the shipyard life, and Billy just couldn't wait to be all torn and tattered, not least because it might save him from being a recipient of journeymen's japes. 'Eh, Wee Yin!' A crowd of seasoned welders would beckon him over. 'Will ye run to the store and get us a bubble for the spirit-level and a pot of tartan paint!'

Eager to please, Billy would unwittingly head off on a wild goose chase. After waiting half an hour in the store when he'd been sent on an errand for 'a long stand' and fending off ridicule when he asked for 'a couple of sky hooks', he decided not to be so easily fooled the next time.

'Scurry off and get some Carborundum!'

'No fucking way,' he contended, soliciting a tongue-lashing from Willie Hughes, who truly did need the oddly named grinding paste.

At the apprentice school, the boys had general schooling and instruction in matters of welding, metallurgy, citizenship, and general knowledge. The apprentices learned, for example, that prefabrication was the most important new development in shipbuilding, and was the speciality of the yard where Billy worked. Instead of building the entire ship outdoors, plate by plate, the welders assembled large chunks indoors in building bays, and then took them outside to be joined to other structures. Other tradesmen generally envied welders: theirs was the newest trade and they were the highest-paid workers in the shipyards.

One afternoon, apprentices to a multitude of trades from all over the Clyde were given time off to attend a screening of the Oscar-winning documentary called *Seaward the Great Ships*. It was all about shipbuilding right there where they worked. They had eagerly awaited being transported to the Lyceum cinema in Govan, but the outing turned into a dreadful shambles. Some of the boys had sneaked a quick pint at lunchtime, and the mood in the theatre was already quite lively. A few minutes into the screening, the narrator intoned the fatal words, 'And then came the welders, the kings of prefabrication.' That did it. A big roar of self-approval went up from the welders.

'Shut the fuck up,' shouted everyone else.

A great shangie started, in which the welding apprentices were set upon and walloped by apprentices from every other trade. The film flickered off to a white screen, the lights came on and the entire audience was ejected from the cinema in disgrace.

Billy's happy band of apprentices lived to fight another day. Their antics were reminiscent of his boyhood cronies and their mischievous games, only now they were playing with grown-up toys. They were always setting traps for people and playing irritating and dangerous pranks.

Wee Lewie, who was usually at the forefront, invented a legendary trick. There were always bits of steel lying around on the decks, and it was the job of an elderly worker to pick them up and load them onto his wheelbarrow for removal. One particular day, he parked his wheelbarrow in one of the building bays and went off looking for scrap. Lewie dragged the wheelbarrow a yard or two and welded it to a strip of metal that was used to earth machinery. After the unfortunate worker returned and filled it with scrap he found the wheelbarrow impossible to lift. Thinking it was now too heavy, he started removing his scrap one piece at a time to try to make it lighter. The wheelbarrow was nearly empty by the time the old man realized it was welded fast to the deck. If only he had scanned the upper deck earlier, he would have spotted five or six apprentices watching him, trying to stifle their laughter.

Another great trick Lewie invented was an extremely dangerous one. He would beg a paper bag from someone's lunchtime sandwiches and use an oxyacetylene torch to fill it with flammable gas, tying it up with a bit of string once it was fully inflated. Then, on a makeshift pulley, he would lower this bomb down several decks to the riveters' fire on the floor of the engine room, where a worker would be heating up the rivets until they were nearly white-hot. As soon as this man turned his back to throw a supply to the riveters, Wee Lewie would lower the bag towards the fire, until boom! It would explode. Charcoal and loose debris would fly all over the place.

Billy found himself in trouble for his own favourite trick, which involved giving people electric shocks. It was a two-man operation. When it rained and there were puddles on the deck, an accomplice would loiter on the deck quite close to a designated puddle. Billy would wait underneath the deck with his welding equipment, directly under this puddle and, when someone was walking through it, his accomplice would signal Billy by knocking twice on the deck with a piece of metal. Then Billy would zap the victim from underneath by creating an electric current through the puddle and giving him a very nasty buzz. Next time it would be Billy's turn on top to see the effect. One of his accomplices in that dastardly trick is now the Lord Provost of Glasgow, Alec Mawson, who used to be a plater. All the apprentices thought this was a scream. The shocked and furious men would try to murder the young perpetrators, and would chase them for miles throwing nuts and bolts, anything within reach, but Billy could run like a deer when he was sixteen. 'If I catch you, I'm gonna hang yer jaw off yer face, you wee crawbag!'

Considering the number of pranks they played, it is amazing Billy was only caught once. There was a beefy caulker called Sammy who wore a Rangers scarf to work, and very unwisely, Billy decided to taunt him up close one day, relying on his swift-footed ability to escape with impunity. 'Eh, Sammy! You're a big blue-nose bastard!' This was the term of insult for a Rangers supporter. As planned, Billy took off like the wind, but he tripped over a bucket and Sammy managed to seize him by the throat. 'You little Fenian tosspot! I've a good mind to wring yer neck!'

Serendipitously, Sammy noticed a pot of blue carpenters' paint lying on the deck, used for marking the next job. In an inspired act of retaliation, he painted Billy's nose until it was completely blue and held him there till it was dry. Billy received his just deserts when he had to walk through the whole shipyard to get turpentine paint remover from the ambulance room. People were laughing for miles.

There was a surrealist sensibility lurking in the minds of the apprentice tricksters. They were fond of daubing the heels of workers' boots with silver paint, achieved by lying in wait on the deck below. The apprentices found surprisingly sophisticated amusement in the fact that, although everyone on the shipyards was drab and dirty, selected victims unknowingly had silver heels.

Less sophisticated was the trick that involved bending a welding rod into an 'S' shape, skewering a piece of greaseproof sandwich paper onto it, then hanging it from the back half-belt of someone's overalls. The recipient would trot around sporting his tail, to the great merriment of the pranksters. It was considered an even greater wheeze to set the tail on fire, so the victim would stride for yards with flames licking up his backside.

Billy looks back and says it was lovely then, being a man in a man's world; but in that first couple of years he was really only a youth in a man's world. Being with men all the time, however, was helping him to become more mature and independent. Even so, Mona still attacked him whenever she got the chance. When Billy arrived home after work, she would start on him with her sarcasm: 'Oh, look who it is! Willie the welder.'

Billy would protest, 'Your father was a shipyard worker!'

'Well, I've got a *profession*!' Mona would sneer.

Billy escaped from the house whenever he could. His father gave him a new bicycle, a deep burgundy Flying Scot, which he once thought was a thing of astounding beauty and grace. He cycled for miles at a time, sometimes way over the hill called the 'Rest and be Thankful' and as far as Dunoon, where he believed his mother lived. He was full of imaginings about her, wondering what she looked like now, and if she had other children. He couldn't remember her face, but he would occasionally fix his attention onto some wild-looking woman in the street and wonder if she were Mamie. The aunts had said she was violent, that she had once turned up at their door with a knife: it was all so confusing. Saddened by feeling geographically closer to her, he would take the ferry across the Clyde to Gourock and cycle the long way home.

Some days Billy cycled to his grandparents' house. Big Neilly would address him on tiptoe with his hands behind his back. 'A pound in the bank's your best friend,' he would say, being given to lecturing rather than conversing. When he showed his grandson his gardening secret of throwing tea and eggshells onto his prized sweet peas to make them flourish, Billy thought he was a magician. In a way he was, for one day he produced a trump card, seemingly out of nowhere. 'Your mother's in town,' he said as Billy arrived for a visit. Big Neilly handed him a written address.

'Is my ... mother in?' Billy gurgled to an unknown man who answered the door to a strange house.

'Come in.'

Just inside, he was utterly shaken to see Mamie standing right there in the dark hallway, wearing a camel-hair coat. She seemed pleasant, not like the demon that had been served up to him.

'Oh, hello Billy,' she said and gave him a little hug. She took him out into the street but he could barely see her in the twilight.

'Well, it's been nice meeting you,' she added quite casually, sending him on his way.

The meeting Billy had been building up to for twelve years had lasted less than three minutes. He was initially just embarrassed. He cycled off home, thinking, 'What the hell was that? What just happened?'

For a number of days, Billy couldn't make sense of it at all, but eventually he began to feel fury. Deep, uncontrollable, primitive rage. He couldn't have articulated it at the time, but he felt cruelly violated in yet another way, robbed of the opportunity to be the 'prodigal' son to a 'prodigal' mother. In the fantasy he'd longed for his whole life, the moment was supposed to be a reciprocal one, where she scooped him into her arms, told him she was sorry for leaving and promised they'd never again be apart. He was furious too, at the divisive lies of his family.

'She's attractive!' He was indignant ... 'She's a nice shape. Brown suede shoes. Hair is nice. This is not the person who has been described to me: some wild woman with a knife. Big fucking anti-climax from where I'm sitting.'

~

Billy became a member of Stephen's Apprentice Boys Club and attended weekend outings at various youth hostels all over the countryside. His cousin John often accompanied him. They would join in the merry throng, peeling potatoes for dinner just like in the army and eating rice pudding, heavy with currants and raisins. The real object of these outings was to keep young apprentices away from the fleshpots of Partick and Govan, in particular to keep them from drinking, which was a major occupation of most Clydeside workers.

Being the tricksters they were, John and Billy got up to a variety of shenanigans in the hostels. One of their favourite tricks was slicing people's bananas inside the skin: holding the banana vertical, they would carefully stick a sewing needle into it at right angles, then move it from side to side so it dissected the flesh. They repeated this at one-inch intervals all the way down the banana.

In another ingenious operation, they would steal a person's egg, make a minute hole in both ends and blow it empty. Then they wrote an 'Excuse me' note on delicately rolled-up toilet paper and slid it inside the egg. People who went to bed with their socks on were prime targets for the cousins. When one of these innocents was asleep, Billy and John would remove one sock and put it on top of the other. They thought it was hilarious fun to watch the victim searching in vain for his missing sock the next morning.

At home in the evenings, Billy and John hung out with girls in the street. Billy fell in love with red-haired Jeanette Canning, who lived next door to John in Drumchapel, and they went for walks together in the woodlands. 'The blood was draining into my willie,' says Billy. Previously he had not been very lucky with girls. At school he had fancied Anne Mallinson from afar, but his only contact had been occasionally swimming with her in the Clyde. Billy had summoned the courage to ask Rena Connell, a beautiful and popular girl, to accompany him to a dance, but she had jived with him once and then vanished; he later heard she married a policeman.

~

Billy was an apprentice for five years. His wages started off at only two pounds, six shillings and five pence, but he was learning a trade so the future looked promising. Billy still hankered after being an engineer, perhaps a marine engineer, but the two certificates he had got from school hadn't helped him to get into engineering. According to Gus McDonald, who worked as an apprentice fitter in the same shipyard and recently took his seat in the House of Lords, the general mood on the Clyde was that Protestants got engineering, and Catholics got the black squad. Billy did know Catholics who became engineers, but they were in the minority. Gus was a big shot in the shipyard, active in the union and quite famous among the boys; Billy has always admired him.

Billy lionized a great many of the more experienced shipyard workers, and was thoroughly amused by others. Hughie Gilchrist was a rogue, an older welder with a hilarious take on life whom everyone liked. He always had salacious stories about attractive women he'd escorted home after the dancing on Saturday night. The man who set up temporary lights for the welders, the 'TL' man, wore a surgical boot and limped around moaning endlessly. As a sideline he sold his fellow workers Embassy tipped cigarettes, which came with coupons except that he kept the coupons. He was a chain-smoker, never removing a cigarette from his mouth long enough to ash it, so there was always a disgusting, long grey stripe on his overalls. Welders said Ash Wednesday had been named after him.

He had a rattling, chesty cough that volcanoed up from the soles of his feet. 'That's some cough you've got!' remarked Billy one morning.

'Och, rubbish!' protested the TL man. 'The graveyard's full of people who would love my cough!'

The men Billy most wanted to emulate were the patter merchants. Some of the men were very funny when they blethered about everyday situations, their work, their mates, or the foreman: 'Watch that sleekit bastard. Never play darts with him. Have you seen him throwing cigarettes at the gaffer's mouth?'

It was survival humour; very accurate and raw. Some of it was racist, some of it about sex, and a lot of it was about religion. Billy found he could get a certain cachet with the big guys through his own comic turns. Jimmy Lucas, Bobby Dalgleish, and Willie McInnes heard him doing his Pilton Road-based impressions of pie-eyed people, singing at parties. 'Eh, Connolly, come here. Give the boys some of that gallus singing.'

Billy's brilliant portrayal of drunken would-be-crooners still has audiences clutching their stomachs. Quite a bit of his comedy, in fact, can be traced to his shipyard days. It gave him an excuse to sit with the fully-fledged welders at lunch, a rare opportunity for Billy to absorb their style, their one-liners and their manliness. They would heat a piece of metal until it was red-hot and toast their cheese sandwiches on it while Billy sat basking in the glow of their approval.

Lucas and Dalgleish were both Protestants from Greenock and, occasionally, they would stage their own mini Orange March, trudging up and down whistling 'The Sash My Father Wore' and 'We'll Guard Old Derry's Walls'. Billy would add to the authenticity of this parade by wrapping a piece of cloth around his apprentice's wire brush and crashing this makeshift drumstick off every metal surface in sight in time to their footsteps.

After they had wolfed down their lunch, Billy and his pals usually played football, but, if the weather was too foul, they would gamble with a dilapidated deck of cards. Three-card brag was a favourite: it resembled poker, at a penny a go. Wee Lewie turned out to be a genius player – a trickster, in fact. He could deal from the bottom of the pack and was always getting caught and having his arse kicked for it.

When they played football, Billy was the goalkeeper. He was chosen for that position because he was a rotten outfield player; however he was brave and funny and a great object of amusement as he belly-flopped in vain. As Billy grew taller and broader, he was able to handle the ball better. To his relief, he shot up rapidly in his seventeenth year. Welders used to pull him to the side and marvel, 'Look at this fucker growing!' They would stand him flat against the wall and look him over intently, as if they could see him lengthening before their very eyes.

Lunchtime football was a riot. There was a mentally retarded shipyard sweeper who got carried away with the excitement of it all. He would appear from nowhere and just dive into the middle of the game, desperate to get a kick of the ball. Everybody loved him and a big roar would go up from the welders when he leapt into the fray, tackling everyone within reach. Just before the summer break, some of the older welders cut the shape of a trophy out of sheet metal and awarded him 'Player of the Year'. He was carried triumphantly around the park, and although he had no idea why, he knew it was a good thing and held the trophy high.

One group of shipyard workers never ever played football. The French polishers, who worked next door to the welding school, were the only women in the shipyard, apart from the office girls. They dressed in overalls just like the men, but wore headscarves instead of cloth caps. Billy and the others were quite terrified of them. The story was, if they caught a young apprentice they would put his willie in a milk bottle and tickle his testicles until he got an erection. The only way the bottle could then be removed was by smashing it. It was just like the myth about Santa: everyone believed it until a certain point.

Women had been useful for labour during the war but were now generally being ousted from the workforce and sent back to the home and kitchen. In keeping with the zeitgeist that emphasized the dangers of working women, there was a great shipyard legend about a crowd of welders who were waiting outside their store for supplies of welding rods, gloves, or helmets. A French polisher was running past, late for work, and one of these welders shouted: 'Don't run dear, you'll heat your water!'

OXYACETYLENE ANTICS

Without missing a beat this girl squawked back: 'Well you won't scald your cock in it anyway.'

Apparently the man never said another funny word his whole life.

5

SHAVING ROUND THE ACNE

It is Bel Air, California in the year 2000. At a dinner party in the very mansion that served as the exterior location for the television show *The Beverly Hillbillies*, Billy is holding court, surrounded by legendary actors and musicians. His beloved friend Sidney Poitier has completely lost his elder statesman decorum, and is rocking back and forth in his chair clutching his stomach and howling.

When the meal is over, we all adjourn down a flight of stairs to an opulent basement and take our seats before a small velvet-curtained stage. The lights are dimmed, and a private cabaret begins. The star is one of Billy's early idols, the jazz crooner Billy Eckstine. He sings his best-known hit 'Passing Strangers' to a small jazz combo, and follows it with 'Cottage for Sale'. In the light spilling from the stage, I catch a glimpse of Billy's face. He is rapt, motionless, and not entirely present. At the end of the evening, I ask him where his thoughts had taken him during the show. 'The Locarno,' he says.

~

The Locarno at Charing Cross was the most sophisticated dance hall in Glasgow at the time. Hundreds of jazzy types jived and smooched around the huge dance floor to the hit records of the time, or to live bands performing on the Locarno's revolving stage. Chuck Berry, with his famous 'duck walk', was Billy's favourite rock 'n' roll artist, but he also adored Bill Haley, the check-suited man who rocked around the clock with his Comets, as well as the stylish glottal-stopper, Buddy Holly. Rhythm-and-blues pianists wailed for his attention: Fats Domino yowling 'Blueberry Hill', the dapper Little Richard with his pencil moustache and Jerry Lee Lewis, with his quiff-shaking gymnastics and downright insanity.

There was a shirt around at the time named after Billy Eckstine, with a rolled, cut-away collar. Whenever he went dancing with Anna Clarke, Billy always wore one of these with a striped, three-button Italian-style suit, a thin tie and flat black Palermo shoes. Remembering his early grooming attempts, Billy still winces. 'I tried to shave round the acne,' he says, 'but I usually looked like a butcher's window.'

Joe West had been courting since he was fourteen and a half, and had shown Billy how to dress and where to get the latest Perry Como hairstyle. The day Billy bought his first Italian suit was a proud one for him. It was a rite of passage for young men in the west of Scotland, getting a first suit on hire-purchase and paying for it out of wages every month.

One day, Billy came home from work to find that Mona had gone through his suit pockets and found an erotic poem some other apprentice gave him. It was called *Mexico Pete and Eskimo Nell*. 'We're going to have to let your father know about this,' Mona informed him in her sly, sadistic way. 'I'm not going to tell you when he'll be informed, so you're just going to come in here every night wondering ... and you'll never know when he's going to kill you for it.' She made him wait roughly two whole years. In the end, William's volatile 'I'm disappointed in you' reaction paled by comparison to the threat of discovery that had been held over Billy by Mona.

At seventeen, Billy was madly in love with Anna. He judged her to be very posh because she lived in a bungalow in Bearsden. Billy appreciated her gentleness and refined way of speaking. Reeking of Old Spice, he took her to the cinema or to local dances, although he could barely afford it because, as well as his suit, he was paying off a BSA 250 motorbike.

It was Marlon Brando's fault: his role in *The Wild One* is surely responsible for millions upon millions of once-loved bicycles being left to rot and rust in lieu of a Harley-Davidson, BSA or Kawasaki. Cycling as a hobby fell by the wayside once Billy became attracted by the exotic appearance of the leather people he saw posing in Jaconelli's in Maryhill or the Hillfoot Café in Bearsden.

The clientele of those cafés, men like Mick Quinn, in his Bronx leather jacket, and Jimmy Hogg, who was the first man Billy ever saw with really long hair, were funny, sharp men who seemed to be magnets for beautiful women. Billy tried hard to be one of the gang, but they hardly gave him the time of day ... in fact they were downright insulting, calling him 'Cinderella' because his father made him be home by midnight. The nickname was appropriate for an innocent such as he. 'I knew nothing about dating,' shrugs Billy. 'I was always wondering what you pressed to make it work, and trying to avoid saying things like "You don't sweat much for a fat girl".'

Paying off the motorbike severely limited Billy's funds. If he and Anna went to the cinema, he had to borrow money for a Coca-Cola, as girls didn't contribute in those days. When they broke up after going out together for a whole year, Billy turned to records by the Everly Brothers for consolation. 'Cathy's Clown', harmonized to the soulful strumming of acoustic guitars, seemed to reflect his teenage angst.

Later, Billy met June McQueen while jiving and he took her to the Locarno and other dance halls that Joe West recommended. Joe also pointed Billy in the direction of the Barrowland Ballroom on Gallowgate. The place is still there with the original dance floor and illuminated red, blue and gold stars adorning a fifties-style façade.

At the top of fifty stairs stood a frightening-looking bouncer with a huge scar on his cheek, watching would-be patrons climb up for a shuffle around the massive wooden dance floor to the live sounds of Billy McGregor and the Gaybirds. If the bouncer saw a punter stagger during the ascent, he would refuse him entry. Some determined drunkards would go back down the stairs, change their coats, then try again.

You had to behave properly inside as well or you would be flung out. Billy remembers seeing his own feet following him down the stairs as he landed unceremoniously on his backside in the middle of Gallowgate. 'My coat!' he protested. The bouncer had heard it all before. 'Gies yer ticket!' he growled. Billy's jacket was soon pitched straight out, down into a freezing puddle.

The Barrowland Ballroom is across the street from the Saracen's Head cider shop, known as the 'Sarrie Heid'. That's where Billy first began to appreciate the taste of a foaming pint of Coates Triple Vintage or, indeed, any old Scrumpy. The Sarrie is generally thought to be very rough now, but I think it's charming, with an intriguing history. Back in the eighteenth century it was a stagecoach inn, visited by Wordsworth and Samuel Taylor Coleridge. Even Dr Johnson, travelling around the Hebrides with his celebrated biographer Boswell, plonked himself down on a chair in front of the hearth and exclaimed, 'Thank God for the sight of a coal fire again!'

Billy's welding pal, Hughie Gilchrist, invented the 'drinking coat' expressly for use in the Sarrie. It was a plastic Pak-a-Mac that buttoned up at the neck. A Sarrie patron wore it to save his good suit from being wasted by splashes of cider that Angus the barman would slosh on people as he lifted eight pints above their heads. Hughie was a practical chap whose other claim to fame was the two-week camping holiday he went on, taking nothing but a bottle of wine, a drinking coat and a spoon.

Drinking cider was only one of several rites of passage Billy achieved in his late teens. At seventeen, he was delighted to have a batch of new apprentices to whom he could appear superior. His jacket was much darker than theirs and he knew the shipyard slang, or 'patter'.

He quickly memorized the insults designed for men of each of the various trades. 'You couldnae tack the high road!' was reserved for welders, while an electrician who fumbled a job was told, 'You couldnae get juice out of a Jaffa.' Metal workers, known as 'platers', were taunted with the jibe: 'You couldnae plate soup', while the ultimate insult for joiners was: 'You couldnae join hands at a party!'

Billy had learned how to glide with ease through the place, working the system as best he could. Now he was out among the tradesmen all the time, mixing with grown men who were talking about adult things such as women and sex. Billy made tea for the older welders. It was quite lucrative, at two shillings and sixpence per man per week. When the tea was ready, he was allowed to sit with them and listen to the crack, or conversation. Hughie, Andy Canning, Danny Lavery, Geordie Laird and 'Dan the Ham' Hamilton would natter about being in the town dancing with women, and how many jars they could swallow apiece. It all seemed incredibly exciting.

Willie McInnes, known as Bugsy on account of his gargantuan front teeth, got him in a corner one day.

'This bike of yours, how much does it cost?' asked Bugsy. He hated his nickname.

'Six pounds a month,' said Billy. 'I save up.'

'I'll tell you what we'll do,' decided Bugsy. 'You get your wages on a Friday. You'll give me one pound ten on a Monday and then, once a month, I'll give you six pounds to pay your bike.'

The system was implemented, and it continued for the next two years until the bike was fully paid up. The point was to ensure that Bugsy always had one pound ten shillings on a Monday to give his wife. Previously, he was liable to drink away all his wages on the weekend and end up broke on a Monday.

One day at the shipyards, Billy and the older men were all sitting at the fire when one of them said, 'Wee Yin! Saw you in the town there Friday night. Were you dancing?'

'Oh aye.'

They hadn't seen him at all. They were just trying their hand. 'Nice bit of stuff you were with, that wee blonde.' Perhaps Billy had been spotted with a girl he was seeing to the bus after the dancing. 'I must say, you were looking a bit shabby. Yer suit was a bit bare-arsed. How old's that suit?'

'About four months.'

'There, you see. How many suits have you got?'

'Just the one.'

'One's nae use. You need at least two. Change them over, keep them good. Stops them getting wrinkled. What are you, an apprentice? No problem kid, we can get you in.'

An expedition was promptly organized to Tailorfit in Glasgow, where they supervised the fitting-out of the Wee Yin. He got a pale blue Italian suit, shoes and socks, a tie and a shirt and felt like a real dandy. The only problem was, the men didn't pay him tea money any more since they said they were making his suit payments. It took Billy about a year to realize they had been paying off Tailorfit at only ten shillings a week and saving a pound. The scam merchants thought it was the biggest joke in the world, and continued to refer to it for years. 'There now, I saw you in town, son, and you looked as sharp as a tack.'

It was an extraordinary society of men, and in a way Billy's first real family. He loved the human variety. Dan the Ham had Tourette's Syndrome. In the middle of a rainy, blustering gale, Billy would be balancing on two planks of wood, thirty feet in the air, when Dan would suddenly start shouting and jumping. 'Hooowahhhh!' Billy would almost plummet to his death. It was a good thing he'd had plenty of training on the Big Sui.

Dan the Ham made very alarming noises. When they all went for a drink on a Friday, though, Dan would miraculously lose his symptoms. After a pint he could talk perfectly normally and even sing his favourite folk song:

'Lassie with the yellow coatie,
Would you wed a moorland Jockie?'

The shipyard workers were merciless piss-takers. Young apprentices learned early on that it was a huge mistake to admit to an interest of any kind. In an indiscreet moment Billy told one crowd of men he wanted to play the banjo, and that did it. Every time he met them, they would sing George Formby's 'When I'm Cleaning Windows' – they didn't know a banjo from a ukulele.

One poor welder from Troon, who perhaps was not as street-wise as the boys from town, enjoyed ballroom dancing in the evenings. Billy witnessed his destruction, one afternoon by the fire.

'I saw you shuffling about there, John, at the bottom of the tank.' Billy could see the poor boy falling into the trap.

'Aye, I was practising,' John replied.

'Oh, practising?'

'Aye, practising my dancing.'

'Aye?'

'Aye, it was a difficult step.'

'Oh, what's that?'

'It's a wee Reverse Birl.' 'Birl' is Scottish for spin, or turn.

The unlucky apprentice became 'The Reverse Birler' from that day on, although, after a while, he was just called 'Reverse'.

As Billy grew older in the shipyards, he became initiated into the ways of the place, and gained a confidence that had previously eluded him. He was mightily influenced by many of his fellow workers, especially one, a sergeant in the Territorial Army. When Billy heard that these part-time soldiers went abroad on exercises, he decided to give it a go and went for a recruitment interview.

'Whatever you do,' warned the sergeant as he led Billy to the red-brick castle-shaped Yorkhill Barracks for his interview, 'don't tell them you want to jump out of aeroplanes or kill people. They'll think you're nuts.'

'Why do you want to enlist?' demanded the Recruiting Sergeant.

'Oh, I'd like a bit of adventure in my life.' Billy has a gift for fiction '... And to serve my country.'

After he passed the colour-blindness and healthy-testicles tests, they put him in camouflage drill and took him up to Kelvingrove Park, where he was asked to run several miles with a full pack in midsummer heat. Billy was one of the fittest specimens and graduated to racing in teams through chemical waste in Springburn while weighed down by telegraph poles.

Undeterred by any of this, Billy moved up from the pre-Para course to the two-week parachute jump course in Abingdon, Oxfordshire, where he learned to pack and check a parachute in the first week and achieved several heart-stopping jumps in the second. His first two were from army barrage balloons and another five jumps were from aircraft. It was thrilling to see the world from the sky. The motto of the Parachute Regiment School turned out to be 'Knowledge Dispels Fear', a notion that might have been helpful back in Stewartville Street. 'It's the ultimate,' he thought, 'it's the Giant Sui.'

During his next three years as a paratrooper, Billy was taught the importance of order and cleanliness and a sense of responsibility for himself and his fellow soldiers that jump-started his maturity. Joe West was amazed that his shy friend had got to the point where he was leaping out of aeroplanes. Billy had never even been in an aeroplane until the day he had to bale out at twelve thousand feet. The whole thing appealed to Billy's *White Fang* sense of adventure, climbing over mountains in the snow and attacking another regiment in the morning. He loved marching to the band, learning to shoot a rifle and sleeping in the rain.

Nowadays, whenever I complain about cold weather, and, having been raised in a sub-tropical climate, I do so quite often, Billy always reorganizes my attire and says, 'There's no such thing as bad weather, only the wrong clothes.' He learned that in the Territorial Army.

Life with the Territorial Army wasn't all outdoor activities. Some evenings, Billy and the other lads went to the seaside town of Carnoustie to drink beer and misbehave. Since the day Billy had dropped in at the Portland Arms in Troon and had his first pint of beer, he had become a pub regular. In The Stag pub one night with a few TA mates, he was urged to sing 'The Wild Side of Life' and was happy to comply. Today, there's a little plaque on the wall in The Stag that reads: 'On This Spot, Billy Connolly Made His First PUBlic Performance.'

In the mess halls, Billy learned to do the 'Dance of the Flaming Arseholes'. When sufficient alcohol had been consumed, there would be a call for volunteers and Billy was only too willing to be one of the madmen who would leap onto the table, trousers down, with a rolled-up page of newspaper sticking out of his jacksie. The end of each wad would be set alight and the nutcases would dance while the others sang,

'Oh the girls in France
Take their knickers down and dance,
Singing Nellie keep your belly close to mine.'

The winner would be the one who pulled his newspaper out last. In the spirit of Cochise, the Big Sui and the cobbler's dunny, Billy never lost a competition.

'You could never accuse him of being shy and retiring,' thought June McQueen, who dated Billy for a year or so, just after he joined the TA. They met in 1963, in Bill McCulloch's Jiving Club near the Botanic Gardens. When June first saw him, Billy was making a lot of noise, singing 'Kelly Please, Please Tell Me' and she was very attracted to him. June was seventeen and living in Maryhill at the time. Billy asked her for a dance, then walked her home that night.

The pair began to see each other three or four times a week for dancing and the cinema. Sometimes they would go out with another couple and the boys would dart into the pub for a quick pint while the girls just kept walking. Billy was always clowning around, giving her piggy-backs and showing off but, after a while, June saw that he had another side that was soft, sensitive and insecure. She felt protective of him. He in turn was kind to her and brought her small gifts including a pink cuddly toy.

June knew Billy had a problem with Mona, so she was apprehensive when she went to his house one evening, bearing a gift bag of sweets for his aunt. Billy had revealed that Mona had ripped up the photo of June he'd hidden inside his record player. Not understanding the full extent of Mona's crazy paranoia, June assumed it was mainly to do with religion; she was not a Catholic and Billy's family seemed to be critical of their relationship when it went on too long.

Mona accurately sensed that Billy and June had begun to enjoy some arousing 'winching' in the movies or up by Loch Lomond and, almost as if she were jealous, she herself began to be seductive with Billy, disrobing on some pretext or another when they were alone together. 'I burned myself today,' she whispered to Billy, 'here ...' she would show him one naked breast with not a mark on it, '... and here ...' she flashed her upper thigh. 'She was exactly like Bette Davis in *Whatever Happened to Baby Jane,*' says Billy now. 'I nearly had to leave the theatre when I saw that movie.'

At the end of Billy's twentieth year, he was awarded his TA Parachute Wings. He immediately presented them to June, who has treasured them ever since. Towards the end of that year, Billy achieved his dream of following in his father's footsteps in the forces visiting foreign lands, when he and the Fifteenth Scottish Parachute Regiment went abroad for three weeks of exercises. They landed first in Orange in France, then in Libya and finally in Cyprus where they spent a week in the Kyrenia mountains. Towards the end of that last week, they were surprised by EOKA terrorists who attacked them in the middle of the night. They had to dive for cover and return fire. It was all very exciting at the time, but afterwards Billy wasn't so sure. 'I hope I didn't hit anyone,' he agonized.

On his twenty-first birthday a couple of days later, Billy performed a striptease in a tent in Cyprus, blowing the light out at the vital moment. Even today, he just loves to show his nakedness to the world and has been seen on British television cavorting bare-arsed all over the world in broad daylight, from the magnetic North Pole to Piccadilly Circus.

When the exercises were over, Billy's regiment came down from the Kyrenia mountains and flopped about on the beach, soothing their sore feet in the Mediterranean. After a few moments of relishing their well-earned relaxation time they noticed an elderly Cypriot walking with his donkey towards them. The donkey was carrying baskets of oranges and they wondered if they could buy some of them. 'President of America ... he ... he ... shot ... he is now dead,' the man informed them.

'Jesus,' they said to each other, 'Kennedy? It can't be.'

They drove to Akrotiri RAF Base where they heard the official news of John F. Kennedy's assassination. They were placed on emergency alert in case a world war broke out. Later, Billy heard that Lee Harvey Oswald had been killed on his birthday. 'America's going nuts,' he said.

~

'May I speak to Billy Connolly?' I ask a hotel operator in Sydney, Australia.

'Whom may I say is calling?'

'His wife.'

It is 20 January 2001. The inaugural ceremonies for the new

President of the United States have just ended.

'How's filming going?' I ask.

'Great. Judy Davis reminds me of your sister. What did George W. have to say?'

'Well, it's at least the appearance of "compassionate conservatism". I liked something he said: "Children at risk are not at fault. Abandonment and abuse are not acts of God. They are failures of love ..."'

'That's nice. It's a shame he keeps electrocuting people.'

Billy began to develop a social conscience in the shipyards. The older tradesmen encouraged Billy and the other apprentices to read political works such as George Orwell's *Animal Farm* and *The Ragged Trousered Philanthropists* by Robert Tressell. They wanted the younger men to have a solid grasp of left-wing politics so they could be more active in the union. The aim, they explained, was not just to achieve shorter hours and longer Woodbines, but to be informed so they could eventually take on the employers and truly represent the working man.

Billy fully embraced the notion. He had a mentor at that time, a shop steward called Bill Adams who spent his weekends camping on Loch Lomond. Bill encouraged Billy to consider trying to get a scholarship to Ruskin College in Oxford and become a full-time union official. As time went by, however, Billy went off the idea because he really didn't much like what he saw of union operation in the shipyards then. In his opinion, there was a bullying element to it.

After returning from exercises with the Parachute Regiment, Billy found himself thinking an awful lot about his time away. 'That was ridiculous,' he decided. 'I'm on their side. I don't believe in colonies and forcing people into living a certain way. Cypriots should decide themselves how they want to live, and if they think armies crashing through the country in the middle of the night is a bad thing, I can't say I disagree with them.' He became disillusioned with the Territorial Army and started to wear a Campaign for Nuclear Disarmament badge on his uniform. He was just becoming a nuisance, so they encouraged him to leave and he did.

Billy entered the Territorial Army a private and he left as a private, but in the meantime he had become a different man. He was fascinated by world events, and couldn't understand why his interest was not shared by all his fellow shipyard workers. The Cuban Missile Crisis had come to a head the previous October and the day the United States and Russia were facing off and the world was supposed to end at 3 p.m., most of the young tradespeople had been chattering nervously and watching the clock. 'Ah, shut up and get on with your work,' chided the older ones.

Three o'clock came and went. That evening, as the workers were all pouring out of the shipyard gates, there was a mad dash for the newspapers. Billy expected everyone to be focused on the afternoon's political negotiations that meant they were still alive, but people just turned the papers over to the sports section. They didn't care what Kennedy and Khrushchev were saying – what was the team for Saturday? Billy half respected them for that.

At the age of nineteen, Billy had started growing his beard. He wasn't sure he could sprout successfully, but he gave it his best shot. By the time he was twenty-one, it was ridiculously long and scrawny, and his new nickname was Ho Chi Minh. Shipyard politics caught his attention. A new union was in the process of being formed. It was called DATA – Draughtsmen and Allied Trades Association – and these men wanted to be recognized by their employers. They asked the members of Billy's union to support them in a strike or some kind of demonstration, so there was a meeting of about one hundred men down by the wharf. The shop steward and his assistant stood up on oil drums, higher than everyone else.

'Speak through the Chair, brother!' was the order. The general mood was one of cynicism. 'Those draughtsmen never helped us! When we were on strike they sat in their office drinking tea.'

Billy had never spoken at a union meeting before, but he decided to strike a blow for socialism. When he put up his hand, people started to titter. 'Well, Ho Chi Minh's going to give us a word,' announced Jimmy McPherson, the shop steward. 'Speak through the Chair, Ho Chi Minh!' Billy was nervous, but he began well: 'This is ridiculous, attacking DATA for not supporting us. An attack on DATA is an attack on trade unionism and we have to stand behind them. We're talking about solidarity here.' People were beginning to murmur agreement,

'Some of our loyal brothers have been saying that DATA never stood behind us when we were on strike ...' Then Billy really blew it. He had been reading a little too much P. G. Wodehouse: '... but in the scheme of things, it matters not a jot.' Everyone collapsed with laughter. That was the beginning and end of his political career.

Billy wasn't the only one who was changing. George Picket very abruptly switched football jerseys from Celtic to support the Rangers team. That was absolutely not allowed. Apparently, George had reached a point where he could no longer tolerate the bigotry of the other Celtic supporters, since he himself was Protestant. George became as strong a Rangers supporter as he had been a Celtic teamster and was pilloried for it, although Billy always admired his bravery.

Out of the blue, Geordie Laird, Danny Lavery and Dan the Ham came in to work one day and announced they had all 'found Jesus'. No one could believe it. Danny and Dan in particular had been wild drinking men and, as evangelists, they were just as aggressive. They tried any number of annoying ways to try to convert their fellow workers, such as sneaking tiny Bible tracts into their sandwiches and toolboxes, or floating them down to the engine room.

Wee Lewie was tragically killed that same year. He had been out drinking, and was hit by a car as he stood on a traffic island. Billy and the others missed him dreadfully. It shocked them all rigid; they had always thought Lewie was the kind of lad who could topple into the Clyde and come up with a fish supper.

A disquieting change occurred at home too. One evening, Billy came home from work and found Mona sitting quietly on the couch. Usually she was in the kitchen but, right now, she was just sitting, staring blankly.

'Hello,' said Billy.

'Hello,' she returned. She seemed quite nice, which immediately made Billy suspicious.

'What time is it?' asked Mona. She had a clock right in front of her, but Billy told her anyway. Then she said, 'What time is it?'

Billy told her again. A few minutes later she repeated the question. 'What time is it?'

She asked again, and then again, six times. Finally she said, 'I've had a very hard day today.'

'Really?' said Billy. 'Why was that?'

'That family along the road. The McKees. They've been listening to me with their tape recorder underneath the floor.'

'Where?'

'Under the floor.'

'What are you talking about?' Billy was looking around, trying to spot it.

'Never you mind. They've been listening to us all along.'

It got very weird. Then William came home.

'Something's wrong with Mona,' said Billy.

She was examined by the doctor, who took her away to be locked up in a psychiatric hospital. That's where she spent the rest of her days.

6

WINDSWEPT AND INTERESTING

It's 4 December 2000. I'm halfway down a glorious mountain in Park City, when I finally attract the attention of my twelve-year-old ski instructor, my youngest daughter Scarlett. She loves to wall-ski, and delights in taking me off the beautifully groomed central slopes, deliciously sprinkled with their famous Utah powder, and in among the pine forests where I am frequently ambushed by a shallow tree stump or curvy, child-grooved tracks too short for my skis.

'When we get back to the lodge,' I tell Scarlett, 'if you like, you could phone your father in New York, and remind him that it's my birthday so he won't be embarrassed that he forgot.'

Billy hates every aspect of skiing and complains bitterly about the tendency of the rest of his family to don 'dreadful suits and plummet down a ridiculously steep hill'. That afternoon, he is in his hotel room getting ready to leave for his show when an authoritative twelve-year-old verbally accosts him.

'Dad! What day is it?' she hints heavily.

'Eh, I don't know ...'

'It's the fourth of December!'

'Oh bollocks, I forgot.'

'It's not too late.' (*Sotto voce*) 'Mum's just in the next room.'

The following week, I am just opening my eyes in bed at Candacraig, our Scottish home, when the upper left arm of a man who has been travelling all night is presented three inches from my face.

'I got your birthday gift,' he boasts. 'Open it.'

'Open what?' I mumble.

'It's the best present you ever got! Roll up my sleeve.'

That wakes me. Underneath the tight sleeve of his 'Still Plays With Motorcycles' T-shirt I unearth a fabulous work of art, fashioned in a Manhattan tattoo parlour some time between Scarlett's phone call and his 8 p.m. curtain. It is a proper sailor's love note: a huge swallow over a blushing heart with 'Pamela' and '4th December 2000' etched onto fancy ribbon scrolls. I am suitably impressed. He'll never forget my birthday again ... unless, of course, he forgets to check his biceps.

∾

Billy had wanted a tattoo ever since dabbities began to lose their appeal. There was a tattooist called Prince Vallar in Anderston, very close to Billy's birthplace. On his childhood Sunday walks, Billy would often stop outside and peer in at the human body-art. Brilliantly illustrated sailors lurked outside the parlour, waiting to have 'S-c-o-t-l-a-n-d' tattooed above their knuckles, or swallows etched on their thumbs like the ones they'd seen at sea, migrating to South Africa. Billy always fancied having a great fanged serpent wrapped around a rampant lion covering his entire chest. In truth, what he really craved was to be incredibly exotic, and that desire has never left him.

Jack's Dolls' Hospital was another stopping point on those Sunday walks. Florence loitered happily, sighing through the window at the intricately painted, reconditioned porcelain maidens. Billy, mean-while, would inspect the instruments in the music shop next door. He had many questions about guitars, but his father called every-thing a 'banjo': a guitar was a banjo, a mandolin was a banjo.

William's musical tastes were limited to the vocal gymnastics of Irish tenors like Count John McCormack, or Canon Sydney MacEwan, who was a Catholic priest. Billy did not find religious performers appealing in the least, being drawn instead to more glamorous types, particularly those who strummed their instruments and looked like they might have plenty of attractive women hanging on their arms.

Billy became passionate about the rich and plaintive tones of acoustic guitars, especially when strummed by the Everly Brothers. The country singers Hank Williams and Slim Whitman had been his idols since he was a small boy, but those tastes broadened to include the rhinestone crooning of Hank Snow, the soulful twanging of Patsy Cline and Skeeter Davis, and the emergent growlings of Jimmy Rogers. He adored Jean Shepard with her whimsical hit, 'I Forgot More than You'll Ever Know about Him'.

There was a Scottish television show in the fifties called *The White Heather Club* that featured the likes of the Scottish tenor Kenneth McKellar warbling popular Robert Burns songs such as *Ae Fond Kiss* and *My Love is Like a Red, Red Rose*. McKellar was hardly Billy's cup of tea, but occasionally the programme would feature Joe Gordon's Folk Four. Joe played evocative ballads on a jumbo Gibson guitar. At the time, Billy didn't know it was folk music, but he knew it spoke to him.

Other folk music programmes eventually appeared on television, such as *Hootenanny* and *Sing Out*. Billy watched eagerly for a group called Long John Baldry and the Hoochie Coochie Men. He would have loved that name for his own band if he had one, and he was crazy about their bluesy noise that was half rock, half blues-folk. Finally *Alex a While* appeared, introduced by two folk-singing brothers called Alex and Rory McEwan, who had top-notch guests such as Archie Fisher and Martin Carthy. Best of all was the night the American star Pete Seeger came on playing his banjo and singing 'Sacco's Last Letter', a song about a note from a condemned prisoner to his son. Billy just bolted upright in his chair. 'That's it! That's the noise I want to make!'

From that moment on, Billy was mad about the banjo and he still is. At work in the shipyards, he was becoming even more of a fantasist. He would sit in the propeller shaft beside the rudder, legs dangling, having a smoke and gazing dreamily up the Clyde. He'd never even lifted an instrument at that point, but that's where he envisioned his first album sleeve.

At the beginning of 1962, the Connollys moved to a tenement in White Street, in Partick. None of the family had enjoyed living in Drumchapel and, besides, it made sense to do as Florence suggested and purchase a flat with money they'd managed to save, instead of always renting. Billy was relieved to be closer to the centre of Glasgow again, and looked forward to a better social life.

There was a communist bookstore called Clyde Books in Argyle Street that had an unusual collection of records for sale, as well as a range of anarchist and communist literature. Billy ferreted out all kinds of little-known banjo and folk-music recordings by gifted singers like Alex Campbell, who lived in France and busked on the street with Derroll Adams, and Ian Campbell from Aberdeen who played with his sister Lorna. All of these artists made records with left-wing messages that ranged from subtle to emphatic. Billy found that a great deal of folk music had a political edge. Some of it protested the plight of workers who were forced to suffer harsh working conditions or meagre wages, some of it expressed anti-war sentiments, while other songs articulated the pain of oppressed peoples. Billy wallowed in an eclectic conglomeration of musical influences that also included Irish rebel songs, and a wonderful folk album by the New Lost City Ramblers that featured superb banjo playing.

Billy became determined to get a banjo. He traipsed up to the Barrowland market where he was tickled pink to find a battered old zither banjo for two pounds ten shillings. He had no idea what to do with it or how to tune it, but he lugged it home and plinked away as best he could. After a few days of this frustration, he came up with an inspired plan. There was an Information Office in George Square, a place where normally a person might pose the question 'Where can I get the bus for Fort William?' or 'Where are the art galleries?' Billy sauntered up to the counter at noon one Saturday, and boldly addressed the pamphlet-touting woman: 'Excuse me, where I can learn to play the banjo?'

She stared at him for a second or two.

'Just a minute.'

She disappeared for a while, leaving Billy to browse the array of coloured brochures for Mackintosh exhibitions and variety shows.

When the woman returned, she was holding a flyer. 'There's a place just two blocks from here: The Glasgow Folk Centre. They teach banjo, mandolin and guitar on a Saturday afternoon.'

Billy could not believe his luck. He hurried along the street and up some squalid stairs to two curiously wide rooms, probably remnants of Glasgow's mercantile past. Billy could hear the tinkling of a banjo as he approached and, with considerable excitement, in he breezed. Guitar lessons were in session in a broad circle at one end of the first room, while at the other end two or three forlorn-looking renegades were messing around on their banjos.

The teacher, a Bob Dylan lookalike, wrestled Billy's ancient instrument from him, tuned it and showed him a basic strum. At last he could get a harmonious sound from his bargain-find! Billy shut himself in his room that evening and practised as if his life depended on it. Something about the playing of this instrument, perhaps the regular strumming and repetition of phrases, was surprisingly soothing for him. From then on, he and his banjo could barely be prised apart. The teenager who had never before been motivated about anything, quickly became a skilled and stylish banjoist, and surpassed his teacher within a mere six weeks. The Folk Centre had an extensive library of folk music, so Billy was able to borrow records and find some new heroes: Lester Flatt, Earl Scruggs and the versatile Carter Family.

In 1964, Billy found his way to a great Monday-night Folk Attic in Paisley. The resident band was called the Tannahills, after a poet from Paisley, and the lead singer was a stocky little man called Danny Kyle. Billy instantly loved him because he was pricelessly funny and told ridiculous jokes, in between his songs. He learned that Danny was on the receiving end of relentless teasing at the time, as people at the club were saying he had waited till his mother had emigrated to America before he'd dared to grow a beard. After the Tannahills had finished their set, Billy introduced himself to Danny; it was the beginning of a lifelong friendship. 'I'd like to learn how to play the banjo well,' said Billy. 'Good idea,' replied Danny. 'Ron will teach you.'

The Tannahills' banjoist, Ron Duff, was a very experienced player. As it turned out, he preferred to play the guitar so, after a month or two of tutoring Billy, he put him in the band. 'You can take over the banjo now,' he offered. 'I'm glad to see the back of it.'

Billy was really still a novice, but at that time hardly anyone in Glasgow had even seen a banjo, so he got away with it. Billy was jubilant, for his career as a folk musician was launched. He upgraded his banjo to a Windsor Monarch and began to play semi-professionally in the various folk clubs around Glasgow. He continued to practise with a vengeance, ever relishing the metallic droning of the instrument. It was like a mantra for him.

When *The Beverly Hillbillies* came on TV, featuring bluegrass banjo played by Lester Flatt and Earl Scruggs, Billy thought their 'three-finger picking' was terribly impressive and applied himself to adding that style to his repertoire. When Billy learned 'frailing', a type of strumming, from Pete Seeger's book *How to Play the Five-String Banjo*, he was dismayed to discover the technique played havoc with his fingernails. This has been a lifelong problem for Billy. The guitarist John Pearse told him that flamenco guitarists strengthened their worn-down nails with layers of cigarette paper and nail varnish, but Billy found that method far too messy. His friend Hamish Imlach advised him to stuff himself with Jelly Babies, presumably for their gelatine content, but that didn't work, and neither did mountains of raw broccoli. Over the years, Billy has tried commercial liquid nail hardeners, silk wrapping and acrylic nails, none of which have been successful. He now applies several layers of Revlon nail repair kit, carries nail buffers, polish and several grades of files with him at all times, and heaven help anyone who asks him to do a household job that results in a broken nail. 'If anyone peeked inside my banjo case,' confesses Billy, 'they'd think I was a manicurist.'

~

'Ya bastard!' It is autumn 2000 and Billy is on the telephone in a highly excitable state. I am arrested, mid-stride, wondering who has wounded him. 'Ya *bastard!!*' he repeats. Now I'm worried. '*Oh!*' he cries in pain. 'I'm so jealous!'

I walk over, expecting to put a verbal Band-aid on a narcissistic injury. He ends the phone call in a strangely amicable way, considering his verbal angst.

'That was Steve ...' he explains. '... Steve Martin. Lucky bugger!'

'Ahhh ... yes ...' I nod sympathetically. 'He's been asked to present the Oscars, hasn't he?'

'No, no, no,' Billy dismisses that scornfully. 'That's not it ... No, he's just been asked to play his banjo ... "Foggy Mountain Breakdown" no less ... on Earl Scruggs' tribute album!'

~

Billy always wanted to be a great banjo player more than anything else. In the mid-sixties he certainly became better than many around him and began to meet really fine players, like Geordie

McGovern who had very diverse musical tastes and applied banjo to other musical styles, such as jazz.

Billy decided to start his own band, which he called the Skillet Lickers after an American band called Gid Tanner's Skillet Lickers. They were all dead, so Billy thought they wouldn't object if he stole their name. The line-up of the Skillet Lickers was Billy, Geordie McGovern, and another great banjo player called Jim Carey. Billy was the least talented player of the three of them, but he became the official banjo player in the band because Geordie and Jim preferred respectively to play the mandolin and guitar.

What was it about the banjo that meant it was so assiduously avoided by everyone around Billy? For a start, many of his friends in the folk scene thought the banjo was not much of a solo instrument, although as Billy noted, it certainly did Pete Seeger and Derroll Adams no harm at all.

'Banjo players' wives are always driven crazy by the noise,' Billy announced to me a couple of years ago, as if he were telling me something I didn't already know. Hearing a single banjo lick being practised over and over again in your house is a truly torturous experience.

'What's the difference between a banjo and an onion?' I tease him. 'Nobody cries when you slice up a banjo.'

'How many banjo players does it take to change a light bulb?' he returns.

'Just one, but he does it over and over again ...'

Billy has his own take on the 'guitar versus banjo' question: 'People play the guitar to get laid, but they play the banjo because they love the sound it makes. You never hear anyone saying, "See that beautiful woman? She's sleeping with the banjo player."' The former American *Tonight Show* host, Johnny Carson, once said to Billy, 'One of the lines you'll never hear in your life is: "That's the banjo player's Porsche."'

The Skillet Lickers became quite popular, but Billy abandoned them in order to join a group called the Acme Brush Company, a laissez-faire band without set members. Billy was always a part of it because he was mad keen, but no one in Glasgow really knew which players constituted the band because every time they played there was a different line-up. The selection process was an interesting one: on any given evening, if you knew the chords you were the guitarist, while if you knew the words you were the singer. Billy loved having the name of that band on his banjo case. Fellow bus passengers would eye him suspiciously: 'What kind of brush is that?'

Billy says he never played in a band with women in it because he was sick of 'Plaisir D'Amour', a high, warbling ballad sung by Joan Baez emulators that he found particularly annoying. He didn't play much with the mainstream men, either. According to him, the traditional English folk singers were a boring bunch, all with tweed Norfolk jackets, beer bellies and glasses. They were always singing about battles at sea, disasters in mines, or cross-dressing eighteenth-century sailors. Songs about beer barrels were popular with them too, and nonsensical farming ditties such as 'Chicken-in-the-Raft', whatever that was; Billy thought it might be a sandwich. Some of them formed groups, sang harmonies and copied Peter, Paul and Mary. Billy couldn't be bothered with any of them; he preferred the less traditional folkies, people with long hair and earrings.

When Billy met Clive Palmer and Robin Williamson, two of the men who later formed the Incredible String Band, he thought they were breathtaking. Clive, a dazzling banjo player, was the coolest man on earth with a very pale face and waist-length, straight hair. He was afflicted with polio in one leg so, as he limped, his hair swung way out to the side like a pendulum. Billy noticed that he frequently keeled over, but, in true Jack Connolly style, he would just pick himself up and walk on down the road.

Clive's preferred form of dress was a pair of army drill pants, tucked into surgeon's wellies, and an enveloping overcoat. He had very exotic friends, like Ricky who wore a great Eton collar outside his jacket. If you go to a Grateful Dead concert, you see the kind of people who were always hanging out in Clive's enormously lofty Victorian flat in Edinburgh. He couldn't afford to heat the place, so he camped in a tent in the middle of the room, complete with sleeping bag and camping stove.

'There's a smell of gas in here,' remarked Billy one day as they were sitting in Clive's tent playing banjo together.

'Oh it's paraffin. I put paraffin in my hair.'

'Why?'

'Lice. Paraffin kills them.'

Clive's partner, Robin Williamson, wore a red velvet cape and had a pet fox. Women were crazy about him, for he was the most beautiful-looking man they'd ever seen. He would walk through Edinburgh looking like a Renaissance painting of an angel, or a noble medieval Knight of the Round Table. He also had a lovely manner and a beautiful voice. Billy reckoned that both he and Clive knew special things about life that came roaring across whenever they sang.

Billy noticed that most folk singers would introduce their songs in a spiritless fashion, by simply announcing the name of the song and where they had learned it. Billy did not want to join the competition to see who could dig up the most obscure folk songs from old ladies in Orkney, or fruit pickers in Blairgowrie. He decided there were too many purists in the scene, 'real-ale types' who disapproved when British people sang American songs. They would inspect his banjo and say, 'Is that a D28, or a D35?'

Billy rarely hid his irritation. 'It's a fucking banjo. Do you play? No? Well shut up.'

When Billy introduced his songs, he tried to find something interesting and funny to say about them. His hero, Diz Disley, used to grab the audience with: 'I learned this song at university, with a record I bought while I was there, with some money I stole while I was there. Some people call it a grant.' Billy, too, began to invent daft introductions to his songs. Most banjo songs he came across had quite banal words set to great tunes, so he would make dark and silly jokes about Appalachian singing, or poke fun at the lyrics. He never gave it much forethought; it just evolved naturally.

In 1965, a folk singer called Jimmy Steel was in the process of showing Billy some fancy banjo licks when he offered Billy an even greater gift. 'I've got a gig on Sunday night,' he said suddenly, 'come along to the Folk Attic and I'll introduce you to the crowd.'

Jimmy began his set by singing 'Kelly the Boy from Killane', and Billy accompanied him in another song. Then Jimmy put down his guitar: 'Billy's going to sing you a song.' So Billy launched tentatively into a song by Jimmy Driftwood called 'St Brendan's Isle', about the saint's journey to America from Ireland in a leather boat. In the song, St Brendan sights an island, but when he steps onto the beach it sails away because it's actually a whale. About a verse and a half in, Billy stopped, completely flummoxed through nervousness. 'I've forgotten the words,' he explained to the audience, as Danny Kyle who was watching from the bar held his breath in horror, 'but it's about a guy who is sailing ...'

Abandoning the song altogether, Billy proceeded to make the best of the situation by telling the story instead of singing. As he waded into the tale, an extraordinary thing happened: instead of shuffling or booing as often happens when an audience notices a performer's mistake, people became riveted by his storytelling, eventually howling at the hilarious way he talked the song through. They'd never seen anyone do that before, not with such aplomb. Realizing he was gaining momentum, Billy embellished the narrative even further and performed a flourish on his banjo at the end: 'Dum diddly ah dum, ding ding!'

It went down a storm. Billy had made the amazing discovery that he could slay the audience just by talking. He was pleased as Punch to gain both admiration and new friends that evening. Danny saw his potential as a performer and realized he had just witnessed a point of evolution, while Davey Speirs, a great friend of Danny's, grabbed Billy on his way out. 'Why don't you come to my house and I'll show you a few chords on the guitar? Some songs just don't suit the banjo. You'd be better with a guitar as well.'

One night in the Paisley Attic, Billy met a splendid, flat-picking guitar player called Tam Harvey. Tam had wonderful hair, way down to his waist, with ringlets at the back and a sparseness on top. Billy teamed up with Tam and began to play the folk clubs with him. They called themselves the Humblebums, a variation on the word 'stumble-bum', meaning 'hobo'.

After a satisfying beginning in Glasgow, the band soon ventured outside the city to towns in other parts of Scotland. Transportation was a problem, for neither of them had a four-wheeled vehicle and hitchhiking was impossible with all their instruments. At that time, Billy and Tam sometimes drank at the Scotia Bar, a wild place in Stockwell Street that is still thriving. In order to buy more drinking time for regular punters, the barmen used to set off the fire alarm, knowing it would be a couple of hours before the engine arrived. Being short of dinner money, Billy and Tam learned that if they turned up at the Scotia at exactly 2.15 p.m. on any given day, they could score what was left of the stew.

'Anybody got a car?' Billy asked the crowd at large one afternoon when he and Tam were desperate for a lift to the Buck and Hind pub in Buckhaven, about fifty miles away. 'Jamie Wark's got wheels,' someone replied, pointing to a man with very long blond hair, in a combat jacket and desert boots, who was drinking at the other end of the bar. Jamie Wark belonged to a group who liked to sing rock 'n' roll and Beach Boys songs at the top of their voices. 'Aye,' agreed Jamie, who turned out to be a welder too, 'I'll take you, if you pay for my petrol.'

So that was it. Jamie became their unofficial roadie. He liked to drive them, never charging any more than basic costs, and it was the beginning of his twenty-year association with Billy. There was always a fight about who sat in the front of his light blue minivan. Only the front passenger was able to sleep; the loser would be stuck in the back with all the equipment.

It was very fortunate that the Humblebums now had the means to travel. Due to the popularity of folk music at that time, bars and lounges throughout the country became transformed into folk venues once a week. Billy and Tam heard there was a pub in Arbroath called The Windmill Hotel that had a lively folk club on a Sunday night, so they took a trip north-east to investigate. There was a group playing onstage when they arrived, but they sought out the club manager and requested a spot. 'You're excellent!' he said at the end of their set, slipping them ten shillings apiece. 'That's all I can give you,' he apologized, 'but if you come back next week, I can give you ten pounds or something.'

It didn't seem worth going home. They skived off work and just stayed in Arbroath, having a lark, living like cowboys. Tam was good at chatting up women so they always had somewhere to stay ... at least that's what I've been told, although it's highly unlikely that Billy was forced to rely on the kindness of Tam's one-night stands. At the end of the week the two sex-crazed ramblers played a well-received gig, said *adieu* to quite a few lassies and left town with change in their pockets.

The word went round that there were a couple of nutcases about who played great folk music, so the Humblebums began to travel around the countryside with a reputation before them. It was quite a circuit: they played Fife, just north of Edinburgh – as the Scottish joke goes, when you cross the Forth Bridge you're in Fife – and then a slew of tiny coal-mining towns, industrial centres and fishing ports, wherever there were folk clubs. Before long, the duo had become sufficiently well known to play the larger towns, which eventually led to major cities. They were becoming more and more confident as their popularity snowballed.

By now, Billy was performing virtuoso banjo solos such as 'Cripple Creek' or 'Down the Road', and humorous introductions ('I'd like to dedicate this to nervous flatulence; it's called "Windy and Warm"'). Billy has recently been heard to lament, 'I used to be a folk singer but I had an awful voice, like a goose farting in the fog.' This is quite untrue: he has a fine natural tenor voice that is very pleasant to the ear. In the Humblebums, he sang popular folk songs and parodies with Tam, while Billy told a few outrageous jokes in the classic format with the punch line at the end, pausing now and again to mime the action.

Although ostensibly part of a duo, Billy can now be heard on audio tapes from the time, taking the stage like a solo artist: 'I'm William F. B. Connolly the Third,' he announces at the beginning of their act. 'Beware of imitations!' At the end of their set, he relegates Tam to his backing instrumentalist: 'I'd like to thank my guitarist, Tam Harvey ... and leave you all with this advice: Lie on your back and you won't squash your nose.'

The music of the Humblebums resonated with the class-conscious sensibilities of their audiences. 'I'd like to dedicate this song to everyone who ends up in the Dunfermline Infirmary after visiting the local police station there,' Billy would proclaim, referring to recent cases of suspected police brutality. 'They usually fall down the stairs.' He followed that with his parody of the Crystals hit 'And then He Kissed Me' that he re-titled 'And then He Kicked Me'.

Billy's social conscience had formed in the shipyards and through his reading, but the folk scene gave voice to it. He did not have to look far for mentors. He and Tam sometimes backed Matt McGinn, who had written some wonderfully funny songs about being in a trade union, as well as more serious songs about the plight of the working man, which deeply touched Billy's heart.

Matt had great taste and great ideas. For example, he sang Irish rebel lyrics to the tune of 'The Sash My Father Wore', which was an Orange, or Protestant, tune. He really wanted people to own up that bigotry was wrong, and Billy was impressed by his stance. Hamish Imlach was another of Billy's folk-scene heroes, a witty and talented blues-and-country guitarist who cooked curries like nobody alive. Hamish had an Indian mother and claimed to have sat on Gandhi's knee when he was a baby. Aly Bain, a phenomenal fiddler from the Shetland Isles who joined the Humblebums for a while, added colour and richness to their music and became a lifelong friend.

It was such a novelty for Billy, having all this support. He felt truly at home in this folk-scene 'family', with Danny Kyle cast as an encouraging surrogate father-figure.

∼

A Hollywood party in 2001, Billy is holding court amidst some of the most controversial and intriguing characters of our time. Our twelve-year-old daughter Scarlett wanders up. 'Dad, who's the guy in the gold wheelchair?' Billy looks over to a man in a moving throne, wheeled by a sinister-looking minder.

'Um ... Oh that's Larry Flynt.'

'Who's he?'

'A guy who started a magazine ...'

'What's wrong with him?'

'Someone shot him.'

Moon Unit Zappa intervenes. 'I used to go to your school. Do they still let you go barefoot and curse?'

'Yes ...'

'I was always dying to go to a stricter school and wear a uniform ...'

Amy, our fourteen-year-old appears. 'Mum ... I was just talking to Peewee Herman. He's rather intense, isn't he?'

Billy stares at his children with an expression of utter panic. 'Fuck,' he turns to Stevie, Frank Zappa's famous guitarist. 'When I was a teenager I just nearly got to meet Jack Radcliffe.'

~

Jack Radcliffe was a popular comedian from variety theatre days. He had turned up at Stephen's Shipyard one day to do some publicity photographs and Billy was thrilled to see him walking by, although by then Billy's true steering lights were younger men who'd made their names in folk music. Of course, Bob Dylan was always 'The Man', but other early heroes of Billy's included Diz Disley, who played guitar like the French gypsy jazzer Django Reinhardt, as well as blues singer Dave Van Ronk and the banjoist Tom Paley, who was one of the New Lost City Ramblers. Billy's unspoken ambition at the time was to become one of them.

Another strong influence at the time was Josh Macrae, who introduced Billy to the thrilling music of Ravi Shankar. Josh was an art teacher-turned-singer who had a passion for the same folk music as Billy. He played a coveted Martin guitar, wore splendid clothes, sang skilfully and was very popular with women.

With every new step, Billy was growing and becoming more educated. He was reading Orwell and Steinbeck as well as poetry by James Hogg, Yeats and Burns. At twenty-four, he started writing songs himself, although Billy now insists they were all 'shite'. Billy's appearance and values were also changing dramatically. In 1965, the gurus of rebellion were touting their causes in both Britain and the United States, with the birth of the Rolling Stones, the Grateful Dead and Timothy Leary. Lenny Bruce, who had been arrested in San Francisco for obscenity in 1961, died of a drug overdose in 1966.

Billy began to rebel against his previously held work ethic and personal style. He was exposed to people who shunned 'working for the man', preferring to 'ramble' through Europe in the summer and play the folk clubs in winter. He took to wearing bow ties, corduroy jackets, boots and Levi's, trying to look more 'windswept and interesting', as he puts it. He was succeeding. People noticed him. He had a beard, his hair was becoming curly and long and he was strolling about playing the banjo, imitating the 'rambling' style.

Florence was pleased to see her brother was finally becoming 'his own individual self'. Billy's aunts and father, however, thought he had lost the plot altogether, running around with little money and very odd clothes. When Billy went to see William in the pub, he was highly embarrassed by his son, the bampot, or crazy, welder with hair like a woman and two earrings, and his drinking pals cracked jokes at Billy's expense. William had become quite a heavy drinker. His children had never seen him stagger when they were growing up but, in 1962, Billy met William at a bus stop and he was too drunk to recognize his own son.

The only family member who seemed to relate to Billy's 'rambling hippie' experience was his cousin. John was really quite brilliant and had done well at Essex University before taking a hated job in London as a clerical officer in the Civil Service. When he returned to Scotland, he had a huge beard and a receding hairline and looked remarkably like the poet Allen Ginsberg.

At school, he had always worn National Health plastic glasses, but currently he sported wire-framed spectacles with a sticker of a bullet hole in the middle of each lens. It was a startling look. People would be shocked when they encountered him at close range.

'What the fuck's wrong with you?' he would snap.

'You've got ... bullet holes in your glasses.'

'And what's wrong with that?'

John loved the folk scene and persistently hung out with Billy and his pals. After a while he took to dressing like Billy, in cowboy boots, Levi's, and a corduroy jacket with a denim shirt. 'Oh, come on!' objected Billy. 'Get your own ideas.'

Over time, Billy became more and more bizarre in his own dress.

BILLY

He turned up to meet Danny and John in the pub one evening, sporting a red-and-black striped jersey, green-and-white striped trousers and a black-and-white vertical striped coat down to his knees, with Lapland reindeer-herd boots that curled up like Aladdin's lamp. When a fellow customer eyed him in disbelief, Billy delivered him a variation on a line from an Al Pacino movie. 'What are you fucking looking at?'

At that, Danny just slid down the wall, convulsed. He pointed out the obvious: 'What do you mean, "What are you fucking looking at?" he choked. 'Look at you!'

Billy and John did not suffer fools gladly and had nothing against smacking them in the mouth. They were both quite violent, as a matter of fact, given to diving on people and giving them a severe seeing-to. People generally expected hairy folk to be far more mellow than that. They were very much products of their childhood environment, where physical and verbal aggression were the first lines of defence.

The two cousins hung out together in the Marland Bar, a bear pit of an Irish pub with weird and volatile customers. The first night Billy found the Marland, he was just entering the glass-panelled front door, when he came face to face with a man being thrown out head-first through the glass towards him. A cheery song by the fireside, led by Hamish Imlach, had never faltered for a second.

Besides original dress, Billy had another idiosyncrasy, one that was related to his earlier abuse. He could not bear to be touched by anybody at all and would jump in the air if another person got within eighteen inches of him. 'Don't fucking touch me! Leave me alone!' Such flinching was quite understandable, considering how often and how brutally he had been attacked and beaten without warning. As a survival mechanism, he had developed an ability to be hypervigilant, that is super-aware of the approach of another, and his body was now wired to accelerate from resting state to peak fight-or-flight mode in less than a second.

According to Billy, it was Danny Kyle who deprogrammed him. Every time it happened, Danny would just collapse with hysterics. 'That's not normal, Billy,' Danny tried to be patient with him. 'You'll have to relax. It's touchy-feely, you know, the way we live. We like to touch each other and we kiss: we're different. You'll have to calm down or you'll always be fighting.' It took a long time.

While Billy was busy becoming hairy and exotic, his 'brother' Michael was lecturing him on how to lead a better life. Michael thought Billy was phony and preferred to hang out with John's brother, Eddy. They wore suits and ties and looked like junior executives. Michael had left school at sixteen, then worked first in a factor's office and later in Dixon's, which was then a photography shop; Michael was crazy about photography. He eventually went to work for the Post Office, where he has held down a job for thirty years. Though they grew up together, Billy and Michael had very little in common.

Mona's disappearance into her impenetrable psychotic world had been very difficult for Michael. He was protected from the truth at first, but it had gradually dawned on him that his mother was not coming back, either mentally or physically. Nowadays, excellent anti-psychotic drugs are available for the treatment of schizophrenia, and people who become afflicted often lead relatively normal lives. At that time, however, the illness was considered a dark and shameful malady, so an improbable and persisting story of Mona's symptoms being due to a 'blood clot' was created. Whatever Michael understood, it must have been very painful to lose her. William became his source of consolation. They had always been close. Michael called him 'Pop' and thought of him as his own father.

When Billy visited Mona in hospital, wearing his oversize duffel coat and looking as hairy as a Highland cow, she looked even more bewildered than before. He was appalled at what he saw in there. The patients sat listlessly on benches against bare walls in a huge, bleak, Victorian ward, mumbling to themselves or rocking silently. Mona would burst into tears and have nothing much to say, then one of her fellow patients would come shuffling up and start rubbing Billy's hair. She was never nasty to him in there. In keeping with the symptoms of paranoid schizophrenia, she thought the family was part of a plot to keep her locked up. 'If you let me out I'll be good,' she would say, but she couldn't remember where they lived.

7

'I WANT TO BE A BEATNIK'

It is May 2001, and the ballroom of the newly renovated Century Plaza Hotel on Los Angeles' Avenue of the Stars is crammed with the newly renovated bodies, careers and faces of Hollywood's 'A-List', all bouncing to Stevie Wonder's live performance of 'Lean On Me'. Billy, in a pink silk Versace suit and black T-shirt, bumps and grinds with Cher, who tells him she brought a video of his movie *Mrs Brown*, one of her favourites, to watch in her limousine on her way home.

Billy takes the stage and I try to recover from the horror of witnessing Billy tell this particular audience an outrageous joke about haemorrhoids.

'Someone ...' I shout in Dustin Hoffman's ear '... should stop him!'

'No, no,' he thoroughly disagrees, 'I was laughing so much I couldn't speak.'

A petite Barbie doll lookalike trots past in a mini-skirt, bra-top and 'follow-me-fuck-me' shoes. Spotting Billy, she mimes obeisance to him and provocatively mouths the word 'Wonderful!' He hardly seems aware of her, so she repeats her circuit of the nearby tables four or five times, deliberately throwing him obvious, seductive glances as she passes. When Billy turns to speak to me, I am expecting a self-congratulatory smirk. 'That woman,' Billy finally remarks upon her presence, 'has one of those tiny Olympus cameras. I think I'll get one.'

~

Billy claims he never notices when women make passes at him. 'It's the last thing I expect ... because I'm not the Kevin Costner type,' he explains, as if that would come as news to the listener. 'I've never been able to chat women up. When I was young, women would be howling at my jokes and I wouldn't know how to make the transition between laughing and "get your knickers off".'

In the sixties, when Billy looked like a hippie but sounded like a welder, he had the impression that women found such a mixture very disconcerting. June McQueen may have been taken aback when he began getting hairy but her response to his outrageous talk was always a trying-not-to-laugh: 'Och, that's disgusting!'

By the summer of 1964, June was worried about the progress of their relationship and didn't want to 'get into trouble', the old euphemism for becoming pregnant. There came a point when Billy thought she seemed to be awfully interested in jewellers' windows and he panicked. June's pride was hurt when Billy started shutting her out. By contrast to June's experience of Mona, Billy had always felt welcomed by June's family. They seemed less bigoted than other folk and he was always up at their house, chatting to her father who worked as a caulker burner in John Brown's Shipyard in Clydebank. Billy, however, still planned to be more exotic than he was, and knew that he was on the wrong track. June must have thought Billy was mad because, when she asked why he wanted to break it off, he replied, 'Because I want to be a beatnik.'

Survivors of childhood sexual abuse often experience sexual confusion in adulthood and Billy was no exception. Billy knew he was attracted to women. He had certainly enjoyed 'getting cosy' with June but, because abusers always design their victims' future sexuality to some extent, Billy had a nagging question about his sexual orientation and was drawn to seek a few experiences with other men to satisfy his curiosity. They were experiences that resembled the furtiveness of his abuse in both style and setting and he found them ultimately uncomfortable and unsatisfying. He eventually came to the correct conclusion that he was definitely a heterosexual man who had simply known homosexual abuse.

~

When Billy first met Iris Pressagh in 1965, he thought she was delightful, very beautiful and, moreover, she never once vomited on him. He was still recovering from an incident in Edinburgh involving a military sleeping bag he'd got inside one evening with a young woman who was feeling a little off-colour. He still deeply regrets tying up the neck of that bag.

Iris reminded him of Cher; there was an album sleeve of the lanky singer in a record shop up near Dumbarton road and Billy was struck by how similar they were. Iris had led a very sheltered life. She had done well at the high school in Clydebank before becoming a kitchen designer and attending night classes at Glasgow Art School. They met at the Polish Club where Billy was performing. Iris loved folk music and fully embraced the folk scene. She even bought an Autoharp and learned to play it. Their relationship grew steadily as they spent time accompanying each other to folk clubs and parties.

At first, Iris's mother and father were not too keen on Billy. As far as they were concerned, there were five main strikes against him: he was Catholic, hairy, a freak and didn't have a proper job. Moreover, they thought he was 'on drugs'. In fact, Billy was far from being a junkie at that time; he always liked to imagine himself sitting happily on the porch of an evening, smoking a joint and listening to good music, but he found he couldn't handle any kind of recreational drugs. 'It's just too profound,' he realized. 'I go places I can't handle.' At the height of the early seventies drug culture, when some high-flyers were snorting, smoking and ingesting the cost of a Mercedes-Benz at a single party, Billy's friend Danny Marcus teased him for having a 'five-cents-a-day habit', although that was enough to have him hanging from the ceiling.

Iris was very accommodating. Billy appreciated that she did not attempt to keep him on a short leash. She barely complained when he abandoned her for long periods of time to hang out with his friends or play music, only phoning her whenever the mood took him. It was an ideal situation for Billy: she put no pressure on him, they seemed to get along and both of them enjoyed a 'wee bevvy'.

Billy had steadily progressed from drinking every now and again, to drinking large quantities of beer as often as possible. During one of his frequent drinking sorties, a theatre director called Keith Darvel approached him. He was directing a play called *Clydeside*. 'I believe you're a banjo player,' he said. 'I'm looking for a musician for my play at the Citz [Citizens' Theatre]. It's about socialism on the Clyde beginning at the First World War. Do you think you could handle that?' 'Aye,' affirmed Billy. He had never even seen a play before. 'Can I bring my friend Tam? He's very good.'

Clydeside rehearsals took place during the day, but it was difficult for Billy to attend because he was still a welder. Billy had already missed several weeks' work on sick leave that year, when he contracted pneumonia with pleurisy and was taken into the same place Mona had gone, Knightswood Hospital. It wasn't so bad to be laid up in hospital. Flora came to visit Billy and, defying the rules, sneaked him half a bottle of whisky. By bribing the porters for empties, he and Willie Bennett, a bookie from Temple in the bed next to him, saved up their daily allowance of Mackeson Stout (its vitamin content was thought to have restorative value) and spent their Saturday evenings in the ward toilets getting pissed on whisky with a stout chaser.

When *Clydeside* came along, Billy was a journeyman welder of three years' standing, whose experience extended beyond the Clyde. He had been hired for a company in Jersey and had worked a six-week stint on an oil rig in Nigeria as well. The war had been heating up in Biafra so, in 1966, welders from all over Britain were employed to fast-track completion of the rig so it could be towed out to sea and out of harm's way. It was exhausting work with little time for recreation. Alcohol was forbidden on the rig, but workers could climb onto a barge and buy Dutch 'Oranjeboom' beer from local people in canoes. When Billy set out to sample shore nightlife, he was tickled to discover that the shabby little shipping town of Port Harcourt boasted a 'topless' nightclub that turned out to be only roofless.

By the time Billy returned from Nigeria, he had become an excellent welder. He had high hopes when he went along to apply for a job at a company called Stewart and Lloyd Phoenix Works in Rutherglen. His fellow applicant was so wasted with alcohol, he was incapable of filling out his form, so Billy lent the man a hand. There was one question Billy balked at: 'What school did you attend?' It was an easy way to flush out Catholics. The pickled Protestant got the gig.

There was life beyond the shipyards, Billy knew it ... still, it was hard to take the leap. Billy's welding pals had been bemused at his 'windswept and interesting' metamorphosis. They absolutely lacerated him but, at the same time, Billy could tell they were ever so interested in his progress. At teatime, they would nudge him to elaborate about his antics in the folk clubs and Billy sometimes sang them funny songs.

Old Bugsy had played guitar when he was young and he always encouraged Billy to pursue his dream of being a folk singer. One day, just before the *Clydeside* rehearsals started, the two of them were standing around the fire when Bugsy suddenly asked:

'What are you doing about that banjo stuff?'

'I'm still playing nights,' replied Billy.

'That's brilliant.'

'I'm going to go professional.'

'When?'

'I was thinking the Glasgow Fair.' This was in about six months' time.

'Och, you'll never do it.'

'What are you talking about?'

'If you plan it six months ahead, when that comes you'll plan it a year after that, and when that comes you'll plan it eighteen months after that. If you really wanted to do it, you'd quit right now.' There was an uncomfortable moment. Then Bugsy spoke from the depths of his own longing: 'There's nothing worse than being an old guy in here, knowing you could have got out when you were younger.'

His words chilled Billy's soul. Billy quit on the Friday, with a good deal of nudging by the foreman who thought he spent far too much time yakking with co-workers. Billy picked up his wages and walked away for ever. The moment he left the shipyards, Billy felt like he had been sprung from jail. His heart had never been in welding.

So Billy played the banjo and Autoharp while Tam strummed the guitar and mandolin for *Clydeside*, which had been cast with some talented actors including Peter Kelly, whom Billy had seen at the cinema, and Richard Wilson, who would later appear in *One Foot in the Grave*. Billy knew nothing about live theatre. He and Tam sat in a corner with scripts they'd been given, but neither of them knew that the word 'cue' meant it was time for them to play. At their first rehearsal, they performed the opening music and, after a scene or two, it was their cue to play again.

'Well?' urged Keith the director, impatiently expecting them to start.

Billy thought he was asking him what he thought of the play so far, so he said, 'It's very good.'

'I'm glad you think so.' Keith raised one eyebrow. 'Do you think we could have a little music?' The actors were all tittering.

Billy said, 'Sure, what would you like?'

'Maybe the piece in the script would be handy.'

The director took them aside at lunchtime for a crash course in stagecraft.

~

After *Clydeside* was over, Billy and Tam continued to ramble around the Scottish folk circuit, enjoying their popularity and getting shit-faced on beer while they were at it. They usually mingled with the crowd after their gig, allowing people from the audience to either ply them with drink or proffer their autograph books.

One particularly wet and stormy evening, after a concert at the town hall in Dunoon, Billy was packing up his banjo when a sweet-faced, middle-aged woman approached him. 'Billy Connolly?' she inquired. Billy was irritated. He'd rather hoped a person who had just seen him on stage would know exactly who he was, but he nodded and took out his pen.

The woman failed to produce an autograph book. Instead, she took a breath and uttered three words that stopped Billy dead in his tracks: 'I'm your mother.' They stood staring at each other for a few seconds. Deeply shocked, Billy moved awkwardly towards her and buried his face in her coat. It was true. He remembered her smell.

They went back to Mamie's house to drink tea and attempt to catch up on the past twenty-two years. On entering her living room, he saw Willie Adams sitting there looking exactly the same as he did all those years ago when he closed the door on Billy's face. Mamie and Willie now had three grown daughters and a son.

'I saw Florence once,' said Mamie. 'Right here in Dunoon. I was waiting for the bus, but then I followed her. Just looking at her.'

'How did you know it was Florence?' Billy asked.

'I could tell from the way she walked,' said Mamie. 'I would have known from a mile away.'

Billy has often thought about the pain she must have suffered, feeling she couldn't speak to her own daughter. He sensed something had gone horribly wrong with her life. He had a romantic notion that she was a tempestuous, free spirit whom others had always tried to tame. He began to get to know her a little, but it was a painful and disappointing process. When Mamie chided him for his excessive drinking, it didn't go down too well. 'What, does she think she's going to be my mother *now?*' he raged. He decided to keep his distance.

∾

Billy wrote a song called 'Back to Dunoon' at this time, but it had little to do with his mother. Instead, it was a satirical jibe at Dunoon residents who lamented the paucity of tourists visiting the place:

'Why don't they come back to Dunoon?
This switched-on scene
Has two pubs, three cafés and a fire machine,
And hills you can walk on while the rain rung doon,
A night life that stops in the afternoon ...
Why don't they come back to Dunoon?'

After Billy and Tam sang this song at the Orange Hall in Paisley, they noticed a man with long hair and an intense expression sitting waiting for them as they came off stage. It was a young musician called Gerry Rafferty. 'I really enjoyed your set,' he enthused. 'It was brilliantly funny. I've never heard anyone being funny like that before.'

'Thanks,' replied Billy.

'We're having a few beers up in the house. You want to come up?'

Gerry sang some of his extraordinary songs. 'Holy shit.' Billy turned to Tam. 'Are they really his?' Gerry seemed dreadfully strange. 'He's the kind of guy you'd expect to see hanging about in the darkest corner of a library,' thought Billy. He liked that. Gerry was a couple of years younger than him, brown-haired with a Beatle haircut and he wore more conservative clothing than Billy. Gerry, on the other hand, thought Billy was a raving eccentric. 'He looked like the Wild Man of Borneo,' he divulges now.

Gerry fell in love with Billy's slant on life and sense of the absurd and Billy appreciated those same things in Gerry. They were kindred spirits, both from the west of Scotland of similar Irish-Catholic descent, and shared a perspective on many things ... parochialism for one, as well as antipathy to the Protestant work ethic, which was truly loathed by both.

The two shared a fury with the hypocrisy and 'mind-numbing conformity' inherent in the belief system of their early lives although, paradoxically, they also shared an affection for aspects of Roman Catholicism, such as certain favourite hymns and some of the Service rituals. Gerry took delight in Billy's 'Jesus' imper-sonations, parodies of the ubiquitous 'Sacred Heart' prints of Christ, looking skyward in great pain and despair. Another thing they had in common was their Boy Scout troop. 'You're kidding!' Billy was amazed. 'I've never met anyone else who was a Peewit!'

But Gerry didn't think the same way as Billy in all things. He noticed Billy's heightened sensitivity to the slightest criticism. 'Why do you bother your arse about that? They're not going anywhere,' he tried to soothe Billy when 'lesser people' nit-picked.

Gerry's musical influences were also quite different, so between them they had a fine collaboration of musical tastes. They both wrote songs but Billy thought Gerry's were much better and was left hoping he'd catch up. When Gerry was writing the popular ballad 'His Father Didn't Like Me Anyway', Billy was writing his own lyrical history:

'Oh I was born in Glasgow,
Near the centre of the town.
I would take you there and show you
But they pulled the building down ...'

Billy had gone to visit a friend who lived in Dover Street. He had a very bad hangover that day and had tried to assuage it by splashing his face in the sink. As he did so, he happened to glance through the kitchen window, just in time to see the house he was born in crumble into dust. The house had been marked for demolition, but Billy's reaction was predictable, for a hippie. 'That's fucking cosmic!' he exclaimed.

When Billy invited Gerry to join the Humblebums, Tam was against the idea. He sensed the chemistry of such a trio would be uncomfortable, and he was absolutely right. For Gerry, the move was engineered to provide himself with a fast track to a recording contract. Billy and Tam had already made one album with Transatlantic Records, whereas, at the time, Gerry lacked an outlet for his songs. Unfortunately for Tam, the other two had so much in common that he soon found himself ousted while Billy and Gerry went from strength to strength, working together for three years and making two fine albums.

Billy's motivational level was nowhere near Gerry's. Billy had always thought it would be rather nice to be famous and maybe rich into the bargain, but above all he still just wanted to be windswept and interesting. He definitely wanted to have better denim than anybody else, to know where to have great boots made and to have a handmade guitar and banjo ... maybe a nice hat too, and swan around looking good, playing well and singing great songs. Gerry was a highly ambitious man who taught Billy an awful lot about being very single-minded and proud of it.

'I'm going to be the very best and don't you forget it,' Gerry would announce. 'Remember where you were when I told you.' He would say that to people. He was far more comfortable in recording studios than Billy, who was always a little in awe of his technical ability.

The two men became very close and even spoke to each other about their respective difficult childhood experiences. Billy confided in Gerry about his relationship with his father and the aunts. On one occasion, he even asked Gerry to accompany him to Dunoon to visit his mother. 'We went to a little housing estate,' says Gerry. 'I sat in the taxi while he went to the door. A woman came to let him in but he was only in there ten or fifteen minutes. When he came out, he was as white as a sheet.' It was a harrowing experience for Billy. Mamie pushed his buttons ... ironically, by running down Margaret and Mona. 'They weren't heroes of mine, but she was in no position to do that,' he complained.

Billy greatly appreciated Gerry's very original sense of humour, although Gerry never displayed it on stage. Before Billy met him, he had worked in a shoe shop. Sometimes he'd turn up at the shoe store all covered with fake bandages. 'I was in an accident last night.' The manager would sigh, 'Then you'd better go home.' That would give him a chance to get away to play a gig with his previous band, The Mavericks.

Gerry was mucking around in the basement of the shoe shop one day when he found a pair of size fourteen hiking boots. He subsequently planned an elaborate scene that had Billy weeping with laughter when he heard about it. Gerry had a friend who happened to be a very small man with tiny feet, and he encouraged him to visit the shoe shop on a busy Saturday and ask for hiking boots. Gerry instructed him to reject any pair of boots he tried, on the grounds that they were too tight. The fellow turned up as arranged, and Gerry began to offer him a variety of sizes, beginning with the smallest. The man actually took an eight, but by the time they got to size twelve, he was still marching around the shop insisting, 'No, no, they're too tight!'

At this point, the place was a mess. There were hiking boots strewn all around the shop. Other people were trying to get shoes fitted but there were huge boxes everywhere and this dwarf was marching round with hiking boots that fitted him like skis. 'No, no, they're still too tight!'

Finally they got to the fourteen, the monster boot.

'Try them on,' urged Gerry.

'Ah, these are great!' the man exclaimed, whereupon he grabbed his own shoes and paddled towards the door. He went flying down the high street.

'Stop! Thief!' Gerry pursued him and wrestled him to the ground, then grabbed the boots and returned as the big hero.

~

Gerry complains that he found his own shyness something of a burden. He admired Billy for his more extroverted approach to life, yet Gerry himself could be courageous, particularly when it came to practical jokes. Gerry was already friendly with Danny Kyle and all three of them were on a Clyde ferry together one day, travelling to a gig. Gerry and Danny became bored so they began to open their instrument cases and take out their guitars. Other passengers noticed and started to gather around, looking forward to some entertainment. The two deliberately dilly-dallied in their task, tuning obsessively and mucking around with capos, so by the time they were ready to play, quite a sizable, expectant crowd had gathered. The two japers then proceeded to sing flat on purpose and got the words of well-known songs like 'Doh a Deer' completely wrong. Danny and Gerry managed to stay deadpan, but Billy laughed so hard, he peed his trousers.

On the road, Gerry and Billy used to amuse themselves by reading newspaper reports of unlikely court cases to each other, like the one about a man who slaughtered animals in an abattoir. In his passport he had described his occupation as 'killer'; still he could not understand why he was refused entry to Spain.

They used to try to find 'Hitlers' in the phone book but they never found one, not even in Germany. They did find the Reverend Wildgoose in Cambridge, and a Harry Banjo in Solihull. Billy telephoned Harry Banjo, but there was nobody home. He always wanted to write a song about Banjo and Wildgoose meeting each other.

Gerry used to phone people at four in the morning to tell them that bricks would be arriving soon. 'There'll be two truckloads of well-fired bricks outside your door in a couple of hours,' Gerry would advise them. It was the 'well-fired' bit that made Billy scream. People would be trying desperately to wake up. 'See you later,' Gerry would say, banging down the telephone. Gerry could keep a perfectly straight face when he did those tricks but Billy was useless. He would crack up and run for cover.

Gerry's greatest improvisation took place in Rosyth. They were performing in a social club near the dockyard and arrived a couple of hours early so they were given an office to sit in. They changed their clothes, tuned up and then sat around with nothing to do. After a while Billy noticed Gerry talking on the phone with the phone book in his hand. He had dialled a number, and the person on the end of the phone said,

'Is that you, Willie Johnson?'

'Yeah. It's me,' said Gerry.

'Well you've got a nerve, phoning here,' the woman challenged him. 'You were supposed to be down here cleaning that chimney at ten o'clock this morning.'

So Gerry launched into a diabolical invention. 'I was just about to come to your house when I was listening to the radio and the new government regulations were being announced, and I realized I would be breaking the law.'

'What do you mean?'

'We need a safety net if I'm going to be on your roof. Have you got such a thing in your house?'

'No.'

'Well, have you got bedclothes and blankets and such?'

'Aye.'

'Well, if you'd bring them out to the front garden, they'll serve as safety nets. Keep the kids off school to hold the blankets. Do you have any scaffolding?'

'What? No! What would I be doing with scaffolding?'

'Well, we need scaffolding around the building. It's the new safety regulations, you see. Look, what about furniture? You could take it outside and pile it up so we could use it as scaffolding.'

'Aye, I'm sure we can do something.'

'But here's the hardest bit,' warned Gerry. 'With the new regulations I'll need another four or five extra men on the roof to watch over me, and we'll need breakfast for seven people. Nothing much. Bacon, eggs, sausage, fried bread and potato scones. Maybe a kipper or two.'

'Well, OK then.'

'I'll see you at ten o'clock in the morning.'

As soon as he'd put down the phone, he lifted it again.

'Hello, is that you, Willie Johnson?'

'Aye.'

'Well this is Jimmy Farrell. Where were you this morning?'

'I'm sorry. I'm up to here.'

'Well you'd better be at my place at ten o'clock tomorrow morning. It's our only opportunity.'

'I'll be there.'

Gerry had arranged a set-up that would have been worthy of *Candid Camera*. He and Billy never went to Jimmy Farrell's place to see what transpired, but for months they speculated about what probably happened in the garden with all those bewildered people running around with furniture, breakfast for seven folk and children kept off school to hold the blankets. If only they could have seen the chimney sweep's face.

$$\sim$$

With Billy and Iris, it was on and off. He had disappeared to Jersey and Nigeria, and Iris was still there when he came back. Then Iris disappeared to pick grapes in France with some friends and when she came back, Billy was still there. He had the urge to break it off but he didn't have the heart. He saw some little signs that it wasn't going to work. She was often plastered with drink, but then so was he.

Both Iris and Billy were still living with their parents. Billy could never get himself together financially, so it took him a long time to extricate himself from his father's place. It was an uncomfortable situation. Out of kindness, Billy was always putting up destitute folk singers for the night. William would walk in at breakfast time and there would be two hairy men in the bed. Billy had taken to wearing patchouli oil, embroidered trousers with high platform heels, beads and earrings. William just didn't have a clue what had happened to his son.

Billy was eventually flung out of the house for not going to Mass. The crunch came on Ash Wednesday when Billy finally exploded: 'What are you talking about? I never go to Mass.' William retaliated, 'Then get out of my house, you communist poof!'

When Iris told Billy she was pregnant, the two of them were in a room in Danny Kyle's house. Billy went through to the living room to find Danny.

'Danny, how do you get married? What do you do?'

'Oh, it costs seven and sixpence. You go to Martha Street and give them the dough. They post the banns, give you the date and you turn up and do it.'

Billy did not expect his family to come. He left from William's house to go to the registry office. When he was dressed he awkwardly faced his father: 'Well, here I go.'

His father gave him an envelope containing twenty pounds. Billy had no idea why. 'All the best,' said William, staying put. His son wasn't being married in a church so he wasn't going to make the effort.

Billy's entire wedding cost forty pounds. The singer Peter Sarstedt had given him some black mohair material that a local tailor fashioned into a smashing suit. Iris wore a white trouser suit with a floppy white hat and looked enchanting. Her mother turned up and so did Danny Kyle and his wife Helen. Gerry was Billy's best man and his future wife, Carla, was Iris's bridesmaid. After the ceremony, they walked to the pub and sang songs together before their evening concert. There was no honeymoon – Iris's parents went on a trip instead, and left the newlyweds alone in the house. After a while, Billy and Iris moved into a small room and kitchen in Paisley, exactly like Billy's very first home. At night they would take some lit coal on a shovel from the kitchen to the fireplace in the bedroom and lie there watching it flickering on the ceiling.

Jamie was born the following December, two days after Christmas. When Billy got up that morning, he phoned his father from a public telephone. 'I'm going up to the hospital to see what the baby is.' 'It's a boy,' said William. Billy hit the roof. William had had the nerve to phone the hospital earlier, pretending to be the father. People laughed at Billy in the hospital elevator. He did look a sight in that environment, with his fringed jacket and beads. He overheard someone say: 'Poor wee wean won't know whether that's its father or mother.'

Billy was very happy. His new son was a beautiful baby with a fine head of hair. They named him James Maxton Connolly after two of Billy's heroes: the Independent Labour Party politician James Maxton had shoulder-length hair and fought for school milk in the early part of the century, while James Connolly was an Edinburgh-born socialist.

William felt sorry for his new grandson. He was mortified when he arrived at Billy's poky tenement and saw Jamie gurgling in a laundry basket and he was utterly shocked to see their décor. Billy had sawn all the legs off the chairs so people sat low to the ground with their feet straight out. Billy thought it was an ingenious design idea of his, but William thought his son was an idiot and very hard up. The walls were orange and purple and Billy had cut shapes out of polystyrene and stuck them on the wall to make an abstract painting. The room smelled of incense, which William obviously mistook for marijuana. 'What a den!' he blasted.

8

'SEE YOU, JUDAS, YOU'RE GETTING ON MY TITS!'

It is 7.15 p.m. on a Thursday night in January 2001. I am over-stretched, trying to write a patient report, prepare a lecture, clean up the dog pee and check on a child's homework before Billy and I leave for a charity event in Beverly Hills. We are due there at eight. Billy pops his head in to remind me that I have just fifteen minutes to get dressed for what will be a very flashy, public event. Twenty minutes later, I climb into the car, breathing heavily. I am now wearing a new outfit that seemed like a good idea a few minutes ago.

'Jesus, Pamsy,' he exclaims, 'you look like you glued your body and dived into the wardrobe.'

I shoot him a look, which causes him to revise his comment.

'No, I mean, you look great ... er, did you try that on in the shop?'

~

In the folk scene, Billy discovered that when he made his highly original observations about humanity, people found him very funny. It was a revelation to him that not only were his singing and playing appreciated, he was masterful at engaging people with his words and body movements alone. He was lucky to have the kind of freedom to experiment that was afforded by the folk clubs. There was no intrinsic expectation that he would do any more than sing a song or two, so he had the glorious luxury of being able to improvise without any pressure. In the process, he made all kinds of discoveries about what audiences found comical. If he spoke explicitly about sex rather than just hinting at it, it could be mind-bendingly funny. When the audience reacted by screaming, he knew they'd never heard anybody saying anything like that before. He was developing an ability to anticipate laughter from an audience but, best of all, when he was unintentionally funny he did not try to prevent or analyse that process.

He began to write humorous, often satirical songs. One was about the familiar Glasgow tenement problem of having an outside toilet.

'Oh dear, what can the matter be
I'm scared to go to the lavatory
I haven't been since two weeks last Saturday
I know who's hiding in there.'

People just exploded and that thrilled Billy. It was lovely for his audiences, too, to see a performer from their own cultural background with whom they resonated. Eventually, Billy began to feel more confident in his ability to slay the audience on any given night.

Billy's most remarkable surge ever in the development of his comedy occurred in 1970, after the Humblebums split up. Gerry was desperate to be known as the great songwriter he was. Near the end of their final tour together, they were avoiding each other's gaze, shuffling their feet in Glasgow's Queen Street Station. Both of them knew it was time to call it quits. 'This is daft,' said Billy.

Gerry went back to London to get his own band together, and build a better platform for his extraordinary songs. His first album, *Stealer's Wheel* was a beauty. Billy was very nervous at the prospect of working on his own, which astonished Gerry, who had no doubt that Billy would go on from strength to strength ... although he would never have predicted Billy's international success. 'It didn't surprise me that he went on to achieve great solo success,' says Gerry today, 'but I was surprised by the scale of it. He was so much rooted in the west of Scotland, I imagined he might not travel very far. I was fundamentally wrong.'

The folk-singing artist Ralph McTell had been signed to Transatlantic Records around the same time as the Humblebums. When he first met them in London, Ralph thought Billy was 'not cool', beneath London standards, an 'exotic hippie person, completely over-the-top in green velvet flares'. Ralph was a denim kid at the time, locked into a Woody Guthrie reverie. He thought Gerry sounded a bit 'Paul McCartneyish' but he loved Billy's banjo playing.

In Ralph's opinion, the relationship between Billy and Gerry became destructive to Billy in some ways. 'Billy's a fine musician,' Ralph says. 'He has a deep, pure love for the banjo and loves mountain music and primitive styles of playing: working-people's music. Gerry, on the other hand, wrote sophisticated, rather urbane songs. Billy is rooted in a different place from Gerry and, during the course of their association, he ended up being punished for it, relegated to doing comic interludes and a bit of accompaniment.'

From Gerry's perspective, Billy was just developing more as a comedian. 'The jokes were getting longer and the musical content shorter and I was frustrated towards the end. At the outset it was just banjo and guitar, but the London recording company formed a band and provided backing groups for my songs. That was difficult for Billy.' Billy simply shrugs his shoulders. 'It was Big Yang and Big Yin,' he says today.

In the last months with Gerry, Billy felt he had become a passenger, and truthfully he didn't like it one bit. To make matters worse, once Billy became a solo act, nobody would employ him; Gerry was marked to become a huge star and Billy to disappear. But necessity turned out to be the mother of comic invention for Billy, for once he was on his own, he had an invigorating surge of energy and began to write prolifically. Not having Gerry, or his songs, to rely on meant he was challenged to create a great deal of new stage material and change the way he played his instruments. Fortunately, he had a wealth of ideas floating around in his head and was turning new influences from his immediate environment into songs, and funny monologues.

He had seen an article in a magazine about the mystery of a grossly injured body that had been found just outside Edinburgh. Investigators had concluded that the victim was an illegal immigrant who had tried to enter Britain by crawling inside the undercarriage of an aeroplane, with tragic results. Billy wrote a song about it called 'Please Help Me I'm Falling', based on a song by Hank Locklin.

The Humblebums had been the opening act for Hank Locklin when he toured Scotland. Hank always had great boots. He used to invite Billy up to play banjo with him in his dressing room because he was dreadfully homesick.

'Boy they're beauties,' Billy coveted his grey hide cowboy boots. 'What are they made of?'

'Elephant's ear,' replied Hank. 'I might forget you, but my boots won't!'

~

Billy's first solo gig was in Musselburgh. It was shaky, but it worked and gradually, towards the end of 1970, people began to employ him on his own, leading to a rapid rise in his popularity. He was different: no one else had his mixture of a very eclectic repertoire of songs as well as hilarious monologues. He needed help with his career, and for some curious reason agreed to allow Doug Mitchell, a stocky, medieval-looking entrepreneur with a past history as a taxidermist, to manage him. Soon, he was flying in the clubs, just ripping everyone to bits and really making a name for himself. One gig that did not go so well took place at Glasgow University.

'No, Doug,' Billy had protested beforehand. 'There's no way I'm going to play that crowd of bastards. Not any more. Students just heckle you to death and vomit in your banjo case.'

'It's worth a hundred pounds,' goaded Doug. 'If they heckle, just leave the stage. All I'm asking is that you try. See how it goes.'

'All right then,' replied our skint hero.

Billy walked on stage the following night, carrying his banjo. He placed the case at the side of the stage, took out his instrument and strolled to the centre of the stage. He didn't even make it to the microphone.

'Get aaaff!' someone shouted.

'Certainly,' replied Billy good-naturedly and left immediately. He still comes across people who whisper in awe, 'I was actually there the night you did that!'

Once the word got out that Billy on his own was a sensation, audiences began to turn up in vast numbers. Television people heard about him, and before long Billy was engaged to sing topical parodies every week or so on a popular Scottish daytime talk show called *Dateline* hosted by Bill Tennant. A month or two after his first appearance, Billy had a panic call from the producers. An antiques expert had agreed to be interviewed on the show, but she had contracted a bad case of stage fright and suddenly withdrawn, so Billy was asked to extend his role by filling in as the featured talking guest that day. It was a riot: everyone in the studio was screaming, cameramen, make-up people, everyone. Billy never looked back in Scotland.

Out of the blue, Billy was engaged to play seven weeks in a couple of Irish bars, the Harp and Bard in Massachusetts, USA, and the Windsor House in Toronto, Canada. For quite a while now, Billy had had a real bee in his bonnet that he could be well received in North America. He subsequently proved that to be true, although his real success there took many years.

News of Billy's outrageousness had travelled across the Atlantic Ocean, and the small audiences in Massachusetts and Toronto loved him. He sang 'What Does a Scotsman Wear under his Kilt?' to the tune of 'Blowing in the Wind', which was the punch line. When Billy returned home he brought Jamie a Mickey Mouse bendy toy and a pair of tiny red, white and black cowboy boots. The boots were far too uncomfortable for a one-year-old and Jamie kicked them off in protest. It was the beginning of his admirable, and persistent, refusal to step into his father's shoes.

Although Billy still had a hankering to fill the shoes of one of the savagely satirical performers, like Matt McGinn, he was happy about the way his comedy was developing. Maybe Matt was more of a mover and shaker politically, but Billy was just making people roar and that's what he wanted. He had no desire to educate or change anybody politically, and he still hasn't. His attitude has always been that if people are changed, moved or educated by anything he does then that's brilliant, but that is not the aim. The aim is to make them laugh. The majority of folk singers he knew were trying to educate people, which Billy thought was a desperate arrogance. He had changed his political stance several times on the way to his present one, so he felt he had no business telling anybody what the right way was. He himself hadn't a clue.

Billy just improvised the shape of his show and varied it from night to night. Sometimes he would sing more because he hadn't much to say. He was not averse to telling an immensely long story with a puny wee punch line, for he realized that punch lines aren't everything. It was fun to tell jokes every now and then. The audiences liked them because they felt safe. Everybody knew when to laugh because there's a pattern to standard jokes, but Billy was attracted to the more esoteric story, where the punch line isn't necessarily at the end. Occasionally it was right at the beginning but he had to tell the whole story to make sense of it. Billy was becoming more of a patter merchant like the ones he'd known in the shipyards.

Sometimes he even borrowed old music hall lines: 'I was just walking home last night, when some bastard stood on my fingers.'

～

By the end of 1971, Billy was really making his way as a solo artist. In January the following year, he received an invitation to perform on television in Ireland, in conjunction with a folk concert there. Just as he was about to leave, he had a phone call from Florence.

'Mona's very, very ill,' she informed him.

'What's wrong with her?'

'Phlebitis,' she answered, 'and there's something horribly wrong with her pancreas. Michael's with her.'

Billy considered ignoring the information, but relented and turned up at Stobhill Hospital to see her.

'Billy's here,' whispered Michael.

'Oh? ... That's nice,' she sighed.

Billy went over and spoke to her. She seemed bewildered, just as she had for many years. He was struck by how small and vulnerable she seemed ... a disoriented little old grey-haired lady, without a trace of monster about her. She died that same night.

'Billy cried buckets at her funeral,' says Michael. Mona's passing created an emotional quagmire for Billy, a mixture of relief and guilt, fury and loss. It seemed as though the first act of his life story had ended, and glad he was to have made it to the intermission.

Billy's concept of his world as a series of theatrical events had formed during his experience with *Clydeside*. He had come to love musical plays. In 1972, in collaboration with a poet called Tom Buchan, Billy created a stage event called *The Great Northern Welly Boot Show*, directed by Tony Palmer. It was performed in Glasgow with mediocre success during an arts festival called Mayfest, but the following year, the director Robin LeFevre reconstructed it for the Edinburgh Festival Fringe. This time it was a roaring success.

'SEE YOU, JUDAS, YOU'RE GETTING ON MY TITS!'

The show was a combination of songs and sketches that told a story about workers taking over a factory that made rubber boots. A talented painter called John Byrne designed the sets and costumes. John looked exactly like Frank Zappa and Billy liked him immensely from the minute he met him. John, who signs his paintings 'Patrick', is thought to be an exceedingly eccentric person, but I think it is his giftedness and intensity that shocks people. Billy's friend Sandy Goudie, another marvellous Glaswegian painter, called on John once in his mother's house in Ferguslie Park. He was shown into a back room where he found John dressed in a starched, white French sailor's uniform. On his head was a white beret topped with a red pom-pom and he was utterly focused on painting a self-portrait. The thing that rocked Sandy was that it was only 8.30 a.m.

John designed some stunningly inventive wellies for the show. There was the 'Jack Buchanan Evening Welly', which had silk lapels, a white shirt and a bow tie. The 'Dixie Flyer' was a cowboy welly with a wheel for a heel and Billy dreamed up the 'Rustic Wishing Welly' that was like a dead tree. The one that stopped Billy in his tracks, however, was a banana boot called the 'Reggae Welly'. It just was the most beautiful, silly thing imaginable.

One night during the run of the *Welly Boot Show* in Edinburgh, there was a delay in set-changing, so Billy ran on stage to appease the audience by performing a piece he had been working on lately. It went down a storm. Billy had been drinking in the infamous Scotia Bar when his pal Tam Quinn wandered in. Tam was a guitarist who played with his brother Mick in a band called The Lagan. He told Billy a joke he'd heard earlier that night, the best Billy'd heard in a while. 'Jesus came into the bar where all the apostles were hanging out and saw them eating a Chinese take-away. "Where did you get that?" he asked. One of them replied, "Oh, Judas bought it. He seems to have come into some money."'

Billy told it to the audience the next time he was on stage. As always, he embellished and protracted the original to a considerable degree, setting it locally. When the audience just exploded, Billy was encouraged to develop it further and further, until eventually it became a set piece called 'The Last Supper and Crucifixion'. The idea was that there had been a misprint in the Bible so Galilee was actually Gallowgate, a street near Glasgow Cross that originally led up to the old gallows. 'Of course,' Billy would say, 'Gallowgate is near the Cross.'

Billy eventually used a picture of the Sarrie Heid as a backdrop when he performed this piece on stage: 'All the Apostles are there, tearing lumps off the Mother's Pride. The atmosphere is getting a wee bit tense: "See you, Judas, you're getting on my tits!"' Billy didn't know it at the time, but the Sarrie was a particularly appropriate choice, since it's believed that in the eighteenth century condemned prisoners once spent their last night there on their way to be hanged.

The piece was wonderfully satirical but it caused Billy a good deal of trouble. He was forced to defend it, as a number of people found it offensive. Some brave clergymen insisted that religion could only gain from it, but others just went crazy and screamed at Billy in stores and bookshops. He always took that as proof that he had hit the target.

Some people physically attacked Billy, notably Pastor Glass, an evangelist who still demonstrates outside various places in Scotland when Billy is appearing. Glass and his followers resembled the cast of *Village of the Damned* and took to hitting Billy with heavy bags of change representing thirty pieces of silver. 'Those people don't blink much,' thought Billy. Billy vowed Glass had a satanic look and was certain that always irritated the pastor. He was a man of the cloth, yet he looked like the devil; Billy was supposed to be the devil but some said he looked messianic.

Predictably, Billy's father hated 'The Last Supper and Crucifixion'. He thought it was blasphemous and often complained about it. He criticized Billy for 'going in the wrong direction' and alienating people. 'When it comes to being funny, everyone's an expert,' thought Billy. His father would listen to Billy's conversation and wait until he heard something he thought he could attack. The thing that most got Billy down was the way William sided with the hecklers. He would say:

'You lost them tonight. They beat you.'

'No they didn't. I won.'

'No you didn't. It went on too long.'

'Fuck, what is it, some kind of football match?'

9

BIG BANANA FEET

It is 1992, in the old Chasen's restaurant in Beverly Hills. The occasion is a birthday dinner for the actor Sylvester Stallone, hosted by the film producer, Leonard Goldberg. I have arrived before Billy, and in the course of surveying my immediate environment, I've noticed that the former President, Ronald Reagan, is dozing off at a table facing the door.

Billy makes an entrance in a green, red, gold and turquoise paisley suit. Reagan catches sight of him and is immediately shocked to an upright, fully conscious state. He stares for a moment in amazement at our Scottish fashion-maven before they exchange smiles (they once had a heart-to-heart about the man's hearing-aid problems). Reagan then turns to make a private comment to his fellow diners, who seem grateful for Billy's wake-up call. 'Is this a dream or my medication?'

~

Sometimes I am wicked enough to take close friends to visit Billy's clothing closet and they always burst out laughing. It is absolutely stuffed with bizarre garments in the most wonderful assortment of colours, styles and fabrics. Billy certainly knows how to cause a stir with his attire. On the American *Tonight Show* recently, the host Jay Leno surveyed Billy's swish Japanese suit and silver-buckled sandals, out of which peeked his toes painted with black nail polish, and exclaimed, 'What are you, Billy, some kind of punk pilgrim?'

Even very early in his career Billy understood the value, to a performer, of cutting a dash. He did not wish to turn up at folk clubs, most of which were held in lounge bars, the back rooms of pubs or function suites, and blend in with duffel-coated people who might nudge him and ask, 'Who's the guest tonight?' Billy wanted to walk into a room in an outfit that identified him as a performer.

Iris began to make Billy's clothes for the stage because shops never carried clothing that matched his outlandish ideas. One favourite item was a pair of wide, deckchair-striped trousers, which he wore on stage with startling T-shirts dotted with gigantic stars and hearts. Billy swooned over clothes in very wild prints, and he took to scouring furnishing fabric warehouses to find the most colourful, flamboyant materials he could, in velvet, corduroy, satin or tartan. Some of Billy's folk-singing pals accused him of becoming too 'showbiz', but Billy in turn found their dowdiness a trifle fraudulent and forced.

Billy liked strange-looking hippie stuff and eventually he wore it in the street as well. He sent away for 'mosquito boots', which were like suede cowboy boots, from the shop Badges and Equipment, in the Strand, London. He tapered and flared some military tartan trousers in which he postured and pranced until somebody dropped a pint on them in the pub one day. After that, they were unbearable, like wearing a hedgehog.

Frank Lynch became Billy's manager. Billy performed at Frank's White Elephant Club in Edinburgh one night and, afterwards, Frank spluttered, 'That's the funniest thing I've seen in my whole life: I'm in pain. Do you want to come and talk to me?'

Frank also owned the Apollo in Glasgow. He told Billy he'd been backstage one night when Status Quo were playing. 'You've got to see it,' he hooted. 'It's really funny. They take off their Levi's and put on their stage Levi's.' But Billy understood it completely. By now, Billy knew all about the importance of changing for the stage and that performing required a heightening of both the visual and the verbal.

Although Billy was basically just speaking his mind when he performed, he found himself in an accelerated state of magnified consciousness that wasn't really him. He was essentially talking about reality, but he found he had to do so in an exaggerated way to make it special. That principle applied to his appearance too. He decided that, first and foremost, a stage performer's hair and body should be clean, unless his grubbiness is part of what he does ... he had seen that working really well and thought Tom Waits did it brilliantly. Tom always looks as if he's been sleeping in the back seat of a car and has just stumbled upon the stage by accident.

Billy decided he would like to be sexier on stage, not like actors and film stars and matinée idols, but to have a kind of rebellious, rock 'n' roll kind of sexiness. He considered wearing a leather suit but he had already tried that on stage and it had been too sweaty and uncomfortable. Maybe just tight leather pants would be the answer, with a twinkling rhinestone at his crotch. He has very sensitive skin, so he decided on velvet. He had some suits made in white and black velvet with flared trousers, which he wore with platform shoes, and a target on his knee to throw it all off balance. He even ordered satin suits, in white, pink and a screaming red and purple, with Lurex stars on his backside like his costume for the *Welly Boot Show*. His sleeves were flared like a wizard's, and the black suit had a hood that went way down past his calves. He designed many of those clothes himself, and was really proud of them.

Billy was crazy about a strange band called the Pink Fairies who were wild and hairy, a bit like the Pretty Things. Two of them wore tights with riding boots, a style Billy really liked. Billy thought big pink or yellow fluffy après-ski boots might be a nice touch, worn with tights or leggings. He would look like he was a roadie for the rock band Kiss. He settled on boots that looked like two giant, half-peeled bananas, a bit like John Byrne's Reggae Wellies.

Frank Lynch had a chain of discotheques and some alumni from the Glasgow School of Art who called themselves 'Artifactory' had created wacky interior designs for the dance houses. In one discotheque, there was a giant Liquorice Allsorts box with candy seats spilling out onto the dance floor, made of pink and black foam. One of the designers, Edmond Smith, was commissioned to make banana boots for Billy's stage appearances. A few weeks later, one of these outrageous pieces of footwear arrived at Billy's house. It just took his breath away, it was so damn clever. 'Edmond, I love that welly,' he cried. 'Could you start on the other?' 'It won't be identical,' Edmond was dead serious, 'but then, bananas never are.'

Delighted with his footwear, Billy looked around for something to complete the outfit. It wasn't easy to find tights or leggings to fit him and Billy could never understand why people in shops looked so baffled at his requests. Eventually he found women's oversized leotards and wore two pairs of tights so they would be opaque. Later on, Alan Jeffries, a young London designer who understood Billy's daftness, made him woollen tights with a design of his face on the rear: a beard hung down like his real one, and a pair of blue eyes peered out from his bum.

Billy was once describing this outfit on a talk show in Canada when he became aware of a fellow guest, the American comedian Robin Williams, roaring at the back of the studio. Billy thought, 'There's that guy, that nutter from the dressing room.' He had been instantly fascinated by the zero-to-sixty-brained, improvising genius in the Hawaiian shirt. They have been friends ever since.

When Billy dreamed up a suit that made him look like a giant pair of scissors, Alan fashioned the outrageous garment. The two halves of the scissors had large red handles that crossed at his crotch, with silver blades going down into the banana wellies. Billy admits he was a little apprehensive the first time he wore it on stage in the second half of his show at the Aberdeen Music Hall. For the first part of the show, he had worn his multicoloured deck-striped overalls with cowboy boots, but during the interval he changed into his scissors suit then nervously presented himself to his manager and stage crew in the backstage area. 'Fucking hell, look at you, man!' exploded Frank.

Billy never referred to his outfits on stage, but he thought his startling appearance helped to give him a licence to be unpredictable and say anything he damn well pleased. His show became half talking and half music and then, in time, his conversation very gradually overtook his playing and singing. It was like the hands of a clock; the next time you saw the show it was different, but you never saw anything moving.

Billy's impression of British comedians in the late sixties and early seventies was that they had little satirical or political edge. Instead, they were talking about their mothers-in-law, referring to sex by innuendo, or making racist cracks about Pakistani immigrants. There was a show on TV called *The Comedians* and the men who received a platform on that show, largely Manchester-based wisecrackers and the Irishman Frank Carson, became the famous bow-tie stand-ups of the time. Billy had little in common with them. 'How do you describe yourself?' he was asked at the time. 'I dunno ... a comic singer ... banjo player.' He really wasn't sure how to answer.

One day, Billy read in the paper that he was a comedian. It really surprised him because he had no idea how a person became one of those. And anyway, where would he fit in, among the bow-tie guys and the remnants of variety theatre? He looked like a hairy freak. He was the wrong age, the wrong shape and too wild by half. His solution was shrewd and required gumption. 'I'll just stay where I am,' he decided, 'and hope the genre gets bigger.' It did.

What Billy created wasn't called 'alternative comedy'. There was no such thing. The press began to take notice of this crazy person with weird boots: 'Is he the new Harry Lauder?' read the headlines. Billy felt insulted. He didn't want to be the new anything. He just wanted to be Billy Connolly, whoever the heck he was. He never really approved of Harry Lauder anyway, wearing a kilt and being a 'Scottish showbiz personality'.

At that time, Billy wouldn't have been seen dead in a kilt: 'I wouldn't know how to tune one,' he told his audiences. Billy's real desire was to be as funny as ordinary people. He thinks it's magical to be in a bar around lunchtime with a bunch of people who are having a get-together. They might be office workers or nurses from the hospital along the road, or men who've been digging a hole out front. Maybe one of them is leaving, maybe there's a birthday, or one of them might have been promoted. Billy says you can recognize this little mob by their explosive laughter. They'll talk away, then Boom! there'll be a huge, backslapping laugh. They'll talk away again, and then Boom! there'll be another. There isn't a comedian anywhere in sight. These are just people talking about their lives and roaring. There's a wonderful, real quality to that laugh that show business doesn't have. It's unrehearsed.

Billy believes the catalyst for that electric hilarity is a particular kind of tension. Perhaps the individuals are oppressed or controlled by someone else, or else they might be bored or frustrated. Whatever the root cause of the tension might be, if it creates some type of siege mentality it will often spark that intense jocularity. Billy seeks it passionately. While acknowledging that it's impossible for professionals to achieve it exactly, Billy attempts to create it spontaneously every time he goes on stage. He retains something up his sleeve in case it doesn't happen, but on those heavenly nights when he successfully puts himself out there on a limb, something happens that rehearsed material can never instigate in a million years. On those magical occasions, he knows he's flying and the audience does too. He comes off stage after those shows and whimpers, 'I wish I was in the audience tonight.'

When Frank insisted that Billy begin to play larger theatres, Billy resisted it but he knew his manager was right. He belonged on a bigger stage and eventually began to appear at the Pavilion Theatre, the Carnegie Hall and the Kings Theatre in Glasgow. After his success in those venues, he realized that it had been an act of cowardice to try and stay where he was. Some people objected to this hairy upstart daring to play venues that variety theatre had dominated for years. Andy Stewart and others had come through that way, yet here was Billy in his weird clothes with a head like Jesus, swearing and talking about farting and shagging.

William's approval was still far from forthcoming, too. William verbally acknowledged his son's achievements only once in his whole life, when the Variety Club honoured him and gave him a statue. It was an enormously satisfying occasion for Billy. People he loved and admired turned up, including several Celtic football heroes. After dinner, Billy spoke to the invitees for a few minutes and was very warmly received. On the way home in the limousine, Billy's father turned to him: 'You were very good.' That blew Billy away. He'd never said anything positive before. William only came to see Billy half a dozen times. One of those times was to watch him play Frosch the drunken jailer in *Die Fledermaus* with the Scottish Opera. At the performance, William passed out in a drunken stupor and had to be woken for the finale. Billy rather enjoyed that.

In October 1973, Billy went to London to do a voice-over for a tourist film called *Clydoscope*, directed by Billy's friend Murray Grigor, a film-maker from Fife. Billy had bicycled the entire Clyde's journey from Lanarkshire to the sea, stopping every so often during the filming to phone Iris who was pregnant again. When Billy sang a song to an image of himself on a gigantic sound-studio screen, he thought it was his original tune, but Billy had unwittingly stolen it from *The Wombles*. Fortunately, Mike Batt, who wrote the song, was merely amused. Billy put the last chord on the banjo, then turned round for feedback:

'How was that?'

Murray was standing behind him with a tray of champagne.

'It's a girl,' he announced.

~

Cara was a stunning baby, and the most pleasant child. She looked like a Smartie, completely round and smiley with the nicest manner. Billy called her the 'sleepy dumpling', which later became the name of his entertainment company. Billy absolutely loves babies. He refers to them as 'talking sausages' and has quite a way with them all. If you ever need a baby to fall asleep, Billy's your man. He has a special technique called 'Sleepy-Toes' that never fails. Cara was always a placid child with very knowing eyes. She listened a lot and giggled a great deal.

Jamie, meanwhile, had refused to go to kindergarten because they made him settle down for an afternoon nap. He was already taking after his father. 'Bollocks to sleep, let's do things!' Billy and Iris were peeling Jamie off the railings to try to get him inside, when Billy remembered his own school horrors. 'What are we doing?' He looked at Iris. 'Let's take him home.'

Jamie's main memory of that time is that everywhere he looked there were extremely hairy people. He himself had shoulder-length hair by the time he was four and was furious with his mother for refusing to take him to the barber. He was frequently mistaken for a girl.

Billy and his family had moved from 'the den' to an elegant and spacious apartment in Redlands Road, well away from his father's place in White Street. William had left Singer's when Mona first became ill, to become a night-shift telephonist at the Buchanan exchange so he could be available during the daytime. Mona had been allowed home occasionally but she could no longer sit crocheting mats and embroidering lovely cushions as she used to. Instead, she wandered around in a state of disarray, while her family exhorted her to wash. Margaret had never married and still lived with William, so she took care of Mona at night.

After Mona's death, Margaret seemed to soften up and Billy became more comfortable in her company. Just before Michael married Helen, a bank teller from south Glasgow, Margaret, or 'Gags' as Michael called her, took him aside. She intended to reveal the identity of his biological father, whom he'd never met, and the circumstances of his conception. 'I don't want to know,' insisted Michael. 'I don't really care. The people who brought you up are your parents.' It was his last opportunity to receive Margaret's information, for soon after her fifty-first birthday she died of cancer.

Returning home to Redlands Road after her funeral service, Billy spotted a couple of fans sitting on his garden wall. Redlands Road was too accessible to members of the general public now that he was growing in stature. He was very grateful for the appreciation people were showing him, but he didn't want them turning up at his door or stealing his jeans from the washing line.

Billy and Iris decided to move to the countryside, to the peaceful town of Drymen just outside Glasgow. At last they had a wonderful garden for the children to roam around in and Billy made them a sandpit. As a toddler, Cara always loved having a job to perform. She trotted off to feed the rabbits, guinea pigs and the donkey they named Booby after one of Billy's roadies, Booby Daniels. Afterwards, she would take a nap in a wheelbarrow.

Billy was happy that his children were having the kind of life he had only dreamed about, but deep down he was hitting a wall, frequently tormented about his own lost childhood. There was a woodland between the house and the road and a river ran beside the house. Jamie was an Action Man fan at the time, so he pleaded for a battery-powered toy dinghy for his Action Man to drive. Shortly after Jamie received the expensive toy, Billy heard a great din in the garden and went out to investigate. Jamie had commanded Cara to launch the dinghy further upstream, while he and a friend waited in the bushes to ambush it with huge, jagged boulders. Billy himself had never had a toy worth anything close to thirty pounds, yet here was Action Man, tragically wiped out by heavy artillery fire.

On the surface, Billy's life was quite jolly, but inside he was lost. When he made public appearances, he arrived to great fanfare. He would open shops and cut ribbons while pipe bands played. A little voice inside, however, kept nagging him. It sounded a little bit like Mona. 'Who do you think you are? You don't deserve this.'

Billy was getting drunk very regularly and was even having blackouts. The trick, he decided, was to never let his hangover catch up with him, just stay drunk. He began to go off on long solo tours of Australia, Canada and Britain, playing ninety nights in each country.

Touring was an interesting phenomenon. After about a month of little sleep, endless packing and unpacking and a brutal performing schedule, he would enter a kind of limbo where life was quite dream-like. The drinking and carousing became normal, while the rest of the world became blurry. Billy likens it to the experience of sailors who spend so much time at sea they begin to hate shore people.

Nobody in that insulated world ever told him he was drinking too much, or that he was too loud or hogging the company. The road, he decided, had its own rules, structure and hierarchy. Everything was provided without any effort on his part. There was never a shortage of cigarettes, cigars or drinks. He met women who wanted to sleep with him, which usually seemed like a very good idea. When he came back from breakfast every morning, somebody had made his bed. Wonderland! He never took stock, because that would bring him back into the real world, and to hell with the real world. The real world was where disease, unemployment and unhappiness dwelled, not to mention having to take responsibility for his actions. Unfortunately, when the tour was over, he was obliged to go home. It was lovely to see his family again, but he could never get room service on the phone.

Touring was not his only activity in the seventies. Billy became a successful recording artist with Polydor Records. Michael had criticized Billy for years about his music and his 'stupid folkie friends'. 'You watch,' Billy had forecast, 'I'll be on *Top of the Pops* one day. You'll be laughing on the other side of your bloody face then.' 'Oh yeah, right,' laughed Michael, 'with your banjo. Terrific.'

Billy's contact at Polydor, George McManus, alerted Billy that the country-and-western singing star Tammy Wynette had recorded a song called 'D-I-V-O-R-C-E', a tear-jerker about a mother who spelled the details of her divorce to protect her child from heartache. In 1975, Billy recorded a parody of her hit, under the guidance of the Irishman Phil Coulter, a music producer who had been working with the popular group, the Bay City Rollers.

'Frank Lynch had been putting the bite on me to see some guy who was funny and played instruments,' reports Phil now, 'so I went up to the Kings Theatre in Glasgow under sufferance, to record Billy's show. We sniffed around each other like two dogs, then I went into my mobile studio and Billy went on stage. Within minutes, I had flung my clipboard away, arrested my stopwatch and had fallen across the mixing desk, which screwed up all the faders. He was the funniest man on the planet and he still is.'

Billy's version of 'D-I-V-O-R-C-E' went gold. It climbed to number one in the British charts, while Tammy Wynette's original version only made it to number twelve. Billy appeared on *Top of the Pops* in a purple polka-dot suit, playing his guitar and singing:

'Our little dog is six years old
And smart as any damn kid

And when you mention the "v-e-t"
He damn near flips his lid.
Words like "s-h-o-t" shot
Or "w-o-r-m" worm
These are words that make him "s-q-u-i-r-m" squirm.'

Frank Lynch thought Billy should play the London Palladium and, to Billy's surprise, it sold out without a single advertisement – every McAnyone in London bought a ticket. The twelfth of January 1975 was a staggering night: Billy had never before heard such noise or enthusiasm from an audience. At the end, the stage crew brought down the fire curtain because they were afraid the crowd was going to rush the stage.

One early morning that same year, a Glaswegian taxi driver was transporting a passenger from his hotel to the airport when he suddenly became aware of the identity of the hung-over gentleman slumped in the back. It was Michael Parkinson, Britain's most famous television talk show host, in the middle of a promotional tour for his biography of the football player George Best.

'You like the funny men, don't you?' assumed the driver.

'I do.' Michael opened one eye.

'D'you know the "Big Yin"?'

'No.' He was irritated. 'What's that?'

'You should have him on your show.'

With that, the driver screeched to a halt, leapt out and disappeared into a shop. When he re-emerged, he presented Michael with a copy of the album *Billy Connolly Live*.

'Play that,' he ordered.

Michael took the record home and stashed it away in his record collection. His son Andrew finally persuaded him to put it on. 'You'll really like it, Dad, play it.' Michael had never heard anything like it in his life. It was 'The Crucifixion', and he could only understand about half of it because Billy's accent in those days was much more raw; nonetheless, Michael began to laugh to the point of losing control. He took the album to his producer, John Fisher. 'This guy's hilarious,' he told John. 'We have to put him on the show.'

In the limousine on the way to the BBC TV studios for his first appearance on the *Parkinson Show*, Frank had warned Billy, 'Whatever else you do, don't tell that joke about the bum. You'll ruin everything.' He was referring to one of Billy's favourite stories of that time. Billy was dressed for the show in a pale brown leather suit he'd had specially made in Glasgow and an obscenely hairy sporran. 'It's hideous,' said Michael, staring at the suit, 'but let him wear it.'

Billy was the first guest that evening. Michael introduced him as 'One of the most original and best comedians I have heard in many a day'. Billy played it safe by opening with a song by Leo McGuire:

'I am heading with my crummoch up from Gretna Green to Skye
But my journey has an element of farce
Cos the calendar has stated it's the middle of July
Yet here I am with snow up to my arse.'

It was a parody of all the 'tartan and velvet' entertainers and the audience loved it. Then Billy sat down and Michael interviewed him. He thought his new guest seemed shy, gauche, and a little wary. 'In those days you really had to get it out of him,' remembers Michael, 'but he was so bloody funny, and he had an extraordinary way about him. People liked him.'

'I hope I can get away with this, it's a beauty,' Billy said suddenly. There was a close-up shot of Parkinson nervously fidgeting with his collar. 'This guy was going out to meet his friend in the pub,' began Billy, while Frank Lynch buried his face in his hands. 'Oh no, Billy, not the one about the bum!'

Typically, Billy couldn't resist. He continued. 'How's it going? Fine. How's the wife? Oh she's dead. What? I murdered her this morning. You're kidding me on! No, I'll show you, if you like. So he goes away up to his tenement building, through the close ...' at this point, Billy smiled indulgently at Parky, 'that's the entrance to the tenement,' he explained, 'and there's a big mound of earth there and, sure enough, there's a bum sticking out. He says, Is that her? He says aye. He says, Why'd you leave her bum sticking out? He says I need somewhere to park my bike.' When Billy delivered the punch line, the crowd just exploded.

'You see him on stage now and he's exactly the same as he was in that studio,' says Michael now. 'He got away with that joke at that moment in time, and he always gets away with murder. Little old ladies come to his shows, sit through a torrent of "f" words and end up wanting to adopt him,' he observes. 'They don't mind what he does because they say, "He's a nice man", and he is. Likeability is an extraordinary gift.'

Billy was grateful to Michael, who had come to his dressing room before the show and treated him like he was Bob Hope, although, as far as Billy was concerned, Michael was the big shot. Best of all, Michael hadn't asked Billy to be funny in rehearsal. Billy is a performer, not a technician. He's always afraid people will lose faith in him in rehearsal, for he cannot shine in an empty room.

Michael thought Billy was 'the genuine article', as he puts it. 'We have a shared background and aspirations ... It was like he was talking about my own life. I saw him as a class warrior. There was a political edge to his humour: it was as if he was saying to working-class people, "Look at me ... if I can do it, you can."'

After the *Parkinson Show*, it seemed as though a door had opened for Billy and a brilliant light shone through. 'It would have happened anyway,' says Michael graciously, but the truth is that appearing on the *Parkinson Show* made Billy a star all over Britain and Northern Ireland. He embarked on a two-month, sell-out, one-man UK tour, which he titled 'The Big Wee Tour'. When the lights came up at the beginning of the show, the audience was greeted by a life-sized cutout of Harry Lauder with Billy's hirsute head stuck through a hole above the neck, singing Harry's own song, 'Keep Right On to the End of the Road'. A blackout followed and, when the lights came up again, Harry had disappeared and Billy was standing on stage alone. 'Friends, Romans, countrymen,' he began, 'I come to bury Lauder, not to praise him.'

By now, Billy was determined to explore every nook and cranny of his ability, whether that meant acting, or writing a book, a play or some poetry. He looked at himself in the mirror one morning and spoke his epiphany: 'Fuck, you can do anything you like! You don't need lessons! You don't need fucking permission! The greatest guys in the world will be happy to show you how. All you have to do is look interested!'

Billy really took to acting. He appeared in a couple of BBC television plays with politi-cultural themes, written by Peter McDougall, a fellow Glaswegian. Like Billy, Peter is largely self-educated and was abandoned by a parent. His father was a seaman whose frequent escapes from the family mirrored William's and inspired in Peter the same type of deep pain overlaid with sullen rage that Billy feels about both of his parents. Peter is a brilliant, melancholic walrus with a fury and darkness as fathomless as Billy's own. 'He is still the tortured soul that he has always been,' says Billy of Peter, 'and the light of truth shines through him like a beacon.'

Peter's play, *Just Another Saturday*, won the Italia Prize and was about the Orange, Protestant order, while *Elephant's Graveyard* tracked the hopelessness of an unemployed man. John Morrison was the leading actor in both but Billy received critical acclaim for supporting roles. Peter was immediately impressed by Billy's innate acting ability and still considers his work in those early television roles to be the best acting he's ever done. 'He had a wonderful stillness,' Peter says now. What ensured Billy's solo comedic success, according to Peter, is his perspicacity, a quality both men share.

The two men embarked on a friendship based on background similarities, mutual admiration and a penchant for getting pissed.

The second time Billy met Peter, he carried the intoxicated writer's comatose body home to rest. Peter was living in London at the time, so Billy often met him in a pub in Little Venice. After a serious skinful, the pair once attempted to enter a nightclub, but were refused entry for being unpleasantly uninhibited. Peter knew a back way in, but it required an athletic challenge involving a Tarzan-type jungle swing across the canal. Billy attempted the manoeuvre with great bravado, fully clothed and wearing the high-heeled clogs he favoured at the time. Predictably, he lost his grip and fell into the canal. When he surfaced and climbed out of the water, he realized that one of his clogs had sunk without trace. Billy began removing his sopping jacket. 'No!' cried Peter. 'Don't go back in!' It was too late. Billy dived back into the putrid canal and searched around in murky water. 'You'd think the Dutch would have invented shoes that could float!' he moaned.

In 1976, Billy wrote his own stage play, *And Me Wi' a Bad Leg*, about tenement life in Glasgow. Bill Paterson played the leading role, and the play was first performed in Irvine, Ayrshire. It was successful enough to go on to the Edinburgh Festival and finally to the Upstairs Theatre at the Royal Court in London. During its run, Billy decided to visit his cousin John, who had moved to Bath. John was even crazier than before and his practical jokes had got completely out of hand. He had taken to riding around in a Bedford van looking for cyclists. He had a long broomstick with a red boxing glove on the end with the word 'BIFF!' written in white paint on the side. He would slide open the door of his van and drive alongside the unfortunate man. 'Hello!' When the cyclist looked in the door and saw the word 'BIFF!' coming at him, likely as not he would cycle into a hedge.

On his return from London, Billy attended the Edinburgh Festival premiere of *Big Banana Feet*, a documentary by Murray Grigor about Billy's previous Dublin and Belfast tour. It presents an artist who is surprised to have filled the halls, exhibiting defensiveness about his proclivity for frank body talk. 'Of course my show's vulgar,' Billy is seen arguing scornfully. 'I do it on purpose. I enjoy it from the stage and they enjoy it in the audience. But I don't think it's rude or offensive because I talk about my willie: fifty-three point nine per cent of the population of Britain's got a willie ... what's wrong with that all of a sudden?

'And when it comes to four-letter words, most people swear,' says Billy hopefully, 'but I happen to think Glasgow people swear better than anyone else in the world. It's like machine-gun fire. You hear it at a football match, usually accompanied by a mouthful of cold pie and Bovril.'

Billy innately understood then what he can verbalize today: 'Anywhere you're vulnerable, you're funny,' he explains, adding a truism that explains an awful lot, including his obsession with cavorting naked in public:

'If your knickers are down, you're funny,' he thunders. 'I *love* life with my knickers down!'

10

STAIRWAY TO HELL

Backstage at an Oscar party in Los Angeles, 1999, I am trying to squeeze my way through a rambunctious crowd of contenders, mentally swearing that I will never again wear an evening gown that features a train at the back. Kevin Spacey steps on it, pulling me up short. At least I think it's Kevin Spacey. I am known for my dreadful errors of recognition, notably mistaking the late Freddie Mercury's hairdresser for the star himself after a Queen concert in the eighties.

I am again jerked to a halt when Geena Davis (surely it is she) sticks her heel right through the middle of my train. A child actor, whose name I definitely don't know, extricates steel from satin. Thanking him and glaring at her, I continue on my obstacle course, searching for my husband. I spot him by the bar, engrossed in conversation with Bill Maher, the quick-witted comedian who hosts the TV show *Politically Incorrect*. Billy is one of his favourite guests on the show, always offering an original and outrageous topical comment.

'Pamela, this is *Bill Maher*.' Billy no longer takes any chances with me.

'Hi, Bill. Um, Billy, Ben's here.'

'Ben who?'

'Kingsley. I've been chatting to him in the back room. Go and say hello.'

While Bill and I catch up, Billy takes off in search of the bald thespian, best known for his stunning performance in *Gandhi*.

'You fucking idiot!' He's back already. 'That's Patrick Stewart.'

∿

As Billy's fame escalated, he began to meet many of his heroes. He was particularly fascinated with rock stars, especially the wild ones like Mick Jagger and Keith Moon. Billy opened for Elton John in the American College in London and came across his old pal Davey Johnstone who had joined Elton's band. Davey is a sweet man and a talented guitarist who had been playing the banjo in the Scottish folk scene since he was sixteen. Billy called him 'The Child Protestant from Edinburgh'.

In July and August of 1976, Billy opened for Elton during his USA tour. Billy learned the hard way that it is not easy to play someone else's audience. 'Hearing them announce my name is like someone saying "Ready, Aim, FIRE!"' moaned Billy at the time.

'Ladies and Gentlemen!' the announcer would boom.

'Whaaaa!' went the crowd.

'Elton John ...'

'WHAAAAA!' The crowd's crescendo lifted towards a peak until he finished his sentence: 'would like you to welcome his friend ... BILLY CONNOLLY!'

'Ooooohhhh ... Boooo!' they would go.

It is unlikely that every stadium on Elton's tour was filled with four thousand stoned Puerto Rican people, 'all holding hands trying to get in touch with the living', but that's what it felt like to Billy. Some nights he won, some nights he lost. None of them really wanted to sit through the antics of a Scottish idiot wearing tights and banana boots.

Billy was assuaging his hangover with a cup of tea one morning when he came across an article about one of his heroes, Tom Waits,

Billy serenades the 'talking sausage'. With Jamie at Mick Quinn's house.

The 'Artful Dodger' look: Billy throws some rubbish into the White Street midden, in an artful photograph taken by Michael.

Some Mariachi band leader is missing his blouse. Pre-Gerry Rafferty Humblebums: Billy and Tam Harvey on stage at the Kelvin Hall.

Billy surreptitiously unzipping his fly while posing for a publicity still with Gerry Rafferty. Taken on Hampstead Heath.

Above: Would you vote for the man on the right? Ho Chi Minh meets Harold Wilson, then Leader of the Opposition, at a Labour Party rally at the Apollo, Glasgow.

Right: No one ever told Billy you're not supposed to wear checks and stripes together! The trousers are red, white and blue and the funky shoes are black and silver. Publicity shot outside Buckingham Palace, July 1974.

Left: Billy, the 'Half-Stoned Cowboy' on his 'Seaside Extravaganza Tour' of 1977. He is wearing the tour T-shirt, displaying a caricature of Billy with a large belly, like the seaside postcard artist McGill's famous image 'Where's my little willie?'

Below: Billy with Iris *(left)* and Jamie, taken by Jamie Wark whose mother is beside Billy.

Left: First day at school. Five-year-old Cara posing in front of Billy's new Mercedes, taken at the house in Drymen.

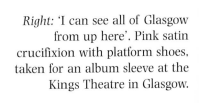

Right: 'I can see all of Glasgow from up here'. Pink satin crucifixion with platform shoes, taken for an album sleeve at the Kings Theatre in Glasgow.

Above: 'Myself, I find those Carmen Rollers very effective, don't you?' The *Parkinson Show*, just after Hogmanay in 1977.

Left: Visual proof that Billy is much smaller in real life! As a 'holier than thou' minister, spoofing the TV epilogue.

Director: Anthony Page. Producer: Bulldog (Danny O'Donovan, Elliott Kastner).

Above: With Richard Burton in *Absolution*, only one of them was 'on the wagon'.

Right: 'Anything that moves is mine', on tour in Ireland.

Above: First meeting: our 'Janet Street-Porter' sketch on *Not the Nine O'Clock News*, just before my 'Janet' teeth fell out and Billy cracked up.

Below: The *Not the Nine O'Clock News* gang, 1980. (*Left to right:*) Sean Hardie (producer), Mel Smith, me, Rowan Atkinson, Griff Rhys Jones, John Lloyd (producer) and Bill Wilson (director). My T-shirt reads 'Honi Soit Qui Malibu'.

in *Rolling Stone* magazine. Waits informed the world that he died on stage every night while opening for another rock band. Tom described it as 'a nightly exercise in terror'. 'Oh thank God, I'm not alone,' sighed Billy.

Despite the difficulty of supporting another act, Billy was learning valuable stage survival techniques and was subsequently sought after to open for other bands. After touring the east coast of the United States with Elton, he opened for Elvis Costello, played a week at the Bottom Line in New York with the Irish band Horslips and supported the jazz guitarist, Larry Coryell.

Billy managed to hold his own with the audiences of all those artists, although sometimes it was pretty alarming. During his tour of Kansas City, Chicago and Boston with Manhattan Transfer, the band got stuck in a blizzard and he had to do an entire show himself. With Dr Hook and the Medicine Show, Billy visited Wilkes-Barre, Pennsylvania, Washington, Atlantic City and Georgetown, and he was relieved to find that at least Dr Hook's audience appreciated him. Billy now bestrode the world like a giant velvet-looned colossus, at least until the day his luggage got lost and he had to go on stage in corduroys with borrowed equipment.

Whenever Billy was in Los Angeles he stayed at the Hyatt Hotel on Sunset Boulevard, known as 'the Riot House', where every rocker in the world had checked in or partied at one time or another. One or two had never checked out. Numerous true tales and apocryphal fables have emanated from the Hyatt. One night, when Billy returned there from his concert he ran into Tony Palmer who had directed the *Welly Boot Show*. Tony was sitting at the bar with a fat, short-haired guy wearing a sports jacket with a Hereford cow badge on his lapel. He looked like a dentist but he was talking about 'gigs' and people hiding under tables in Greece.

'Are you in a band?' asked Billy.

'Yes,' he replied. 'I'm a drummer.'

It was John Bonham, from Led Zeppelin, better known as 'Bonzo'.

'Wanna go to a party tomorrow night in my room?'

He was on the same hotel floor as Billy.

'Is that your bodyguard at the end of the hall?' inquired Billy.

It was. The next evening there was a long line of bizarre people along the corridor outside Bonzo's door. Periodically, a man came wandering along and sectioned off part of the queue, saying, 'All right, everyone up to here, in you go.' They were changing the guests every fifteen minutes. A man sat at the door with vials of amyl nitrate that he smashed and held up to each guest's nose as he entered the party room.

'We've got a gig tomorrow night,' said Bonzo. 'Do you want to come?' Absolutely Billy wanted to go. He couldn't believe it. Elvis Presley had lent Bonzo his gold Lincoln Continental to travel as far as the private Star Jet. That luxurious aircraft whisked them to San Diego where a motorcycle escort met them and escorted them to the gig. On the way, Bonzo was roaring at Billy's story about an English saxophone player called Jimmy Jewell who had gone on the road with Gary Glitter's *Rock 'n' Roll Circus*. The show was dying everywhere and Jimmy hadn't been paid for weeks, so he got up in the middle of the night and raided the petty cash box. He skipped off, leaving a note inside saying: 'Goodbye, cruel circus, I'm off to join the world.'

Best of all, Billy met Jimmy Page, the most mysterious man alive in rock 'n' roll. Jimmy, who was an Aleister Crowley fanatic, wore velvet pants with weird signs and stars on them, which everyone assumed had deep and portentous meanings. Legend had it the pants were transported by vestal virgins who'd been flayed on the way to the gig. When Billy met Jimmy, however, he had the sacred pants in a plastic Safeway's bag.

On the way back, Bonzo told Billy about the time he fell asleep during a performance of their most famous song, 'Stairway to Heaven'. The drums didn't come in until three minutes into the song, so Bonzo nodded off. It was pure luck that he woke just in time.

Billy is the only person in the world who ever interviewed Bonzo. He agreed to talk to Billy for a show on Tyne-Tees Television called *All Right Now*, but just before the interview he became really nervous and shovelled down a two-course meal of cocaine and brandy.

'OK,' Billy improvised, 'we'll do a non-interview. I'll ask long, rambling questions and you nod, shrug and look bored. Then we'll go and have a proper dinner.'

Billy seemed to gravitate towards convivial fellow performers who were also party-minded. One such person was Brian Connolly, singer with the Sweet, who had long blond hair and the shakes, while another was Les Gray, from the band Mud, who was afflicted by psoriasis and wore gloves over his flaking skin in case he snowed on people. Mal Kingsnorth, Billy's sound engineer, referred to them as 'Shake 'n' Vac'.

Billy had developed a piece of comedy about the children's television puppet characters Bill and Ben, the Flowerpot Men, smoking marijuana. It always went down well with his British audiences, but any drug reference was a sure hit on both sides of the Atlantic. Of course, the mid-seventies rock 'n' roll scene was very much a drug culture and the audience wasn't the only group enjoying an alternative reality. As Billy says now, 'It snowed in 'seventy-six.'

One of Elton's roadies introduced Billy to cocaine during their tour. It's not surprising that Billy became very drawn to that particular drug, for it has a very interesting effect on people like him who have difficulty concentrating. Instead of amping them up in the usual way, such stimulants can have a paradoxical effect and actually help them to concentrate. Unfortunately, his cocaine abuse escalated along with his alcohol abuse, and didn't stop until after he met me. His ambition was always to use it and have some left in the morning, but that never happened.

After the tour with Elton, Billy made a unique album, produced by Phil Coulter, called *Atlantic Bridge*. Half of it was recorded at Carnegie

Hall in Dunfermline where Andrew Carnegie came from and the other half at Carnegie Hall in New York. The *Python* star Eric Idle came to see Billy in New York and brought Paul Simon and Mick Jagger. The next day Eric phoned. 'Why don't you come round?' he suggested. 'I'm talking to Mr Jagger.'

It was the beginning of a great friendship with the *Python* star. Eric had been to see him before, usually in London with Peter Cook in tow, but Billy had always been very wary of them. 'I'd always been scared of people with tertiary education and high intellects in case they found me wanting,' he explains. 'I thought they viewed me as just a welder who knew a few jokes.'

'He was pure joy,' says Eric. 'Breathtakingly honest. We went backstage and there he was in his banana boots. The next day he came round to my hotel room and entertained us for three hours telling us stories of Scottish bank robberies. We all howled the entire afternoon ... he was extraordinary.'

Back in London, Elton phoned Billy while he was in the process of having a sepia photo-portrait taken by the photographer Terry O'Neill. 'Maureen?' That's what Elton calls Billy. 'Want to come and hear my new album?' Billy went out to the Mill Studios, already bomb-happy on wine and cocaine, then continued to party when he got there. Elton played him one of his latest tracks then left the sound suite briefly to confer with a studio technician. When he returned, he found that Billy had collapsed onto the floor. 'Jesus! Somebody wake him up! Get help!' People frantically tried to revive him, imagining he had passed away. When Billy came round he was embarrassed about all the fuss.

'I'm perfectly fine,' he informed them. 'It's happened before ...'

'But you can't accept that sort of thing happening ... you just died!'

'Fuck,' Billy shrugged his shoulders, 'that's what life's like.'

~

'Dad, did you ever meet Jimi Hendrix?'

Our teenager Amy is playing an air guitar, wearing head-phones and sliding around adopting seventies rocker poses.

'Yep.'

'You're kidding.' The action stops. 'What was he like?'

'I really don't know.'

'What d'you mean, you don't know ...?'

'Well, now, this is why you must never take drugs. After he died, I met Jimi's roadie in LA. I said, "I wish I'd met Jimi. I thought he was brilliant," and he said, "You did. He was very fond of you." Apparently we had a great night together in the Speakeasy in London ...'

'Oh, Dad ... what are you like!' Amy is rolling her eyes.

'Which proves my point ...' insists her father '... if you remember the seventies, you weren't there.'

~

Billy is one of the lucky ones, for some did not survive the effects of the seventies. The night before Billy left for one of his tours of the Australian continent, he was out on the razzle in London with Keith Moon. Keith seemed surprisingly abstinent. 'I'm only doing brandy suppositories these days, dear boy,' he said.

'I'm going to Australia tomorrow,' Billy informed him in the course of the evening.

'Then tell them from me to fuck off,' replied Keith. He'd had a run-in there with the press. When Billy arrived in Australia the headlines seemed to scream a warning to him. Keith had died that night.

'Fuck,' thought Billy, 'maybe I'd better take it easy.'

Billy toured Australia for the first time towards the end of 1976. He was glad to find that continent to be a lot more fun than Nevil Shute had described it. In the main, his concerts there were extremely successful, but Billy tells a dramatic story about getting beaten up on stage during a show in Brisbane. In the story Billy has told thousands of people, the audience didn't just boo him off, they actually booed him on. 'Oh, come on,' protested Billy, dodging well-aimed missiles, 'at least give me a chance to bore you first ...'

Then an irate man ran towards the stage shouting, 'We didn't come here to listen to this filth!'

'So ... where do you normally go?' inquired Billy.

He took a swing at Billy but failed to realize that Billy's chin does not reach the end of his beard and completely missed.

'Is that your best shot, pal?' taunted Billy.

'No!' said the man, and nutted him.

Billy fabricated this story, partly because he thought if he told the truth it might cause trouble and partly because it made people roar: 'It was living proof that Brisbane people interfere with kangaroos,' he jibed afterwards, obfuscating what had really happened. Billy had in fact become the target for religious persecution by a pocket of Scottish religious bigots in the audience, who shouted anti-Catholic curses and Rangers FC war cries. The whole thing got completely out of control, and Billy had to come off stage. 'Fuck!' He was distraught. 'Is the whole Australian tour going to be like this? I can't leave ... I haven't even earned my fare back.'

Fortunately his show in Canberra the following night was a very different experience. He has always teased Canberra folk for the clichéd notions, probably envy-based, that are held in other states about the lack of soul in their capital, but he was relieved at his warm reception there. It was followed by equal success in Sydney and Melbourne, and subsequent visits to all Australian cities, including Brisbane, have been just dandy.

On one occasion in Sydney, just before Billy was due to play the Opera House, he recorded a marvellous television interview with Michael Parkinson. 'Eh Parkie,' said Billy on their way back to the Sebel Town House, which at the time was the Australian equivalent of the Riot House in LA, 'I think we'll have a wee dram.'

The pair had become great mates. Billy has always highly valued his friendship with Michael. 'Just think of all the great people he's met,' Billy always wonders, 'yet he chose me as his friend.' 'He is everything in a man that I like,' says Michael. 'He's incredibly masculine, funny and liked a drink'.

Their love affair came close to being consummated that evening in Sydney. The Sebel Town House bar was closed so they drove to a 'dive' in King's Cross where they found the entire Queensland rugby team had also gathered, for a post-game beer. The shortest team player was a steak-fed mountain and each one sported a badly shaved head and an attitude to match. Michael felt a shadow looming over his face as one of these monsters squeezed himself threateningly between him and Billy, facing him square-on.

'Hey, Parko ...' That was what they called him in Australia.

'Yes,' replied Michael nervously.

Before the rugby player could continue, Billy's voice rang out insolently from behind him.

'See you!' He was actually addressing the hulk. 'Why don't you fuck off!'

It's a miracle they got out of there in one piece. They were both truly pissed and heading back to the Sebel Town House when the driver suddenly alerted Michael.

'He's gone.'

'What do you mean, he's gone?'

'He's got out of the car!'

The vehicle had stopped for traffic in the middle of King's Cross, a five-way thoroughfare as busy and dangerous as the Place Charles de Gaulle in Paris. Michael was horrified to see Billy standing smack in the middle of the Cross, doing an arm-flailing, Fred Astaire-inspired dance.

'Puttin' on my top hat ...' sang Billy, 'I've pudding on my top hat ...'

'Billy, Billy, Billy ...' Michael had braved the side-swiping vehicles to try to coax him out of harm's way.

'I've seen him,' announced Billy, mysteriously. His eyes were gone.

'Billy,' Michael pleaded, 'come on back to the car.'

'Eh Parkie,' he proposed, 'can you dance?'

'Yes ... on occasion ... but ...'

'Can you take the woman's part?'

He whirled Michael around in a bizarrely rhythmic fashion until a couple of approaching policemen sent them scurrying for safety.

The following night Michael had grave concerns about Billy's ability to give of his best, but despite the odds he gave the best performance Michael had ever seen ... or at least that's what it seemed like through the filter of Michael's own sore head. 'You bastard,' said Michael.

∾

The idea of doing the unexpected always had great appeal for Billy. 'I know. Let's tour the seaside in winter!' he said to Frank one day when he was back in Britain. Frank was very dubious. Summer was traditionally the time to attract audiences to those seaside towns. To everyone's surprise, the off-season 'Seaside Extravaganza Tour' worked extremely well and established a precedent so that others soon followed suit. The seaside audiences loved Billy's new rendition of 'Half-Stoned Cowboy', written by Seamus Healy, that parodied Glen Campbell's hit 'Rhinestone Cowboy'. It was Billy's latest spoof of the American country music he loved. Such pieces gave him a chance to play great music and be funny at the same time.

It was during the tour that Frank Lynch mentioned, 'Hey, a guy wants you to do a movie with Richard Burton.' Billy had never been in a movie before, yet his first scene in *Absolution* was with this celebrated actor. 'Hi Fiddle Dee Dee,' thought Billy, 'an actor's life for me!' Billy thought Richard was magnificent and they quickly became friends.

'Do you know Ronnie Fraser?' asked Richard. Billy liked Ronnie. He was a piss-artist with a face like a dartboard. The two actors had been drinking buddies before Richard went on the wagon.

'How is Ronnie these days?' inquired Richard.

'I believe he's got cirrhosis of the face,' replied Billy.

In the movie, Richard Burton played a priest who found Billy's body in the forest. When they were filming the forest scene, Billy had to lie perfectly still wearing 'dead' make-up, half-covered with leaves. Richard approached the body, to play the emotional moments of discovery and a realization that he knew the killer. As the Welshman leant over Billy's shallow grave, his face betrayed a moving depiction of horror. When the camera closed in on Billy, however, the body had a difficult time keeping still and a huge grin soon spread across its powdery face. Richard Burton had begun to sing at the top of his lungs: 'I Belong to Glasgow'.

Shortly after Billy's movie debut, Frank Lynch booked him to play a week at the famous Roxy, a rock 'n' roll venue on Sunset Boulevard in LA. Phil Coulter was there on the first night. 'I saw him die there: it was painful. He came out and sang the Welly Boot song and, at best, they must have tittered. He soldiered on manfully for maybe fifteen minutes. I could see he was giving them his best shots, but he just couldn't get through to them. He finally picked up his guitar and said, "Fuck this, I'm off." There was a major row backstage and I thought he was going to throttle Frank. The week was cancelled.' 'I went down like a burning Spitfire,' Billy joked afterwards.

Despite his American disaster, Billy's popularity in the UK expanded until he was achieving bigger tours than most artists dream of. He was eventually playing eighty-nine nights on a single tour, whereas most rock bands did ten or so. Established comedians only played nightclubs with a few hundred seats and perhaps the London Palladium if they were lucky, but Billy was selling out rock venues. The record for the Apollo in Glasgow had previously been held by Status Quo, who had managed five nights. Billy did twelve.

Billy's new confidence was apparent from the moment he stepped on stage: 'Right. So first I'm going to tell you the rules so you know how to behave. There's a code of behaviour at my show. This is not your folk singer ... I'm a showbiz personality ... I've been on *Swap Shop*. Anything that moves is mine!'

Anyone who dared come in late was mercilessly harangued by Billy. A man who dared go to the toilet might find on his return that he had been the object of ridicule during his entire absence, with Billy leading the crowd in a verse or two of 'The Happy Wanderer' and inventing every possible sound effect from his bathroom experience.

In the process of building his concert audience, Billy had to be away from Iris and the family a great deal. By the end of the seventies, the couple was in serious trouble. Each had a problem with alcohol, although neither could see it; most of the people they mixed with got pissed on a regular basis. Billy's astounding rise to public attention had been extraordinarily difficult for Iris. When she first knew Billy, he was not long out of his welding boots and now he was one of the most famous names in the country. Iris never liked show business. It is a discomfort shared by the spouses of many famous personalities. As one Hollywood woman who is married to a movie star has observed: 'Wives are superfluous.'

Iris's underlying resentment towards Billy came out when she threw him a surprise thirty-fifth birthday party at the Salmon Leap. 'An extraordinary amount of drink had been consumed,' reports Ralph McTell. A huge chocolate cake was wheeled out. 'Billy Connolly ...' announced Iris, imitating Eamon Andrews; 'this is your ... cake!' She pushed his head into it and Billy retaliated in kind. Soon an unbelievably messy skirmish was underway. There was cake everywhere, on the walls and in the carpet.

'The Scots seem to have a more aggressive sense of fun,' observes Ralph. 'I left my jacket there, all covered in chocolate icing and just scarpered. Truthfully, I was a little worried. Perhaps the skean dhus [Scottish daggers] were coming out next!'

Iris had much to cope with and Billy was hardly ever there. Billy himself thought the two had very little in common once the bells had stopped ringing and they were alone in a room together. In fact, nothing in life seemed permanent to him. It was delightful to have fame, but that, too, seemed temporary. Frank Lynch moved to new pastures in the United States and Harvey Goldsmith took over, with his employee Pete Brown acting as Billy's day-to-day manager. Pete was a skinny man with a cheeky face who accepted the tiresome role of babysitter to his newest client.

Although Billy had had more than enough proof that he was exceptionally good at what he did, he still felt like a fraud sometimes, a welder who hadn't yet been found out. He was still convinced that, any minute, somebody was going to tap him on the shoulder and say, 'Well, I hope you enjoyed yourself, because Monday morning you've got your working boots on. You're a welder again.' On the other hand, it was wonderful to have such success. It gave the lie to the people who said he was stupid. 'You can't be stupid and sustain it,' thought Billy. 'You can be stupid and make it, but if it isn't born of brightness it will dim like a shooting star. Pfffttt!'

Deep down, though, he still had his doubts, and was bitterly disappointed to discover that fame was a hollow victory. He had thought all his worries would go away once he was successful and had some money, but they refused to evaporate. He was particularly worried about money because he was terrified of being famous and broke at the same time. That would be like going to hell. His underlying insecurities disappeared when he was drunk, but came raging back in the morning, so Billy took to asking for the wine list at breakfast. After his show at night, he would go to the nearest bar and ask for a pint of wine. Ten bottles later, he was ready to start a fight. 'I spent the whole time battering people I liked and singing with my arm round people I loathed,' he remembers.

One night after 2 a.m., Billy was so pissed he couldn't find his way out of a London phone box. Luckily, he was able to remember Pete Brown's number, so he managed to call him for help.

'It's not that difficult,' said his manager, forcing himself awake. 'There's only four sides and one's got the phone on it.'

'I cannae ... find the door ...' repeated Billy, utterly gone.

'Billy ... where are you?' insisted Pete.

'I'm eh ... I'm ... och, somewhere in London,' he was barely coherent.

'Read the address on the notice by the phone.'

'I cannae focus,' Billy was about to pass out.

Fortunately, our hero is a creature of habit. Pete willed himself into his car and drove around all Billy's usual haunts. It was miraculous that he actually found him and managed to drag his comatose body out of its red-box prison.

'I was just enjoying a wee snooze,' complained Billy.

~

'Good news,' announced John Lloyd, who co-produced the popular new BBC 2 topical comedy show, *Not the Nine O'Clock News*, starring Rowan Atkinson, Mel Smith, Griff Rhys Jones and Pamela Stephenson. 'Billy Connolly has agreed to come on next week's show.'

'Brilliant!' enthused the three boys.

'Who's Billy Connolly?' I inquired.

~

Billy knew who the artist known as 'Pamela Stephenson' was. The first time he saw me, in the summer of 1979, I was upside down on a television screen. George McManus showed Billy a video of *Not the Nine O'Clock News* at Transatlantic Records and he thought it was excellent. In the clip, I portrayed a television newsreader in a sketch about a world gravity shortage. They'd filmed me hanging upside down then shown it the right way up so my hair was standing on end. Billy thought it was the most stunning effect, seeing the drink of water spilling up in the air and the phone receiver flying up off its hook. But when the two show producers, John Lloyd and Sean Hardie, asked him to be a guest on *Not the Nine O'Clock News*, he was ambivalent. 'It's the hottest TV comedy show around,' he conceded to Pete, 'but maybe I shouldn't do it. I'm not very good at sketches.'

We didn't usually have guests on the show. We impersonated pretty well everyone who was famous at the time, so it wasn't necessary. I had neither seen nor heard of Billy, but was curious to meet the man who was so revered by this bunch of talented, too-cool-for-the-room funsters who poured scorn on most people. In their presence, I was a kind of female *Crocodile Dundee* character, which embarrassed me. In vain I tried to hide my profound ignorance about British society, politics and the people I impersonated.

We all turned up at Billy's Three Kings Yard flat in the autumn of 1979. He greeted us at the top of the entrance stairs in Levi's, a satin tour jacket and cowboy boots. I was speechless with surprise. In my working life I was mainly surrounded by youths, but here was an alpha-man, a crazy, hilarious, sensitive, charismatic savage. I was desperately wishing I had worn something more feminine than my jeans and oversize man's tweed jacket and tie.

Billy, apparently, had a terrible hangover that morning and found it hard to be a good host. He had some beer in the fridge, but last night's brandy had left him with an adding-up dysfunction and he couldn't work out if he had enough for everyone or not, so he offered nothing. 'Anyone else desperate for food?' he asked. We all piled into a taxi to go and eat lunch at Geale's in Notting Hill, where Billy delivered the final coup de grâce by eating his grilled Dover sole with his bare hands. What an animal! I was thrilled.

Billy left convinced he had offended me on two counts. In the first place, he had noticed my eyes popping out of my head when he ate his fish with his hands. His friend China, an engineer on a Clyde paddle steamer called the *Waverley* had influenced him in that regard. Some years earlier, Billy had filmed *Clydoscope* on that boat, the last ocean-going paddle steamer left in the whole world. When lunchtime came around, he and the film crew got a measly fish supper. The Glasgow 'fish supper' is usually haddock or plaice, fried in batter, with chips – an extremely greasy affair that helps to explain why the city became known as the heart-attack capital of the world.

'Don't eat that crap,' objected China. 'Come on down with me to the engine room where the boys are.' So Billy followed him down below, inside the black-and-red painted hull with its decorated wheels, to where the crew congregated in a dark place without portholes. They were given a whole herring each and two giant boiled potatoes, a meal that suited Billy just fine, but he was not given any eating utensils. When he requested knife and fork, the crew burst out laughing and made fun of him in Gaelic before wolfing into the herring and potatoes with their fingers. From that moment on, Billy was inspired to copy them.

His second perceived faux pas in Geale's was a curious one: 'I really don't like the name "Neville",' he suddenly announced. 'It's a terrible name.' Billy now thinks his ostensibly casual words were portentous, because in truth he had never thought such a thing in his life. The only Neville he'd even heard of was Nevil Shute, so he has no idea where his remark came from. Apparently, I looked at him as though I'd been shot and said, 'My father's name is Neville.'

In the show, Billy played the Ayatollah Khomeini, running in slow motion towards me while I sang a love-song to him dressed as a terrorist. It was a terrific piece of satire, but that week the Iranian Embassy was blown up, so for reasons of taste the show had to be ditched until the following week. Another of our scenes, where I played the media personality Janet Street-Porter, would have been innocuous enough to air. Barely intelligible, in huge, fake teeth and a red wig with giant spectacles, I conducted a mock interview:

'Tonight I'm talking to Billy Connolly, the well-known Scottish comedian.'

The cut-away shot of Billy shows him trying to control his laughter as my 'Janet' teeth began to fall out.

'So, Billy, do a lot of people have trouble understanding your accent?'

'Eh? Sorry?' asked Billy, as if not understanding Janet's.

After the taping of that show we congregated in the green room for some horrible snacks and a drink. I sensed that Billy had not been too impressed with me. I felt hurt when I noticed him saying goodbye to everyone else and avoiding me. He left with Pete Brown, then a Mick Jagger emulator in a fur coat. Seconds after leaving the room Billy ran back, sucked the beer off his moustache and gave me a little peck on the cheek.

'Cheerio,' he said. 'You're great. Keep it up.'

Bastard clearly hated me.

11

CAPTAIN DEMENTO AND THE BARRACUDA

'So, what exactly was wrong with me?' pouted the author defensively, twenty-one years after their first meeting. 'What didn't you like about me at first?'

'I thought you were way out of my league. I imagined posh Oxbridge guys would be more your line of country. I thought you were a beautiful woman and very bright ... but I thought if you fancied anyone it would be some kind of big-shot braniac like a Peter Cook type. Some guy in a blazer from Hampstead ... everything I'm not. Never gave it another thought.'

'Good answer!'

~

Of course, there was the rather important reason that Billy and I were still married to our first spouses when we met, although both of those relationships were falling apart. My former husband, Nicholas Ball, was an ardent Billy Connolly fan. He took me to see him in concert a few months after we did *Not the Nine O'Clock News* together and I saw Billy on television rendering his fellow *Parkinson Show* guest, Angie Dickinson, completely speechless with his line 'as useful as a fart in a space suit', but it wasn't until nearly a year later that I met Billy again. By then, Nicholas and I had separated. I was filming at a greyhound track in Brighton with the *Not the Nine O'Clock News* crew, helping to create a tasteful little sketch that involved Epsom salts, racing humans and moving toilet bowls. At the end of a hard day's funnywork, I was jumping out of the wardrobe trailer when a teenage autograph-hunter stopped me. 'Billy Connolly's in town,' he announced, apropos of absolutely nothing. 'He's playing the Dome.'

Billy wasn't there by the time I arrived unannounced to visit him at the theatre, but Jamie Wark let me into a sparsely furnished dressing room that was half-full of instrument cases. Outside the stage door that same autograph-hunter was lurking. 'Pamela Stephenson's in there,' he said to Billy, again apropos of absolutely nothing.

'Really?' Billy replied. That very afternoon, he had been taping Noel Edmonds' radio show.

'What kind of women do you like?' Noel had teased him.

'I think that Pamela Stephens is very nice,' returned Billy, getting my name wrong.

'Oh yeah, you and ten million other folk,' retorted Noel.

I sat on Billy's hand-basin while he prepared for his 'Big Wee Tour' show. He thought I looked like a ridiculous little goblin, perched up there in my red trousers. He told me all about his current desperate unhappiness, that he felt his marriage had collapsed and he was trying to leave Iris but she refused to accept that and kept calling him, saying, 'Where the hell are you?' I took all this with a grain of salt, but I just couldn't leave his side. He seemed to be filled with terrible hopelessness. We went to his hotel, where he proceeded to drink thirty brandies. I was afraid for him.

If we had wanted to announce to the world that we were in a hotel together, we couldn't have found a better place. Quite apart from our celebrity, we were two hairy people wearing loud clothing ... at the time and place of the Tory Party Conference. A hundred thousand people had marched to Brighton to demand jobs, and most of them were chanting outside our window when we woke up the next morning. There was a gang of workmen belting nails into adjoining corridor walls, while the hotel staff scurried around in a panic because the IRA had threatened to bomb the Tory-ridden building.

'All those speech defects in one town,' Billy complained, as I tried to hide. Jamie Wark had barged in without knocking and was crashing about the room searching for guitars and banjos. The two of them seemed quite comfortable with this embarrassing scenario. 'Thatcher ... all those people I hate are here ...' Billy continued, as if nothing was the matter.

'Oh, I get it,' I thought, thoroughly humiliated. 'Jamie's no stranger to finding Billy in bed with some woman ...'

'... all in their blazers talking shite ... and Denis Thatcher even said "Good morning" to me when I arrived. I was so taken aback I said "Oh! Good morning!" in return rather than kicking his arse, which I should have done, but there you go ...'

'Billy!' I hissed, 'tell him to leave NOW!'

I'd made a terrible mistake. Engaging though he was, he was also a pitiful, self-destructive drunk who was likely to be Big Trouble. That was apparently a 'brandy tour'. Whenever Billy went on tour he would choose a different 'tour drink'. He'd had the gin tour and the white wine tour just prior to that one. On the road he tried to keep his spirits up, in more ways than one. He also had a tour voice, a tour dance and a tour name, which at this time was 'Captain Demento' while his sound crew was 'The Flying McNalty Twins'. You can imagine how delighted I was to hear that I had received the honorary title of 'Tour Pull'. I had never been treated like a groupie before, but then, I'd never behaved like one.

The man was a total nightmare. I met him again at the Carlton Hotel a week or so later. When I arrived, he was watching a football match and refused to speak to me. 'Ssshh!' he kept saying. 'In a minute.' I was furious, until I again saw his vulnerability and sweetness. Despite his shocking, chauvinist behaviour, he was really wonderfully kind and his terrible sadness melted me. But after a couple more meetings, during which he again consumed outrageous amounts of alcohol that altered his personality for the worse, I decided I couldn't save him. Severing contact was hard, because I was deeply drawn to him. It felt as though we were joined at the wound. He had unresolved issues of abandonment and abuse, and so had I; he had always been punished for being 'stupid', and I had always been punished for being 'bright'.

As Christmas of 1980 approached, I decided to run away to Bali, a place where I had always found peace. This time it eluded me. My first visit to the island had been in 1974. While Billy was careering round the world on his ninety-day tours, I was swaying to the sounds of gamelan orchestras, squelching through rice-fields and observing curious trance dances in the monkey forests of central Bali. It is a magical island, the sweetest-smelling place on the planet. Intoxicating jasmine incense, the perfume of luscious fruits, fragrant leaves and grasses, fresh chopped coconut and clove cigarettes are fanned through the air by giant palm fronds or the delicate wafting of silk or cotton sarongs worn by both men and women. Time creeps as slowly as the giant snails that crossed my night path to pluck a perfect Frangipani flower for my supper-time hair-do.

At that time I hated Christmas. The Balinese are Hindus, so I had imagined a paucity of sacrificed evergreens dotted with tinsel, but I was wrong. I languished on the beach in the shade of the biggest Christmas tree in Indonesia. As 1980 came to a car-horn-honking finale, not even the delicate, ornately clad teenage Legong dancers with their intricate head and finger movements could take my mind off my problem.

As a human being, Billy was thoroughly intriguing. Culturally, we were worlds apart and his accent was so thick I barely understood a word he said. Even when I did discern his words, his phraseology was terribly confusing. For example, I had taken his statement, 'I want to be myself,' to be a cry for self-discovery. Instead, it turned out to be the Scottish form of 'I want to be alone' ... in other words he was telling me to skeddadle.

'Is it really my task in life to help preserve this National Living Treasure?' I kept asking myself. The healthy answer would have been 'no', but that at the time my grandiosity, as well as my attraction to him, told me otherwise.

Trying to distract my thoughts from the Scottish beastie, I set sail on a jukung, a small, wooden vessel with a triangular sail. I was searching for Komodo, the island habitat of real-life 'dragons', prehistoric lizards that had intrigued me since childhood. I was unwittingly retracing my own family history on that sea voyage for, as I later discovered, my great-great-grandfather, Captain Samuel Stephenson, who was a master mariner, also sailed right there in the Flores Sea in 1821 on his way to the Molucca Islands. In poorly charted waters on his own ship, the *Rosalie*, a section of his crew rose up against the rest, killing several men and taking possession of both ship and cargo. Only one crew member escaped back to Jakarta, then known as Batavia, and he reported that Samuel had been thrown overboard and lost at sea during the mêlée. When news of the mutiny reached his native England, his seventeen-year-old son and heir, Samuel junior, began to make plans to sail for Batavia in order to secure his father's Javan assets. It was young Samuel's first excursion to the Southern Hemisphere and one that must have inspired his interest in the region.

A few years later, probably around the time Jack Connolly's predecessors were making tracks to Scotland from Connemara, my great-grandfather emigrated to New Zealand on a single-decked schooner called the *Fortitude*, followed in 1840 by his mother, Ann, on the *Deborah*. They settled in Russell, in the Bay of Islands, where the young Samuel Stephenson opened a trading station at Okiato. He is still remembered as a historical character from New Zealand's history, a pioneer merchant whose partner, Captain Clendon, was a signatory on the Treaty of Waitangi that pledged peace between the Maori people and the newly arrived Pakehas (Europeans).

In 1844, Samuel married my great-grandmother, a half-caste woman with a distinguished Maori lineage, who had both a Maori name, Hira Moewaka, and a Pakeha one, Ada Charlotte Macauliffe. Her Pakeha father, Captain Macauliffe, was presumably Scottish, while her Maori mother was called Ehaku. The two were married first by Maori rite in 1844 and then, some eight years later, they again solemnized their union in a Church of England rite at the Chapel of Waimate in 1852. By then, Hira had borne Samuel a number of children. Henry, who eventually bought the historic Pompallier House in Russell, was born later, while my grandfather, George 'Octie' Octavius, her eighth and youngest son, was born in 1868.

My father was the youngest of Octie's seven children, born in Opotiki in 1916. In adulthood, he became a zoologist, sharing an interest in rare frogs with a Fijian-born colleague, Elsie Thomas, the daughter of a Methodist missionary. The two married in 1947 and were expecting me when they each obtained their doctoral degrees at University College, London, in 1949. We lived in Auckland until 1953, when we relocated to Australia so my father could take up an academic post at the University of Sydney. That is how my two younger sisters and I came to be brought up in the luscious harbourside city of Sydney, as Australian citizens.

I grew up in the arid suburb of Boronia Park, the Drumchapel of Sydney. When my family moved there, to a three-bedroom, concrete-clad bungalow, Boronia Park was a new development, a sparsely landscaped desert, dotted with mound-dwellings of indigenous giant, red, biting ants. The few eucalypts and scrub bushes that remained after the bulldozers left were home to fierce magpies, striped goannas and funnel-web spiders. We became accustomed to leaping over venomous black and brown snakes that lay sunning themselves on our path to the nearest bus stop. A million cicadas hummed evensong to us, while a friendly kookaburra sat on our landscape-blighting, rotary clothesline, waiting to be fed leftovers from our dinner.

Taming that wasteland was a backbreaking job. My parents planted tough desert grasses, sunset-hued Hibiscus and poisonous, fire-resistant Oleander bushes, and they watered the garden early and late. Sydney is a thoroughly humid place: her heatwaves are only bearable if you happen to be near the coast, however our house was inland. Bushfires raged throughout the summer, filling the sky with eye-smarting, throat-catching smoke. While Billy was freezing in the Stewartville Street kitchen, my sisters and I lay breathless in the sweltering room we shared, sticking our legs up flat against the cool, concrete walls and fanning ourselves with the *Australian Women's Weekly*.

Respite came every year when we returned to New Zealand for the Christmas holidays. We stayed in my grandfather's home near Auckland. My sisters had to share a bedroom but I always won the sanctuary of my father's tiny boyhood chamber, in which hung an illuminated certificate of appreciation that was presented to Octie when he retired as the postmaster at Opotiki. In our lazy summer days, my cousins and I would lie in the orchard squishing ripe peaches, apricots and plums down our throats and would race each other past the tallest, white-capped waves on Takapuna Beach.

I was stricken with polio when I was a toddler in Sydney so, in the hope of strengthening my limbs, my mother took me to ballet lessons in the elegant suburb of Hunter's Hill where there were better houses. Ironically, these had been built a century ago by convict labourers from places like Glasgow, fashioned from the same fabric as the tenements, yellow and red local sandstone. I passed them every day, then scrambled to finish my homework on the Hunter's Hill ferry as it ploughed its way across the glorious Sydney Harbour on my way to school in the centre of Sydney.

CAPTAIN DEMENTO AND THE BARRACUDA

My parents held positions at the Universities of Sydney and New South Wales during my entire childhood. Those institutions must have been 'publish or perish' places because I always remember my parents working at a frantic pace to complete research and write up articles for scientific journals. Academic success was a requirement in our family. My sisters and I were given a solid, classical education at the Sydney Church of England Girls' Grammar School, then a rather formal establishment for young Australian ladies with a strict code of conduct and dress. Ties were worn at all times, even in the crazy temperatures of our sub-tropical summer, while hat and gloves were obligatory for the journeys between home and school.

Schoolwork was never a challenge for me, in fact it bored me, so I spent most of my time writing plays and performing in drama projects. After attending university and then the National Institute for Dramatic Art, I eventually had a successful career as a performer in Australia before making my name in Britain on *Not the Nine O'Clock News*.

Thousands of young Australians end up in Bali every year. In that Christmas of 1980, the place seemed more crowded than usual. I was refused entry to Komodo on grounds of safety, for the 'dragons' had recently devoured a Japanese tourist who got too close with his Nikon. Apprehensive about seeing Billy again, I returned to London bearing an intricately entwined, black seaweed bracelet for his beer-lifting wrist.

'I guess,' Billy had said to me before my departure, 'if you're falling in love with a drunken weirdo, you've got to give it a great deal of thought.' Billy had to give everything a great deal of thought. Just after I returned from Indonesia, he called me from a police station. He had turned up drunk at the house in Drymen and Iris had locked him out. While he was conducting a one-man riot, a police officer turned up and took him off to jail. The policeman, a delightful fellow, got Billy out of the cell for a game of darts and later sneaked him back home.

'I can't go on like this,' Billy told me on the phone. 'I can't bear it ... there's no future. Any time I think of the future I just want to die.' That kind of hopelessness is very dangerous, for it frequently precedes either a deliberate or an 'accidental' suicide attempt. Billy decided to join me in London, although I was ambivalent about that idea.

Billy had verbally and emotionally separated from Iris, for they had become antithetical strangers to each other, but he had not permanently moved elsewhere. For three years now, he had rented a serviced flat at Three Kings Yard in London, but he returned to Drymen from time to time. No clear arrangements had been made for the children, although Billy's irregular visits were not terribly different from the way it had always been since he had begun to tour extensively. His career path had necessitated long absences from home and it still does today. I envisioned that we too might end up on different parts of the globe most of the time, but Billy had an extravagant idea of being a 'house-husband'. 'I'll be like John Lennon,' he promised. 'I'll just stay at home and cook and raise children.'

∼

Germaine Greer once told me she thought women's love and ambition are very closely linked. After my return from Bali, I became worried about a forthcoming stand-up performance at the Comic Strip in London and decided to share my concern with Billy. He asked me a very perceptive question: 'Does it feel nice when you're on stage?' The question surprised me, for I had never really thought about it (I had been performing on stage since I was five years old). 'Yes ...' I answered, although I knew it was not always pleasant. 'Good,' he said. 'You'll be fine then.'

Our on-stage experiences turned out to be very similar: a period of intense fear and panic followed by a heady surge of adrenaline, then a highly enjoyable rush of endorphins and finally, if all went well, a powerful sense of validation. The good feelings would last for a few hours after the show, but in the morning there would be a sense of loss, an uncomfortable physiological experience of our bodies still being over-pumped with adrenaline, torturous regrets about imperfections the night before and renewed anxiety about the next performance.

Billy had learned to deal with his morning-after blues by consuming vast quantities of alcohol the night before, which in a way made sense since drink does help the body to eliminate excess adrenaline. As excruciating as the performing cycle was, I couldn't bring myself to imbibe the way he did and preferred not to wake up with breath like a burst lavatory.

At the time, I was conducting a search for careful professional management, and I eventually signed up with Harvey Goldsmith. His employee Pete Brown engineered both of our careers for a few years from then on, so Billy and I were bound to spend time together no matter what happened personally between us.

When Billy embarked on a Middle East tour in the summer of 1981, Pete and I flew to Dubai to join him for a few days. I love the silence, the architecture and the searing, dry heat of desert cities. While cooling off in the swimming pool of the Dubai Hilton, I watched builders erecting a huge outdoor arena for Billy's show. The evening's performance was patronized by thousands of expatriate British people, many of whom worked in totally 'dry' Middle Eastern areas. During this visit to the Arab Emirates, a more moderate part of the Arab world, they took the opportunity to imbibe alcohol at a startling rate in order to make up for lost time. Many had started drinking on the plane and hadn't stopped since, so there were puking punters everywhere you looked. Some were just lying on the grass completely unconscious. Billy pointed to one paralytic body during his show. 'Aye,' he remarked pointedly to the upright members of his audience, 'if you can lie on the ground without hanging on, then you're not drunk.'

I was hand-on-heart breathless, seeing him perform in this situation. At last I fully understood what all the fuss was about. 'The man's an absolute genius,' I thought, coming rather late to the exact same conclusion thousands of others had beforehand. His words seemed to have come from nowhere. He hadn't prepared anything. He spoke about events that had occurred very recently, only now they had moved from the mundane to the screamingly funny. The previous week, Billy had performed for workers at a refinery on Das Island in the Gulf of Arabia, so he created a spoof comparing their situation to that described in the then popular prisoner-of-war novel *Camp on Blood Island*. He impersonated all the workers marching to work, whistling the 'Colonel Bogey' march from *Bridge on the River Kwai*.

When I'd seen Billy in Brighton, his show had been quite theatrical, especially at the end. There had been confetti bombs and Billy had appeared in a teddy-boy outfit at the end with a rock band, singing Hank Williams and Buddy Holly songs. He had performed an outrageous parody of 'Tell Laura I Love Her' in which he'd ripped his shirt ('very labour-intensive, sewing on all those buttons every night,' he'd complained) and whipped himself with a black leather cat-o'-nine-tails that Jamie Wark had found in a local sex shop. But here in the desert, he was naked, unsupported and incomparable.

I felt quite envious; all my working life I wrote, studied and practised before going before an audience. Billy had this gift of spontaneity that I knew I would never have. It was almost eerie, like the trance dances I'd witnessed in Bali, weird and powerful occasions when the difficult Legong was danced by young girls who had never been trained to do so. The Balinese believe that during those ritual performances they receive messages from 'heavenly spirits' who prompt their movements. I imagined some wickedly funny angels always whispered in his ear.

Billy has an extraordinary motoric intelligence. His body was speaking the most hilarious truths, so knowledge of his language was unnecessary. From my grassy vantage point, watching both show and audience, I could see what the audience missed: Arab people hanging out of every window on the side of the hotel that faced the stage. They were absolutely out of control with delight whenever Billy performed one of his physical pantomimes. It didn't matter that they lacked a point of reference for his description of a little old lady in a fat coat flying out of a Glasgow city bus or a drunken Frank Sinatra wannabe at a party in Govan: they just exploded at whatever was communicated by his rubbery body.

I was on a break from *Not the Nine O'Clock News* a few months later, when Billy called me from Hong Kong, a place he adores for its food and exoticness, especially the Chinese apothecaries with their curious wares. 'If ever you're in need of a ground-up tiger's willie, Hong Kong's your place,' he advised me. Billy was tickled to discover that the Hong Kong tramcars were the same ones he'd known in Glasgow when he was a boy. The 'caurs' had been sold, transported abroad and repainted with strikingly colourful Chinese advertisements for ginseng, gelatine and hairspray.

Billy was flying out of Hong Kong on his way to Los Angeles when one of the plane's engines blew up. Billy didn't notice, for he was a little under the weather, attacking the miniature brandies and listening to Eric Clapton on his headset. Flying had never been his favourite pastime. 'Turbulence must be the best laxative known to man,' he says.

The sober passengers around Billy shrieked in alarm as the plane's shaking escalated to a body-lurching peak, prompting the pilot to announce they would need to land in Tokyo. He had been in touch with the emergency services and said there was no need to be frightened for they would probably be able to make a perfect landing. Fortunately, they did.

The passengers spent the night in a Japanese hotel before boarding the same plane in the morning with a new engine. That was not the end of their crisis, though, because about half an hour out of Narita Airport there was another ominous bang, indicating that another engine had blown and they had to return to Japan for the second time.

'We can't land with all this fuel, so we're just going to have to dump it in the bay,' explained the pilot. 'If you'd like to go to the back of the plane, you'll be able to watch it being jettisoned.'

'I think I'll fucking give that a miss,' said Billy.

This time, the atmosphere was considerably more tense. I had given Billy a paperback copy of *The Dharmapada*, a collection of Buddhist writings, which he happened to have been reading on the journey. For several years now, I had embraced the Buddhist philosophy and had suggested to Billy that Buddhist meditation practices might be very useful to calm his anxiety, help him focus and cut down on his brain-chatter. It worked well for him, especially a practice called 'The Mindfulness of Breathing'. The logic of *The Dharmapada* was extremely comforting to him, helping him to accept what was happening and be at peace with it. As Billy's plane approached Narita Airport for the second time, there were hordes of ambulances and TV crews waiting there for the crash that never happened. After about four hours in the airport, the passengers were offered a no-brainer. 'Would you all prefer to have the original plane with a new engine, or a completely different plane?'

Not too surprisingly, they all voted for a new one. After their third take-off, there was a wild party in the first-class cabin. A drunk American woman with little grasp of the situation kept saying, 'I don't care what happens as long as I get back in time to watch the Royal Wedding on TV.' Her husband was walking round with a bumper sticker Billy had given him stuck to his forehead. It read, 'I may be old but I still get hot.'

In extraordinary times, people try to make sense of a senseless universe. 'This whole thing's probably my fault,' confessed the American next to Billy.

'How's that?' asked Billy.

'I'm jinxed. I crashed my helicopter four times when I was in 'Nam.'

'If I get out of this alive,' returned Billy, 'I'm going to tidy up my life a bit.'

12

'THAT NIKON'S GOING UP YOUR ARSE!'

There is a prone man chortling in our living room, half-hidden by a couple of Labradors. Billy loves to watch American television evangelists whipping up the emotions and endorphins of their massive amphitheatre audiences.

'Look at the "Honest, I'm not bald" hair-do on this one!' he yells. I race in just in time to catch Benny Hinn lunge at a frail-looking Asian woman and forcibly slap her into the ready arms of his trusty henchmen. 'For fuck's sake,' Billy protests, 'the poor wee woman could snap like a twig. He needs his head read.'

'It's dinner time. Come and sit down.'

'Hang on,' he pleads, 'I'm desperate to see if that big, ugly woman with the giant pink hair comes on. The one who matches her Bible cover with her dress!'

'God talks to me ...' booms Benny Hinn to fifty thousand hysterical worshippers.

'God talks to you?' Billy is shouting at the television. 'Go knock on the door of any mental institution in the country and tell them that. They won't even let you home for your pyjamas!'

≈

Billy's own close-call-with-his-Maker experiences on the aeroplane jolted him into awareness of a need to make proper arrangements for his children and move on. He returned to Drymen, but he had trouble finding Iris who had found her own solutions to Billy's departure, hiding away with her brandy in the tree-house. Billy did not realize that, now he was gone, she would retreat there for days on end while Cara and Jamie were left to fend for themselves. He emphasized his love and commitment to the children then returned to London with a heavy heart. If only we had known how bad things were then, for all three of them.

People in Britain were beginning to gossip. Billy Connolly was often in the company of a thirty-one-year-old, New Zealand-born Australian (incredibly, I share a birthday with Mamie) who had turned up in London four years earlier on her way around the world and was now making her name on *Not the Nine O'Clock News*. Our private turmoil was bound to become public; it was just a matter of time. The excrement hit the extrusion device in August 1981, when Billy's separation from Iris became headline news. I had moved into a house belonging to the playwright Julian Mitchell in Ovington Street, Knightsbridge, where we tried to take cover from the barrage of media interest, personal attacks and moral outrage. Neither of us had any idea of how to deal with it, but we came up with various lame strategies that included hiding, water-hosing those who door-stepped us and disguising ourselves. Billy even hit a photographer with a loaf of French bread he'd bought for our supper. It bounced off his head like a walking cane.

Meanwhile, far more serious harassment was occurring in Drymen. As the children walked around the town, they were accosted by journalists. Cara remembers her mother standing with a tabloid newspaper in her hands, laughing. 'Isn't this hilarious?' she was saying. 'Now Pamela Stephenson has to cope with your father!' Billy flew back to Drymen to soothe the children again. He missed them desperately and it was not easy to keep in touch because, when he called Drymen, the phone was rarely answered.

People in the public eye who become romantically involved don't have the luxury of being able to court the usual way. Instead of spending relaxed time learning about each other, our task became to defend ourselves emotionally and physically against the world, in particular the media. We managed, however, to get a weekend respite in Marrakech, wandering together beneath peaceful orange groves and gorgeous sunsets ... before Billy got a tummy bug and began exploding from every orifice ... but then he's just a born romantic.

After that, I became pretty busy with the final series of *Not the Nine O'Clock News*. The Ovington Street house had a fine, well-equipped kitchen, so I encouraged Billy to spend time cooking while I was away working during the daytime. In contrast to the notions held by some societies, Scottish men consider household cooking to be an extremely manly activity. Billy discovered Julian Mitchell's cookbooks, which were all for the advanced culinary artist, and, undeterred, he attacked the classic French dishes.

'How does this look? Is this all right?'

He was holding up the finest, thinnest example of a crêpe I'd ever seen.

'I'll be making soufflés tomorrow,' he announced.

I was astonished by his talent as a chef. Cooking turned out to be very calming for him, a meditative activity. He approached the preparation of each dish as if he were Rodin setting free a masterpiece from a chunk of marble and was always a little reluctant to allow it to be scoffed until I'd recorded its visual finery with a Polaroid camera.

We were under siege by door-steppers in Ovington Street for months. 'God knows,' said Billy, 'it's hard enough without people spying on you as you're trying to keep your soul together, trying to keep in harmony with the rest of the fucking universe. They sell pictures and stories of your life and don't share the money. I heard Ken Dodd pissed in a bucket and threw it out the window on them. What a jolly idea!'

Billy and I were sleeping in late one Sunday morning in September, when the phone rang and rang. 'It might be Cara or Jamie,' I said. 'Better answer it.'

'Good morning, Pamela,' said a familiar voice. 'This is John Cleese.'

I obviously took too long gathering myself enough to be able to speak.

'You know ...' He seemed to think he had to explain who he was, 'the bloke from *Fawlty Towers* ... I'd like you to do a sketch with me in the *Secret Policeman's Other Ball*.'

Billy had appeared in the original *Secret Policeman's Ball*, a live benefit concert in aid of Amnesty International, starring the best comics and rock musicians around. 'You should do it,' he advised me, recounting a backstage conversation between John, Peter Cook (whom he regarded as the funniest person in the world) and the actress Eleanor Bron, who had been one of Billy's fantasy women for years.

'What this show needs most,' John had complained, 'is new satire. Come up with something for tomorrow.' Peter took up the gauntlet. The Jeremy Thorpe trial was dominating the news at the time and it happened that the judge's summing up had generally been criticized. He had seemed to be very biased against gay people, leading the jury in a shockingly inappropriate way. Peter wrote a piece called 'Entirely a matter for you' that satirized the trial, and performed it in the show the following night. Peter, as the discriminating judge, delivered the brilliant line that Billy still quotes at every given opportunity: 'A tissue of odious lies has issued from his slavering lips ... but that, of course, is entirely a matter for you.'

John Cleese and I decided to perform a sketch in which we played a couple of belligerent strangers at a bus stop. 'Give me a pound or I'll take off my clothes,' we taunted each other, both ending up in our underwear. We rehearsed in John's back garden, while bemused neighbours peered out of upstairs windows. Billy performed some solo stand-up for the show and Rowan, Mel, Griff and I offered a scene from *Not the Nine O'Clock News*. At the end of the first night, Billy and I were walking hand in hand backstage in the dark, giggling. We thought we were alone, but a London voice came out of the shadows behind us. 'So!' said Eric Clapton, who was performing a guitar solo in the show. 'You two really are in love!'

'Cover for us, Eric,' I pleaded. 'There's a squillion photographers outside.'

So Eric and I exited the theatre arm in arm, and Billy followed a few minutes later. As I was getting into a car, I heard a crash behind me as well as a great deal of shouting and swearing. 'I hope you've got Vaseline on that Nikon, because it's going up yer arse!'

The next day, there was a cartoon in the papers of Billy having a tantrum and exploding cameras outside the Drury Lane Theatre. The caption read, 'He's normally such a funny bloke.' On grounds of grammar as well as inaccuracy, Billy took great exception to being described in a newspaper article as 'the punch-prone Billy Connolly'. 'I'm not punch-prone,' he protested. 'I punch other people.'

It was a very stressful time, living under negative public scrutiny, and we were both getting very jumpy. For Billy it was worse because the press had replaced his early tormentors. They became contemporary projections of William, Mona and Rosie, leading to a repetition of his childhood sense of terror and hopelessness. Even today, he is easily wounded by unkind words, especially from strangers. Quite understandably, he feels that, after everything he'd gone through, it's time he was allowed to live his life without being under constant attack.

We began to form an escape plan. 'I will arise and go now, and go to Innisfree ...' Billy began his favourite poem and I finished it. He was delighted that Yeats' *Lake Isle of Innisfree* was my favourite too. Living 'alone in the bee-loud glade' certainly seemed like a great idea from where we were sitting.

'Maybe we should take a cruise or something,' I suggested.

'Fuck no. Cruises are like prison, with the possibility of drowning ... I know! Let's drive down to Brighton, to the seaside!'

The seaside has always been a place of happiness and safety for Billy. On his family holidays in the Scottish coastal port of Rothesay, he had a respite from his father's molestation, for he always had his own bed. We jumped in the car and set off, scarcely reaching the end of the street before we were assaulted by a blinding flash. The paparazzi were obviously in hot pursuit. 'Bastards!' cried Billy, but it turned out to be lightning. We didn't get to Brighton in the end because we couldn't find it. We ate fish and chips in a terrible transport café then turned round and went home: we were a mess.

～

As I began work on a new *Superman* movie at Pinewood Film Studios, Billy was asked to take over the lead, from Simon Callow, in a J. P. Donleavy play called *The Beastly Beatitudes of Balthazar B*, which necessitated his learning the entire play in just a couple of weeks. I could see that he was really struggling with it, cramming day after day without a break. 'The mind doesn't work like that,' I told him. Even then I was passionately interested in psychology and neurology. 'The brain doesn't respond well to constant learning without a break.'

'But I open on Friday ...'

'You're not doing a thing tomorrow,' I insisted. 'Cara and Jamie will be here and we're all going on a picnic!' We ate egg sandwiches and chocolate Olivers in Richmond Park. When he opened, not only was Billy word-perfect as 'Beefy', but he received considerable critical acclaim for the role, as well as prudish alarm and embarrassed giggles. Resplendent in his birthday suit, a pair of work boots, goggles and a kinky set of chains, he leapt on stage in the third act, screaming: 'Good evening, ladies!'

On a few of his non-matinée days, Billy appeared on Kenny Everett's TV show. He and Kenny, who both sported massive beards at the time, shared a penchant for dressing up as women and referring to each other's 'delicate problems'.

As Billy's West End run progressed, the *Superman* shoot moved to location in Canada. I began to notice my own stress level was high, and I did not have Billy around to read me a chapter of Roald Dahl's *BFG*, which always soothed me. Finding a gap in my schedule, I asked members of the cast for 'quiet week' suggestions.

'Las Vegas,' joked Richard Pryor.

'Green Turtle Cay,' suggested Christopher Reeve.

I flew off to the latter, wishing out loud that Billy could join me there.

'I've not got long,' he said, 'I've got a gig, you know.'

Billy actually flew to meet me in the Bahamas for a day. It was the stupidest, most romantic thing in the world. Billy had never snorkelled before, so I showed him how and he took to it like a drowning tomcat. I was beginning to understand how terrified he was in the universe. He often referred to John Lennon as a kindred spirit, remarking that Yoko had forced John to travel round the world alone in order to conquer his fear of it. He seemed to be giving me permission to push him into new territory, so I did.

We were in the sea, just off the Bahamian coast. 'It's an amazing world down there,' I said. 'Preparing to dive! Follow me!' I led him on an underwater cruise past flirtatious angel-fish, giant crustaceans and exotic live coral.

'That was brilliant,' he shouted when we surfaced. 'Hang on, I've got to adjust my mask.' I turned round and was horrified to see that not only was he about to brush past some stinging fire coral, but a giant barracuda had decided to follow him. I waved him towards me, trying not to induce alarm. He thought I was being jolly and waved back.

'Yowee!' he yelped as the nasty little polyps took hold.

'Shiiiiiiiiitttt!'

He'd seen the big fish.

'It's safer in the Gorbals,' he said.

~

External environmental threats seemed mild compared to Billy's battle with his internal demons. Unfortunately, alcohol had more than a disinhibiting effect on him: it turned him into a mean, violent, out-of-control nutter with psychotic rage, frequent blackouts and memory loss. Apparently, no one had ever challenged him about this before and I tried hard to figure out why. Perhaps they were too frightened of him, too in awe of him, too drunk themselves to notice, or had something to gain from his loss of control. Certainly, Billy exhibited classic defensiveness the first time I brought it up. I'd had no experience with addiction so I got hold of the alcoholics' bible, the *Alcoholics Anonymous Big Book*, and read it cover to cover in one sitting. I learned that I could not help him unless it was his desire to heal, and internalized the wonderful phrase, 'Detach with love.' The next time he became insane with drink, I faced him the next morning. 'I'm not sticking around,' I announced sadly. 'You're ugly when you drink: ugly and abusive. I care about you, but I'm not going to watch you continue to self-destruct. Goodbye.'

Billy's fear of abandonment helped him in this moment. 'OK,' he said eventually, finally perceiving a link between his alcohol abuse and a possible loss of personal happiness. 'I'll stop for a whole year and then we'll see. Fair enough?' 'One day at a time' as the twelve-step people say, was good enough for me.

'I decided to stop drinking while it was still my idea,' he correctly tells people (for I couldn't have challenged him successfully unless he was ready). His alcohol abuse was a symptom of underlying problems: depression, anxiety and trauma – all, of course, related to his childhood experiences – and, as he began to heal, he became naturally temperate.

He gained an interest in being physically healthy too, stopping smoking and eating better. Some people sneered at the very sudden change in him, but those were people who, for their own reasons, felt strangely comfortable with Billy's self-destructive path. Perhaps, by comparison, it made theirs seem less drastic. Perhaps they erroneously thought he would no longer be funny. People all over the world loved to swap stories about their legendary night out on the town with Billy Connolly and were thoroughly pissed off when it all stopped. On the other hand, those who actually cared about him were relieved and knew he now had a shot at longevity.

Understandably, some of his friends were very wary of me. What exactly was this overconfident 'Sheila' with a penchant for outrageous on-camera stunts doing with Billy anyway? Was it all a giant publicity exercise? Perhaps I would keep Billy away from his friends. Michael Parkinson, for example, wondered about my motives and, knowing Billy was 'a handful' (he had witnessed many of Billy's debauched evenings in Tramp's nightclub in London), worried that I wouldn't be 'up to the job'. Peter McDougall and Ralph McTell both independently worried that I would be somehow 'eclipsed'. These were all very reasonable concerns, from people who barely knew me.

As a direct result of his sobriety, Billy's involvement with his children grew stronger. At eight years old, Cara was a delightful little girl who always wanted to come with me to my matinées of *Pirates of Penzance* at Drury Lane and sit right in the front row. She idolized her father and would sit on his lap for hours, just staring at him. Jamie at eleven was a different kettle of fish. Fiercely loyal to his mother and furious at his father, he avoided me at first and it took us a while to become close. The children began to stay with us a great deal and they responded well to the structure we offered them. They liked the really simple things like our talks together, being given clean towels with an order to bathe, and watching shooting stars in the garden on summer evenings.

Billy and I bought a house in London that was originally a

warehouse where fish were distributed. 'The Fish Factory' was protected from the street and had an inner courtyard, so at last we were able to have some privacy from strangers. On 24 November, Billy's fortieth birthday, I arranged a party for him. At the time I didn't understand quite how much it meant to him that his birthday was celebrated, but he was clearly thrilled.

I had hired a Pope look-alike, a Welshman called Mr Meredith, who came up on the train all the way from Wales. He jumped out of a cake wearing his mitre and robes and blessed the crowd of well-known faces peering at him. He later became less interested in popish activities and more interested in downing a few beers, then he chatted up the girls from the punk band Shock who had large, revealing designer holes in their clothing. The scene intrigued jazz musician George Melly.

'Look!' he nudged Billy. 'It's the Temptation of Saint Anthony!'

After the party, I approached the birthday boy.

'What's your favourite girl's name?'

'Daisy,' he replied instantly.

Just a few weeks after that, Daisy was conceived. By then, eleven-year-old Jamie and eight-year-old Cara were regularly spending a lot of time with us and our lives together in London were very happy. In a very understandable effort to be loyal to their mother, the children had not been able to tell us that things in Drymen had been getting worse and worse. Unknown to us, Iris's alcohol use had reached the stage where she was having severe withdrawal symptoms, blackouts and episodes of delirium tremens, witnessed by both children. She desperately needed treatment and her children needed protection. One weekend when Cara was staying with her grandparents in Glasgow, she had gathered up the courage to say to them, 'I don't want to go back to Drymen.'

When we told the children that we wanted them to live with us for the time being, Cara was delighted. Two years earlier she had looked at Billy with her big, sweet eyes and asked, 'If you leave, can I come too?' Since then she had written innumerable letters asking him the same thing, but had always torn them up. The writing had, though, been on the wall from the very beginning. Billy had even composed a song in 1969, the year Cara was born, that went:

'I'm leaving you now I'll be gone for a while
You're never going to see daddy's loving smile
Don't say, "Oh no!"
When the sun comes up I'll be leaving,
I don't care if your heart's grieving,
I'm following the things I believe in,
Don't say "Oh no!"'

Jamie wasn't entirely happy about moving to London. He knew things were far from fine at Drymen but he'd become accustomed to the inappropriate freedom he'd been given there. He'd had little supervision for years, which he then thought was a good thing and he had assumed the role of Cara's protector. Now he would have to go to school every day.

Billy felt very bad for Iris, but he knew he was doing the right thing. He wanted formal custody of his children primarily for their safety and well-being, yet to achieve this he was forced to go to court to fight a nasty, public custody battle. Billy was dreadfully anxious: a court reporter had come to our house and sat there for days, just watching our family interaction. Billy cooked a meal one evening and Cara had started picking out the mushrooms.

'If you don't eat them,' he joked in a funny voice, 'I'll thrash you within an inch of your miserable life!' He was performing a savage, comic replay of his own food-battles with Mona. We all laughed, until we saw the court reporter making a note in her booklet. 'Oh, fuck,' said Billy when we got to bed, 'she thinks I'm a child-beater.'

I barely recognized him when he went off to court in Edinburgh in a sober, grey suit and neatly trimmed hair and whiskers. 'Please don't thump any journalists today,' I pleaded. To our enormous relief the judge ruled that the children would be better off with Billy and me. We tried to ignore all the ill will and ignorant nastiness that came our way after that. We couldn't explain the situation to the world so we just had to set about creating a proper, permanent family life for the four of us.

I was eight months pregnant and the size of a bouncy castle when Billy offered me a 'by the way' that had me shrieking for an emergency appointment with my obstetrician. 'You were *how many* pounds at birth?' I puked, '*Now* you tell me you were an eleven-pound baby?' Genetics being what they are, my ensuing Caesarean section seemed like a dandy way to have his baby and, a week later, Daisy was plucked from my womb on 31 December 1983.

Famous people seem to get treated differently from others in medical settings. 'Wanna watch?' the surgeon asked Billy. He leapt at the chance: 'It's not every day you get to gaze on your wife's bladder for God's sake,' he explained to me at the time. 'I've seen more of you than you've seen of me,' he is now inclined to boast. 'I've seen your pancreas!' He really is a sick bastard.

Daisy was a beauty, weighing in at nine pounds ten ounces. Her father whisked her off to the surgeons' changing room, where he was so pumped with endorphins he performed a twenty-minute stand-up routine for the entire hospital while I lay freezing in the corridor on a tin trolley. 'Stop that!' I moaned. 'Get me drugs and blankets!'

Everything we'd been through at last seemed to make sense, except that Billy, who had been temperate for over a year, thought – wrongly – that he could now drink with impunity. I didn't know what to make of it. He had certainly proved he could stop completely when he put his mind to it and he never drank heavily around me or the children, but when he was out with his mates, moderation was a serious challenge.

The day after Daisy was born, Billy began a diary that he

continued for four years. He chose a beautiful leather book from
Smythson of Bond Street, designed for aristocrats. It's a hoot to read
his entries under headings like 'Pheasant and Partridge Shooting
ends'.

1 January 1984

I was wakened by a phone call from Pamela in hospital. She
sounded a million dollars. What an improvement, she must be
really healthy which is more than can be said of me. I'm suffering
from the mother and father of all hangovers. Jesus, what a price
we pay for that one night of debauchery!

2 January

A family again at last! The difference in the house is
extraordinary. I think we are going to be very happy here, all five
of us!

Billy was doing his best to deal with all the stresses in his life. It was
not easy and, emotionally, he was flipping from one extreme to
another.

4 January

I got up and made French toast muffins for the kids. When I got
out of the door there was a photographer there who kept
telling me to smile. I told him to fuck off or I would break his
jaw. Pam was looking great, so was Daisy. I changed her for the
first time. I'm a bit awkward but Pam thought I had done well.
When I left the photographers tried to pose me with a book
called *Non-Violent Childbirth*.

Billy looked forward to introducing Daisy to his father and siblings.
Florence cooed over her, but William, who still lived in the tenement
flat in White Street, greeted us briefly then turned on the television

and sat with his back to us all. Not long after that meeting we heard he'd had a stroke, which left him quite bereft of speech and balance. The left side of his brain was affected so he couldn't write with his right arm and he dragged his left leg. When Billy visited him in Gartnavel Hospital, he was very struck by his father's appearance, lying there in the ward with Florence and a priest by his side. 'He's small,' he thought. 'All these years he seemed like a big guy, even when I got taller than him ... but now he seems shrunken.'

He waited until the priest left before he approached William and spoke close to his ear. 'Celtic won on Saturday,' he lied, 'four-nil.' He could have sworn he saw a flicker of triumph in the dazed man's eyes.

13

LEGLESS IN MANHATTAN

It is 11 July 2001. Billy, or rather, the newly dubbed 'Dr Connolly', parades around Glasgow University in a splendid academic robe of scarlet and purple silk. Moved by the occasion, I am grateful for the robustness of my waterproof mascara, for I had to fight back tears of pride throughout the ceremony. A strange voice calls from behind us. 'Dr Connolly?' We both turn around. Another of the University dignitaries is approaching Billy to congratulate him on receiving the honorary Doctorate of Letters.

'I had expected you would be *much* taller!' she gushes loudly. I move swiftly to intervene as I hear him mutter: 'And I expected your arse to be much smaller ...'

~

Decorum, academic or otherwise, has never been a feature of Billy's personal or public behaviour. It is impossible to predict how he will react in any new situation, although he certainly recognizes incongruity when it hits him between the eyes. When Billy started work on the film *Blue Money*, in 1984, he played a sleazy man with horrible teeth, and was asked to hitchhike along a motorway while a cinematographer filmed his progress from a distant flyover.

Billy thought he would be the last person to score a lift, trudging along in his ragged get-up with an inflatable woman over his shoulder. He called her 'Olga', a pink vinyl orifice-bearer draped in a leopard coat. 'You'll never believe this, Pamela,' he exploded. 'Two trucks actually stopped for me. I had to explain and wave them away.'

The experience somewhat tarnished the 'rambling man' fantasy of his folk years, although *Travelling Man* became the title of Billy's simultaneous film development project with Ray Cooper for Handmade Films. That movie presented him with a rather different set of challenges, for it never materialized; however, Billy found Ray an inspiring person to be around. Ray is also a musician: a masterful percussionist who performs with Elton John.

In 1983, Billy took me to visit Ray in his modish converted warehouse in east London. George Harrison was sitting in his living room, hungry, so the four of us went for a Chinese meal at a local restaurant. A man from another table approached us while we were eating to ask Billy and me for our autographs, ignoring George. George didn't seem to care, but we were mortified. 'He's a fucking Beatle for God's sake!' Billy whispered.

To make matters worse, the man innocently inquired if there was anyone else in the vicinity he should ask for an autograph. Billy saved the day. His social skills are idiosyncratic, but frequently inspired. 'Well, George here used to play for Manchester United ...' The man still looked blank ... 'and there's a Chinese waiter over there who used to play for Celtic!'

~

Billy was thrilled that he was in demand for more movie roles, but he also understood the limitations of the motion-picture medium. He had seen comedy work wonderfully well on film but he also knew that the technical requirements of movie making could sabotage a perfectly hilarious performance. One of Billy's earliest film comedy successes was in the movie *Bullshot*. He loved his character,

Hawkeye MacGillicuddy, a blind man whose adoration of his former superior officer prevented him from acknowledging that his disability had actually been caused by his incompetent boss.

The story's irony reminded Billy of the British class structure that so often seems to create emotional ambivalence between groups. He also loved the darkly comic idea that his sightless character didn't just tiptoe along the road timidly avoiding harm. Rather, he was a contradiction, a blind bully waving around his white stick at the perfect height to cause mayhem, whacking people off their bicycles. There was a touch of the cartoon character Mr Magoo about him ... as well as a touch of Billy's cousin John.

At one point, Hawkeye is standing in a garden receiving orders barked by his commanding officer: 'Dismiss!' Hawkeye snaps to attention, takes a sharp left turn, then marches over a wall and straight into a tree. This particular classic piece of physical comedy has been shown in the United States as a 'blooper'. 'I must have been doing something right,' Billy says nowadays, so pleased with himself. 'They really thought it was unintentional.'

Billy's infamous piece of real-life, unintentional comedy was staged on location for his next movie, *Water*, on the sweltering tropical island of St Lucia. Shortly after Daisy was born, Billy was cast as a 'singing rebel' in the film, crafted by the amiable masters of comedy-writing, Dick Clement and Ian La Frenais. In a typical movie-madness scenario, the backing money dropped out just before Billy got on the plane, only to be reinstated just after he arrived. Billy, however, was oblivious to this off-screen drama because he had fallen off the wagon with quite a thud. For months he had been promising himself he would take it easy.

3 April
Jesus I'll have to stop this self-inflicted punishment. I should never leave home again without a letter from my next of kin, or a note from a priest assuring everyone that I'm unlikely to bite their pets.

He had a proper skinful on the plane to St Lucia. When he got to his hotel, a familiar American man was sitting at the bar. 'Dennis Dugan?' Billy recognized him from a television series he'd loved called *Richie Brockelman*, about a broke detective. The two had a few supplementary bevvies, then joined Michael Caine and other members of the cast and crew to reconnoitre the island for a decent meal.

They had a jolly evening, then travelled back by bus through a part of the island that features steep cliffs on either side of a jungle road. As they careered along, Billy thought it would be a merry wheeze to cover the driver's eyes with his hands. 'I'll guide you,' insisted our drunken control-freak. 'Left ... right ... more right ...' It was a game he had apparently played with his London driver: God knows how they managed to survive. Michael Caine apprehended Billy just in time to save the bus from plunging down a bottomless St Lucian ravine.

> *7 May*
> I woke up feeling like death. I've fucked the issue for myself.
> Michael Caine had to get me out of trouble, the whole bit. I feel
> like a real prick.

Michael could see that Billy was in trouble. He spoke to him about his death-wish drinking and Billy took his words to heart. He would try to drink moderately like Michael did. When I arrived at the hotel in St Lucia some days later, carrying a napping Daisy, a gentle, dark-haired woman knelt down to retie one of the straps of my leopard sandals. It was Shakira Caine, Michael's wife, the most exquisite woman in the world. She looked at me pityingly and I wondered why. Only years later did I hear about Billy's arrival-night craziness.

Being on St Lucia with a new baby was a challenge for me, for the hotel had no walls. Our room was open to all kinds of elements and, magnificent though it was, huge flying, crawling things presented omnipresent threats. We spent most of the daytime trying to keep Daisy cool beneath a giant mosquito net, then, as the evenings progressed, we lay gazing at the most bewitching night skies we'd ever seen.

In mid-June, when the *Water* location had moved back to England, Billy drove to Devon late one night to be on set the next day. He was tired. Around 2 a.m., I received a terrible phone call.

'Mrs Connolly?'

'No, but that'll do.'

'This is the police. I'm afraid Billy has been in an accident ...'

My heart stopped.

'Is he ... OK?'

'We think so ... but they're doing a brain scan ... he was knocked unconscious.'

Billy had left the road and somersaulted a few times, totalling his car near Weston-super-Mare. It was very fortunate that he'd not been drunk because the police came to his hospital bedside and breathalyzed him. The following twenty-four hours were agonizingly suspenseful but, mercifully, he regained consciousness.

'D'you think they'll let me keep my Advanced Motorist Certificate?' Billy asked when he came to. He behaved as though he could always get another brain.

20 June
I wish the pain would go away. My eyes look like I should be auditioning for Hammer films, not Handmade.

Billy had sustained considerable physical injuries and his prognosis was uncertain, so the filming had to be put on hold until he recovered. It was remarkable that he'd survived such a colossal impact of metal and tarmac; when I helped him wash his hair, I kept finding little bits of Volkswagen embedded in his scalp.

In true Cochise fashion, he rapidly bounced back to health and, after only one week, he was well enough to attend the soundtrack recording session for *Water* in George Harrison's home recording studio. Billy drove nervously up the impressive driveway belonging to Friar Park, the Harrisons' colossal red-brick, Victorian gâteau, counting no less than nine busy gardeners on the way. The grounds were spectacular. 'Fuck,' he said, 'I don't feel quite so successful around George.'

Billy has always been fascinated with the behaviour and lifestyles of other well-known people, particularly rock 'n' rollers. We had been chuckling about Keith Richard arriving late for a recent dinner party at Langan's. 'Keef' had peered at us painfully from behind his 'piss-off' shades and complained, 'I hate these breakfast do's!'

Billy was interested to see how many giants of rock 'n' roll would appear in time for the official soundtrack recording start at 8.15 a.m. in the studio. In fact, every one of them did: Jon Lord from Deep Purple, Ray Cooper, Ringo Starr and, of course, George. It had not been at all easy for Billy to get up in time. Not even his recent narrow escape had deterred him from further engaging in risky behaviour.

10 July
I feel really bad today. I completely overdid the drinking last night at Peter McDougall's. I can't even remember driving home. I once again have huge blank spaces towards the end of the evening. I don't know how I behaved and I'm frightened to call in case I was over the top or rude or whatever. I wish Pam would call from New York.

I had become a cast member on *Saturday Night Live*, a famous comedy show on network American television, whose alumni included Eddie Murphy, Chevy Chase and John Belushi. This meant I had to spend a great deal of time in New York. Billy did not want to move there, so the whole family travelled back and forth across the Atlantic over the ensuing seven months. I rented an apartment in

Manhattan, in a mysterious 'Knights of Pythian' building that resembled a set from *Aida*.

John Reid began to manage Billy after he turned up on the *Saturday Night Live* set and offered to manage me. I had a better idea: 'No, John,' I replied. 'You should manage Billy. He needs better management and you two are a great match – you go way back.'

Billy's contract with Harvey Goldsmith had expired. 'I'm not planning to re-sign,' Billy had faced him. 'In fact I'm going with John Reid.'

'That's fine with me,' Harvey had said. 'You're not funny any more.'

Billy had known his new manager since John's early days selling clothing in Glasgow. Reid had managed Elton John for years and is a highly creative man. At that time he sometimes engaged in a frustrating behaviour Billy referred to as 'sleeping for Africa', where he would follow a binge of partying with a period of comatose withdrawal when he couldn't be reached. 'I tend to like people who are a bit erratic,' says Billy, 'and anyway, I always admired John's courage and intuitive judgement.'

Pete Brown's brother, Steve, who already worked for the Reid Organization, became Billy's day-to-day manager – a gentle Renaissance man who continues to be a respected, insightful voice of calm and reason in Billy's chaotic professional life. For Steve it continues to be quite a challenge. 'Billy is full of contradictions,' he says. 'He's the most gregarious person I've ever met ... he'll talk to everyone in a restaurant, invite relative strangers backstage and give another hour's performance while we're all desperate to go home ... yet he barely has a friend in the world and sits alone in his hotel room.

'He panics in a clothing shop because he can't bring himself to spend a hundred pounds on a shirt, yet he'll give away sixty thousand pounds for a local hospice without blinking an eye. He has the worst memory in the world for certain things – I'm terrified of giving him his passport because he'll lose it – yet mention a song from the sixties and he'll recite every word.' Billy has his own rationale for the latter anomaly, 'I have a drunk memory, and a sober one,' he explains.

Billy is usually loved by the people with whom he works, but, on occasion, the welder in him returns. When he recorded the television show *An Audience with Billy Connolly* for London Weekend Television on 3 October, a drunken technician approached him, stinking of peppermint. He pointed to Billy's Autoharp.

'We need to hear a level on that thing.'

'What thing?' Billy was affronted by the man's ignorance. He was also very nervous about the show, as many of his famous peers would be in the audience.

'That thing there.' Billy thought the man needed an attitude transplant.

'Well you go away and find out what it's fucking called and then I'll consider giving you a level.' The man never returned.

Billy had asked for a painted backdrop depicting an audience of people who cheered whenever he faced them. It had been provided for him, but in his nervous state he'd forgotten all about it and failed to look round even once. As usual, Billy hadn't planned a show, but on the spur of the moment he decided to talk about a pharmaceutical product that had recently grabbed his attention: Incontinence Pants. He proceeded to mime the antics of a man with such a problem, getting ready for a night-on-the-town with a seventy-gallon capacity in his trousers. The picture elicited tear-producing howls from the likes of Ringo Starr, Joanna Lumley, Robbie Coltrane and Bill Wyman.

Billy had completely seduced his celebrity audience, prancing around the studio stage beneath his name written in eight-feet-high pink lettering. 'What a bloody relief,' he said when it was over.

~

BILLY

Cara and Jamie absolutely loved New York and Daisy was the toast of the Rockefeller Center. She was a superb traveller all round, if you discount that one teensy flight when she vomited on Joan Collins. Billy was also quite given to vomiting at the time. His much-quoted stage piece about throwing up 'diced carrots' became a reality, for he had adopted my vegetarian-ish diet, more for convenience than for anything else. I found myself hoping Billy would just stay in London, for he had taken to arriving in New York absolutely legless.

11 October
I got thoroughly pissed on the plane on red wine I would normally use to wash the car with and poured into New York like a fucking idiot, proceeding to make a total arse of myself.

12 October
Having thoroughly embarrassed everybody and argued violently and foul-mouthedly with perfectly normal people in a restaurant, I am now, not surprisingly, in the baddest of bad books! I made up my mind today to admit to myself that I can no longer drink.

13 October
Pam and I had a long talk about my behaviour. I had very little to say.

28 October
All my pals were away. I called everyone, Jamie in New York with Pam, Cara in Scotland. It only served to make me lonelier. I wanted to drink, but I fought it and won.

30 October
I proceeded to get merrily pissed.

LEGLESS IN MANHATTAN

15 November
Made a total arse of myself. I feel fucking weak and stupid.

24 November
Pam made me breakfast in bed, treatment that surely befits a man who has just turned forty-three. Dear God, forty-three. I must say it's a real pleasure to have reached such a great stage in the game. I honestly thought I would be dead and gone by this time, but here we are and bloody glad of it.

1 January 1986
I woke, for the first time in my adult life, on New Year's Day without even a hint of a hangover.

Billy finally quit drinking on 30 December 1985. He has been sober ever since.

14

THERE'S HOLES IN YOUR WILLIE

In summer 2001 at 7 a.m., a green and white box beside our bed is emitting an unholy noise. To me, that is, the noise is unholy: Billy would regard it as the most sacred of all sacred noises, for it is 'The Fields of Athenry', one of the famous songs sung at every Celtic Park football match. This tinny rendition of the Irish emigration song is Billy's latest attempt at a timely awakening. It emanates from a Celtic souvenir alarm clock that lights up to reveal a 3-D mid-match scene in all its green-striped glory.

Billy sits up and zaps the alarm. 'I'm going back to my natural wake-up call,' he announces.

'What's that?' I wrench myself upright.

'Before I go to sleep, I tap myself on the forehead with my index finger, once for every hour until I reach the time I want to wake.'

'Has it ever worked for you?' I ask hesitantly.

'Nooo,' he hedges, 'but then, I'm a man of unusual ability. I know things that would confound medical science. For instance, next time you get a cut, get a dog to lick the wound ... It'll heal in no time ... you just watch!'

≈

I can't deny that Billy is a man of unusual ability, but he also has some quaint, hand-knitted notions about life. On his 1985 extended tour of Britain and Ireland, he choked in a fish restaurant and subsequently performed two of his Irish shows with a fishbone firmly lodged in his throat. 'Get yourself to the hospital in Dublin, Billy,' I insisted over the phone. He was in great discomfort but had thought he'd let the bone 'work its way out naturally'.

Billy had thought of naming that tour 'Effin' blindin' ', but John Reid came up with 'Wreck On Tour'. Billy has always put a great deal of thought into his tour titles. His favourite was 'Rebel Without a Clue', and was accompanied by a spoof of the James Dean poster from *Giant*, with a banjo around Billy's neck instead of a rifle.

At the end of 1985, the whole family spent Christmas and New Year in Australia before Billy began the antipodean leg of 'Wreck On Tour'. Billy adores my home city of Sydney for its colour, its style, its art and its people. He feels a deep connection with Sydney's convict history, and will often stop on our walks around The Rocks area and scrutinize plaques and commemorative statues, searching for evidence of the earlier inhabitants of the place and all their pioneering hardships. He also feels great empathy with the Aboriginal people he has met during his many journeys around Australia. Through his own tormented beginnings, he feels an intuitive kinship with exiled, pilloried or disenfranchised peoples everywhere, from eighteenth-century convict settlers in New South Wales to the famine-stricken people in Mozambique today, and even with his fellow Celtic supporters.

We rented a beach-side house and Billy, who doesn't swim too well, spent his days lurking in the shallows while bronzed Sydney surfers cruised out to the farthest surf line for the risky business of negotiating the Ninth Wave. Billy hates sand. 'I rub on suntan oil, lie on the sand, then along comes a gust of wind and pppffttt! I look like a doughnut,' he complains. 'What's more,' he continues, 'as a species we just don't belong in the sea. There are things that bite, sting, hurt the soles of your feet and yet we keep going in there.

When are we going to take the hint that the things that live in there don't like us?'

Sharks are omnipresent around Sydney beaches, although some of them are harmless. When a shark is spotted, hovering helicopters alert the beach authorities, who sound an alarm so swimmers can head for the beach. The helicopters chase the man-eating cruisers out to sea and, when it's safe, people can swim again.

Billy came back for lunch one day, furious. 'People are so inconsiderate,' he said, 'always letting off their bloody car alarms. It gets everyone in such a panic. Every few minutes, hundreds of them rush out of the water to see if it's their car that's being broken into.' I didn't have the heart to tell him it was the shark alarm he was hearing. He found out a few days later. 'Fuck,' he said. 'How does anyone in Australia ever live to a ripe old age?'

Celebrating Christmas in a warm climate is enjoyable and familiar to me, but Billy found it very strange at first.

31 December
The evening was lovely. There was a fireworks display on the beach and a lot of happy noises from the surf club, but not one accordion, Scottish tenor nor squeaky soprano. Lovely.

On 23 January 1986, he flew to Perth to begin his Australian tour. He spent the eight-hour journey wide awake all the way and was pleased to have a good book. 'Wouldn't it be good if we all had ideas as good as Howard Hughes?' he mused. 'Of course he was a bit of a space cadet, but I can't find fault with the idea of being transported around in a drugged state.'

Apparently, Hughes preferred to be injected with a sleeping drug in his bed at home and to wake up in his country of destination with no conscious memory of the flight. 'It's a brilliant idea,' Billy decided. 'In my humble opinion, the guy was years ahead of his time

... but then ...' he poked at his wilted lettuce, 'maybe he just had a pathological hatred of aeroplane food.'

When Billy returned to Sydney, a city blessed with the light from the ocean, he lazed around on the roof of the hotel for most of the afternoon, listening to an album of didgeridoo music by Gondwanaland. He was trying not to think too much about the gig, just lying there with all that magical noise in his ears and toasting like a crumpet. The famous crooner, Al Martino, was sitting beside him at the pool. 'It's so weird,' thought Billy, 'to be sitting beside him ... all those years ago his records were so popular in our house.' Billy had even sung 'Here in My Heart' at his sister's wedding. Florence had married Ian Dickson in 1966 and now had two children, Stephen and Andrea.

~

Billy has always loved the company of creative people, especially visual artists. He met up with Mark Knopfler, who accompanied Billy on stage one night at the Sydney Opera House. Mark introduced him to the Sydney artist Brett Whitely and the three men met up in a hotel bar, where the topic of conversation shortly became 'favourite words'. Mark had just produced Bob Dylan's album *Infidel*.

'What's your favourite word?' he had asked Bob.

'I'm not sure,' replied Bob, 'but my least favourite word is two words.'

'What are they?' demanded Mark.

'The words "Excuse me ..."' said Bob. 'Especially when you hear it from behind you.'

Billy, Mark and Brett were roaring over this when a little fat guy approached them from behind for an autograph. 'Excuse me ...' he said, surprised by the stomach-clutching hilarity his two words seemed to inspire.

Billy was tremendously flattered to see a photo of himself on the wall of Brett Whitely's stunning studio. Creatively, Brett was one of the most impressive men he'd ever met but unfortunately he was addicted to heroin. Billy often connects with that kind of edgy darkness in a person, especially when it is accompanied by an apparent lust for life.

Brett had a remarkable gift for animal impersonations. He imitated a bowerbird coveting a blue marble for its lover's nest and snatching it under its wing: a cocky, darting, excellent mime. Brett had visited a Tasmanian Devil in the Toronga Park Zoo in Sydney and had thrown a coin into its cage so it would protest. 'Aahhh!' When it opened its mouth, Brett could see its vermilion palate and he drew a beautiful sketch of the creature in that position.

'Do you do the same show every night?' Brett asked Billy.

'No,' he answered, 'although there are favourite things I talk about for a while until I get bored with them.'

'OK,' said Brett, in disbelief. 'I'm going to come to the show again tonight. Bet you five dollars you can't do it without one single thing the same!'

Billy took up the challenge. When his pal turned up in the dressing room after the next show, Billy could see he was impressed.

'That was amazing!' he exclaimed. 'Here's your fiver.'

'Thanks,' said Billy, pleased and relieved.

'See you tomorrow night then,' said Brett.

'Oh, fuck!' thought Billy.

Billy normally invents his show freshly from night to night, although there are often chunks he likes to do throughout a particular tour. Since he is highly distractible, he has trouble staying with one subject for very long and it's always amusing for the audience to watch him lose track. 'I do the *Readers' Digest* form of comedy,' he explains to them. 'I begin, then it says "continued on page seven" but I just keep going straight through! You daren't come here pissed!'

Sometimes he forgets to tell the end of a story or joke he has begun earlier in the show. At the finish, people in the audience will be shouting at him: 'What happened to the guy in the bathroom with holes in his willie?' Once it happened when he was on tour in Morecambe, and his reply was, 'Come to Blackpool tomorrow night and I'll tell you the rest of the story!' Right at the end of his Blackpool concert, there was a plaintive cry from the same man, all the way up the back. 'Billy! You promised! What happened to the guy in the bathroom?'

Billy loses track of time when he's on stage. On several occasions, he has misread his watch and performed an hour longer than usual. On one famous occasion, he performed over four hours at the Sydney Opera House and his audience ended up being locked out of the car park: the man just loves performing. If you turn up in his dressing room at the end of a show he'll do another ninety minutes for you ... he just can't help it!

Whenever I attend Billy's show at the Sydney Opera House, I love to wander backstage. In the mid-seventies I was a member of the Sydney Theatre Company, whose home was in the Opera House Drama Theatre, so I am familiar with the artists' Green Room. It is always delightful to see an assortment of opera singers in fantastic costumes and grossly exaggerated make-up, tuxedoed musicians and actors in Shakespearean costumes, all clustered around the backstage monitors with the sound turned up full blast, watching Billy's show being relayed from the Concert Hall. There are gasps, roars and body-rocking. Some seem to have difficulty tearing themselves away, even though they are due on stage in their own theatre any minute. Angry stage managers are wont to appear from time to time, in order to issue a stern reprimand to a wayward 'Connolly fan', missing from the crowd scene in *Turandot*.

After Sydney shows, we love to meander round The Rocks, dine on the waterfront then get up before noon for a cappuccino at the Bar Coluzzi in King's Cross where a lively collection of people gather: stockbrokers, politicians, surfers, writers and artists.

Another extraordinary friend of Billy's, Jimmy Boyle, turned up at Billy's concert in Adelaide. Billy had recently opened his Gateway Exchange, a place in Edinburgh where troubled young people can receive some help. Jimmy himself was a product of the notorious Gorbals area in Glasgow. He was sentenced to life imprisonment for murder in 1963 and jailed for many years, incarcerated in a cage inside a cell where he engaged in a 'dirty protest', smearing himself with excreta so his jailers would keep their distance.

Eventually he was taken into the Barlinnie Special Unit, which had been set up especially for persistently violent prisoners. It was a progressive regime, where the men were permitted to live together like normal human beings, make their own food and have a greater degree of freedom within the confines of the Unit. They were given psychological treatment too and the scheme worked like a miracle for Jimmy. He took up sculpture and writing and was outstanding at both.

Billy met Jimmy when he was invited to visit the Unit. He particularly enjoyed Jimmy's company and the two have been friends ever since. After he was released in 1982, Jimmy became hugely successful. 'It's funny talking to a guy about his tax problems when you can't get it out of your head that he used to be a prisoner of Her Majesty,' observes Billy. 'Looking at him it's hard to believe that he was once considered the most dangerous man in Scotland.'

Tortured people find each other. Billy, Brett and Jimmy had suffering in common, but it also makes perfect sense that, being exceptional himself, Billy would gravitate towards other people who have experienced remarkable events or made extraordinary choices in their lives. Anyone who comes to public attention, either by fault, design, or birth, comes into this category, although Billy loves to meet any interesting, likeable person. 'Beige people', as he refers to them, are not his cup of tea. Nor are those without a sense of humour.

Every now and then, Billy takes a sudden and seemingly random dislike to some poor bugger. It always took me by surprise, until I realized that his overreaction can usually be traced to early scenarios. Overbearing women with red hair will remind him of his Aunt Margaret. A reserved Catholic man with a thick neck will trigger defensive behaviour in Billy and so will anyone from the media who attacks him or catches him by surprise. It's never pretty, watching his limbic system gearing into overdrive.

Even in nature, Billy can be partisan, favouring anything but the beige. His idea of a pretty sight can be seen from Palm Beach Head in New South Wales:

> *9 January*
> Last night was without doubt one of the finest sights of my life. I was watching TV with Cara. Just having a nice wee time bitching about the people who were doing their best to entertain us, when the biggest lightning storm I have ever seen started. At one point the entire sky lit up with white dancing light behind the clouds, which was then superimposed with pink (yes pink!) forked lightning covering the entire sky. I was so moved by the experience, another example of the magic of this extraordinary place. I love it.

A month later, Billy was gazing at far more placid skies in New Zealand, the land of the long white cloud. It took Billy a couple of days to mellow out enough to enjoy the place.

> *2 February*
> Auckland. Unfortunately it is Sunday and all the shops are shut. I'm desperate for nail polish, batteries and a Turkish Delight.

When he's on tour, Billy eats lightly during the day and relies on having a main meal after his show at night. Nowadays he can get a late curry anywhere in the country, but when Billy first began to perform in New Zealand, in the early eighties, he was annoyed to find that few restaurants stayed open late enough for him to eat at 11 p.m. In Wellington he discovered one late-opening joint, a Greek restaurant with a belly dancer, but was a little embarrassed to be the only one in the place, night after night, with the big New Zealand 'lassie' wobbling her tummy all over his baklava. 'She must have thought I was a nutter,' he worries.

3 February
There is absolutely nothing to do but go for a walk. I went down to the wharves to see the round-the-world race yachts. Pam's Uncle Bill, who is in charge of the whole affair, showed me around the place. Brave buggers, those yachtsmen: rather them than me.

When Billy called me from New Zealand, he was panicking because he had heard one of my more conservative relatives would be in the audience.

'Don't worry. All my folks are extremely broad-minded,' I lied.

'Oh good,' he said hopefully, 'then maybe they'll take me fishing.' He got his wish.

Billy will do anything to have a tussle with a trout. Whenever he plays Hamilton, he stays in a lodge two hours away from his gig so he can 'Spey cast' into a salmon river. He was chuffed to have a fly named after him, a gold, black and green creation of an Irishman, Peter O'Reilly, but Billy has yet to catch a fish with it.

Putting on his waders and standing waist-deep in a New Zealand stream, as well as absorbing the gentle atmosphere of the sparsely populated places, does seem to have a calming effect on Billy.

5 May
The flight to Christchurch was lovely. There's a big green park in the centre of town. I strolled around it for a while. There's such a soothing peace here.

His new-found mellowness was antithetical to the volatile mood Billy likes to be in for his shows, so he was glad to hear of a little dissidence shaking up the country.

6 May
National Day in New Zealand. The Maoris have taken to demonstrating at the National or Waitangi Day celebrations because they can see no reason for celebrating the loss of their land. I can't blame them.

One of the longest shows Billy has ever done in his life, over four hours, was performed in New Zealand. In mid-flow in a Dunedin concert, he happened to glance at his watch. 'Look at that!' he cried. 'It's eleven-thirty. I better get off ... or ...' a new plan was forming, 'I've always wanted to come off stage on a different day than the one I went on. Do you fancy it?' A huge roar went up from the crowd, so he stayed on stage until a minute after midnight.

~

'Oh, my God!' cries Billy. He is staring at a colour photograph he's just dragged from a padded envelope, postmarked March 2001, Wigan, Great Britain, sent by a fellow welder from those days, Barry Duffy. The scene is the oil rig, Ocean Master Two, somewhere off the coast of Biafra in 1966. Thirteen scruffy-looking individuals are clinging to a crane, which is winching them to a few rounds of lager after a hard day's welding.

Billy has spotted himself in the foreground, the filthiest and cheekiest-looking of the entire bunch, who appears to have just uttered a sly joke. I peer at it, waiting expectantly for Billy to comment on his old mates' current doings or his physical environment. In this moment, however, Billy is oblivious to everything except his own lithe, twenty-four-year-old physique. 'Look at my wee skinny body,' he exclaims in wonderment. 'I'd better start getting out on my bike again!'

~

Billy always returns to his biking with a feeling of owing loyalty to an old friend. It was just like that in 1986, when the end of Lent had signalled for Billy an increase in excessive eating rather than the customary denial. I had sawn him in half in a sketch for the Comic Relief Concert, but the result was not a reduction in size, but rather two dwarves wearing 'Billy Connolly' beards.

Ready for a spot of self-imposed purgatory, Billy decided to attempt the London-to-Brighton Charity Bike Ride. Eric Clapton's manager had turned up backstage at the London Palladium the previous November, after one of Billy's fourteen sold-out shows, with a gift from Eric: a complete set of new Campagnolo bicycling equipment. Trying out all that lovely gear, Billy gingerly took a little training spin round Richmond Park but was knackered by the time he got to Ralph McTell's house. Billy has always loved and admired Ralph, whom he judges to be a talented musician and true family man.

Despite Ralph's protestations, Billy loves to tell people about the time the folk singer got lost while driving Billy from Putney to Knightsbridge. After half an hour of frustration, Billy exploded.

'Fuck it, Ralph,' he flew at him, 'didn't you write "Streets of London"... "Let me take you by the hand and lead you through the streets of London"...?'

'Promise me,' laughed Ralph, 'you'll never tell anyone.'

Ralph was always flattered that Billy sought him out. 'He doesn't suffer fools gladly,' Ralph remarks. 'He's got his own logic that sees him through. I find him insightful, intelligent and spiritual ... my "Dreamtime" song came from talking to him about Australia. He walks the earth like a man and goes home on foot ... and he doesn't need the protection of roadies and minders.'

Happy in the rice fields of
Penestanan, Bali, 1980.

A cleaned-up version of
Billy's former self: at a
movie premiere, Piccadilly,
1983. I borrowed the dress
from Zandra Rhodes, but
found out afterwards I'd
worn it back to front.

Left: 1983: Introducing our first born, Daisy, taken at the Fish Factory.

Below: The whole family in Fiji. A little too much Kava Kava had caused my headdress to slip.

Above: Humblebums III? PR shot with George Harrison for 'Parents For Safe Food', a campaign I launched, at Gruntfuttock Hall.

Below: Duelling duo: Scarlett *(with guitar)* and Amy *(with banjo)* at Gruntfuttock Hall in summer, 1995. Billy's snowstorm collection is hanging on the wall by the curtain.

Mozambique, 1998 – or 'Nose and Beak' as it was christened by Daisy.

Above: A scene from *Brigadoon*: Billy and
his sister Florence at her son's wedding.

Above: Lunch with Mattie in London,
Ontario, 1998.

Below: Sporting a velvet coat in the team colours,
Billy opens the new Celtic grandstand, 1999.

Mail muddle pending: The Doctors Connolly! Glasgow University, 2001.

Ralph discovered this fact for himself one busy night at the Half Moon, a 'villains' pub' in Putney. He had forewarned a couple of drinking buddies that Billy might drop in: 'My friend's coming tonight. If you see people coming over to bother him, will you ask them nicely to leave him alone?'

Apparently, the hard men were happy to act as unofficial bouncers. Ralph tucked Billy up at the top end of the bar out of the way, so if anyone seemed to be making a bee-line for him, Ralph's gang could intervene: 'Leave the man alone,' they would insist in that quiet, dangerous way.

After an hour or two of peaceful drinking, Billy surprised everyone by complaining to Ralph in the tone of a disappointed child at an unattended birthday party. 'For fuck's sake!' He was terribly miffed. 'Where *is* everybody?' He went pouting off to the toilet, with Ralph close behind. While Billy was 'pointing Percy at the porcelain' as they say in Australia, a man came in with a sheet of paper and asked him for his autograph.

'Would you mind signing this?' he asked.

'Aye,' replied Billy, turning round quite affably, 'if you don't mind holding *this*.'

∾

After stopping off at Ralph's house for a cup of tea and a chat, Billy headed off to cycle a circuit of the park but, by the top of the first hill, he thought he was going to perish. The penny had dropped. 'I'll have to get a great deal fitter than I am at the moment,' he warned himself. 'I've got a month, though.'

The big day of the ride to Brighton arrived on 15 June. Billy warmed up at Clapham Common with fifty thousand other cyclists. He was probably the only participant who had been sponsored by Elton John at a very generous one hundred pounds per mile for the charity. He had a cup of tea with the organizers, was rude to the press and set off at a goodly lick. To his great joy, he found he was fitter and faster than he'd imagined and actually reached the finishing line.

While Billy was slimming down, I had been steadily progressing in the opposite direction. On the second day in July 1986, Billy dropped me at the Portland Hospital, then drove off to attend a party at Mick Jagger's place. Bastard: I always enjoyed seeing Mick and Jerry. Towards the end of one evening we spent in their company, Mick's legs ceased to work due to an excess of something or other. As we said goodbye, we noticed that Jerry glamorously draped herself over him, posing for paparazzi as the couple swept off to their limousine. 'Will you look at that!' exclaimed Billy, terribly impressed. 'She's actually carrying him to the car.'

Amy was born on 3 July, weighing seven pounds, thirteen ounces. We gave her a Maori middle name after Hira, my great-grandmother, and Billy was delighted to be a father of another baby girl. 'Scottish men think they're even manlier when they have daughters,' he insisted. A couple of weeks later, I made up for missing Mick's party with my own wild night.

17 July

Fleet Street has discovered from some prick at Annabel's that Pamela, Fergie and Princess Diana were out on the town disguised as policewomen, having a great laugh and causing harm to no one. We're under a state of siege. The telephone never stopped ringing from dawn to dusk with the bastards desperate for details. I managed to last the whole day without pounding anyone.

The last thing on earth that Billy expected in his life was to be invited to a royal wedding, that of the Duke and Duchess of York, a jolly pair we had met at a charity event in Scotland. Billy looked particularly handsome that day in his Moss Bros morning suit. By contrast, I was in post-birth mode and in the middle of my bad-hair decade, desperately trying to sneak unnoticed out of the service for an in-car baby feed. When we arrived at Westminster Abbey, a 'look-it's-Billy-he's-one-of-us' cheer went up from the crowd in the street outside. Florence watched the event on television in her Glasgow living room with a party of friends. 'That's my little brother!' she marvelled. She was so proud.

The television coverage of that wedding reached countries most people have never even heard of, but only Irish people caught Billy on Gaye Byrne's TV talk show, the *Late Late Show*, just as his Irish tour was beginning. Sporting a maroon and white polka-dot shirt, Billy instructed viewers on his now-famous 'drunk singing'.

'You just need to know three new words,' he said. 'The first one is "erufor". It doesn't mean anything. The next is "seeroobee". Then you put together any three syllables you like.'

The studio audience crooned with him: 'Erufor ... seeroobee'.

'For the second line,' he continued, 'change them round and keep singing higher. At this point your friends will all be joining in. They'll think they know it.' Billy then announced to Gaye that he was inspired to try to find his grandfather's birthplace. He knew roughly where Jack had been born, somewhere on the Connemara coast, near Galway.

Billy's charmed version of a bush telegraph worked, because a girl turned up shortly after that, at Billy's Galway concert, with a letter and some photos of her own cottage, which she believed to have been Jack's. She claimed there was an old man in the village of Ballyconneely who remembers the Connolly family leaving early that century.

Billy has always been intrigued by the idea of Irish people choosing to settle in Scotland, Canada or the South Island of New Zealand. 'I love Ireland,' he tells his audiences, 'there's something very alive about the people. "Come on, I know an even colder place than here where it rains all the time ... head for the black cloud, chaps! East Virginia? ... too warm ... let's go north to Canada! Or south to Dunedin drizzle!"'

Struck by the similarity between 'Ballyconneely' and his own name, Billy set out to find Jack's village, but he only got as far as Clifden, a market town set in the middle of gorgeous countryside. Depressed, he returned to the hotel. The broad landscapes were enchanting, but the unending dereliction of the towns was ubiquitous and saddening.

In the middle of May, young Jamie arrived to spend time with his father and the two of them set off early to find the elusive village, the car radio tuned to a Gaelic station that presented haunting traditional Irish vocal and fiddle music. This time they drove through startling scenery and eventually did find Ballyconneely, just a few white cottages with black roofs set into the land on the Atlantic coast. Billy felt lost and unsettled, with jumbled feelings of displacement, echoes of the past and yearnings for clarity all churning around inside him. In the end he spoke to no one in the area, but at dinner that night he discussed the curious logic and use of language he always hears in the Irish countryside generally. It always makes him roar.

'You're the spitting image of yourself,' someone had said to him in a pub near Ballyconneely. A woman wanting bacon in another village, was berating a salesperson: 'What kind of post office is this, with no rashers?'

~

We had moved to a Thames-side house at Bray in the English countryside. Billy has never forgiven me for taking off for Australia immediately after the movers dropped their last box in the new place. He made the best of it, though, and began to unpack the kitchen china with a maximum of grumbling.

Life at home was something of an anticlimax for Billy after touring, on and off, for the past three years.

> **18 May**
> Back home at Bray. The girls don't allow me to sleep much. I feel as if I am put-upon by everyone, a typical after-tour feeling. A cold panic as one realizes that there is no room service on the telephone dial, no tea and biscuits at the lift of the phone. When I woke it was like the middle of the night, and it was! Pam was asking me to do the dawn shift, it was only five o'clock in the morning for God's sake. I got up and did my best, feeling like I'd been hit with a truckload of gravel.

Re-entering family life after a long tour is always a challenge for Billy but, at that point in our lives, his post-tour tiredness wasn't his only family concern. He put up with my antics much like the weary father of a wayward teenager.

> **3 June**
> This morning I was informed that Pamela had gone to the hairdresser to get her hair dyed pink because she is standing for one of those loony parties for Parliament. God help us all! We'll need it!

I was the local candidate for the 'I Want to Stuff a Blancmange Down Terry Wogan's Y-Fronts' party. Billy turned into William when he saw me sprouting candy-floss hair. 'You're a fucking bampot!' he shook his head in disapproval.

Billy's managers, John and Steve, arrived one day to talk him into taking the enormous step of playing the Royal Albert Hall ... and had a good laugh when they caught him vacuuming. 'You're becoming such an old housewife!' John accused him. Billy didn't care. He always enjoys the feeling of achievement he has after giving the house a rubdown. He wondered, though, if he would get the same thrill from giving the Albert Hall a thorough, comic dusting down, or would the illustrious venue prove to be too big for him?

It is an odd-shaped venue in which to perform comedy and Billy obsessed about its size until Steve, with a stroke of genius, arranged for an eight-foot screen to be placed on the stage above his head so people could see him in close-up. It worked like a dream. Billy was even able to do quite subtle comedy in that situation, including a set piece about baby-monitors, in which he did a priceless impersonation of a sleeping baby: 'Don't buy one of these intercoms,' he advised his audience. 'Babies pretend to be dead. They're bastards and they do it on purpose.'

Billy manages to tell the audience what they are thinking, even before they are aware of it: immediately after announcing that he was going to offer them 'A guide to more fulfilling masturbation', he spoke their fears. 'I know, you're going "Oh no, Billy give us a break. I'm with my girlfriend. If I laugh, she'll know I've done it!" Well, don't worry. I read that sixty-eight per cent of all British men masturbate on a regular basis. How do they know? Did it show up on the Richter Scale? Nobody I ever ask ever does it!'

At the end of the 'Billy and Albert' show, Billy farewelled six thousand aching people with: 'It's been a pleasure talking to you ... Don't worry. I'm the one going to hell.'

After his objectionable Elton John tour days, Billy had never thought he would enjoy playing to six thousand people but, from 4 July 1987, he filled the hall completely for six nights: a stunning achievement for a comedian. Altogether, more than thirty thousand people turned up. Billy fully appreciated the Albert Hall's history and unique majesty, the like of which he'd never experienced. Lending contrast to all that grandeur, our Billy did his damnedest to upset the ghosts with his irreverent ravings. Best of all, when he went on stage the very first night, in his black and white suit, he was tickled to find that the entire audience was equally flash, wearing Albert Hall tea-cosy hats. Billy enjoyed the joke just as much as they did.

Billy still wears a tea cosy on his head whenever he gets the chance. Our family motto has become: 'Never trust a man who, when left alone in a room with a tea cosy, doesn't try it on.' The Romans never used tea cosies, so it is quite impossible to translate the motto into Latin. The best I've been able to do (although I'm open to suggestions) is: *Hominem Iniocosum Non Diffidite* (Never trust a man who lacks a sense of humour).

Billy loves his tea cosies, aprons and onion-goggles, the accoutrements of a man who likes nothing better than to be up to his elbows in flour. Our first Christmas in Bray, he forgot to buy presents for the kids, but made up for it by cooking Christmas dinner single-handedly: a delicious 'fishy pie' and a Scottish plum pudding called a 'cloutie dumpling'.

I stupidly pushed my luck by sending him on a shopping errand for props, for my forthcoming tour, as soon as the shops opened in January:

Shopping List
One telescopic fishing rod
One Japanese tea tray
Two guardsmen's helmets
One plastic hairy chest
One false moustache (ginger)
One mallet
Four dozen condoms

'Fuck, Pamela,' he complained, 'some women just want butter and a tea loaf!'

15

PALE BLUE SCOTTISH PERSON

Minutes after the game in April 2001, Martin O'Neil, lauded manager of Celtic Football Team, is stepping sure-footedly out of the locker-room showers. He wraps a towel around his waist and marches swiftly around a bend in the tiled corridor. He is astonished to see Billy standing there waiting for him with his friend Russell Kyle. As the proud recipient of a 'Seat for Life' in the grandstand, Billy is often at Celtic Park when the team is playing, but Martin hadn't expected to see him in the men's room.

'I saw you running about naked in Comic Relief, my friend,' he reprimands Billy. 'Do you want to see what a real one looks like?'

'Och, give me a break,' protests Billy, 'I was freezing at the time.'

~

Billy's yardstick for virility and achievement has never been his genital size – he's always been perfectly happy about that – but rather it has been a question of his ability to seduce the good people of North America. 'I always thought if I didn't make it in the USA it would be half a career,' explains Billy. 'It's such a large part of the English-speaking world.'

His experiences opening for Elton John and others left him with an uncomfortable sense of impotence; the very expression 'opening' conjuring up wimpish images and an ardent desire to overcome his Amerectile Dysfunction. The Viagra he needed for America was some means of raising his professional profile, not his penis. Billy's first assault on America began in March 1987, when he embarked on a tour of the US and Canada.

When he began his tour of Canada, Billy was worried that he would be portrayed as a 'Scottish shortbread type' but, for the first time ever, he had a real sense that it was the Canadian people who were out in force to see him, not just Scottish expatriates. His standing ovation in Cornwall, Ontario, and the lakeside town of Kingston furthered the thrilling feeling that his audience was building in that country. Billy's babysitter from Dover Street, Mattie Murphy, was in the audience one night. She had emigrated to Canada with her family many years earlier and settled in London, Ontario. At first Billy did not remember her, but the way she talked about him and Florence as children, as well as Mamie and the other Dover Street dwellers, brought back memories he'd long forgotten.

When I saw Billy's final American show of the year, at the Lincoln Center, I was thrilled that it was a triumph. Afterwards, at a chic New York hangout called Nell's Place, run by an Australian pal of mine, I observed Billy reclining happily on a velvet sofa with a Perrier in his hand. After his self-imposed 'manhood' challenge, he certainly looked like a person who'd managed to get it up.

In order to promote his USA tour, Billy had appeared on various American chat shows. From his very first spot on David Letterman's popular late-night TV show in New York, Billy became more widely recognized by members of the American public. A Greek parade was in full swing one day in New York and one of the bands had split from the main marchers and was huddled outside Billy's hotel door. When the bandleader recognized Billy, he gave him a warm 'Hello!', which chuffed Billy to the knickers.

'I feel more at home in New York than I do in Bray,' he

announced. 'It's my spiritual home from home.' In truth, Billy hated Bray. It was hard for us to find a place that afforded us privacy while also offering him a chance to mix with local people. Bray seemed to be the domain of relocated wealthy people, so there weren't many real locals in the area.

Early on in our relationship, I had little understanding of either his cultural background or what he needed socially in order to be creatively fed. However, I now realize the notion that a comedian who becomes famous loses touch with his audience is, at least in Billy's case, quite inaccurate. Billy and others used to fear that, after his lifestyle changed so dramatically, his audiences would balk at jokes about shopping at Liberty's. But Billy is not reliant on jokes, or even on subject matter. He always finds the points of contact with every audience. No matter what part of the world he's in, he can always find gut-busting common ground about having children and hating tyranny, about current politics, sports and the wide variety in life and the human condition ... from his anarchic, philosophical or bizarre perspectives.

When he first started to perform solo in the sixties his range of subject matter was limited and full of fairly culture-specific scenes, but very funny. I always love his early stories about Glasgow parties, lively pictures of tenement chaos and drunken mayhem. There are budgies, bagpipes, constables and cursing; and fish suppers catching fire.

The more Billy travelled, the more he had to talk about: 'Aeroplane toilets are made to frighten you. There's no window, no safety belt. You go in and "Oh, for Christ's sake, a wee beige jobbie!" You flush and flush with all your might. Sometimes it goes under that shelf bit and hides. There's no way you're going to bare your bum to this wee beige jobbie that belongs to someone else. And you can't leave. You can't say to the next person, "Oh by the way that's not mine." They'd say, "Is that right? ... Yours got your name on it or something?" Where do all the wee jobbies go? Three hundred and forty people on a jumbo jet for seven and a half hours. That's an awful lot of jobbies.'

As Billy continued to experience different cultures and meet a wider range of people, he was able to increase his audience and expand the range of comedy topics that connected with most people. But he is not funny because of his subject matter; he just *is* funny, as well as provocative, no matter what he talks about. Sometimes it's just too much for me. 'Shut up and make me a cup of tea,' I plead.

~

Billy's initial US tour was a satisfying New World beginning. Back in the UK, he had been the host of Nelson Mandela's Birthday Concert where he'd met the American comic Whoopi Goldberg. Even before they met, I had taken him to see Whoopi perform on Broadway during my *Saturday Night Live* days. In July 1991 she invited him to share the limelight in her HBO special on American cable television, performed live at the Brooklyn Academy in New York. 'The audience that night just loved him,' says Whoopi. 'He was so refreshing and so much fun. He got to them in the way no one had ever done.' She seems to understand Billy: 'Incredibly sensitive is a word I would use to describe him. I think people forget that, in order to do great comedy, you have to have that tragic streak in you.'

Billy thoroughly approves of New Yorkers: 'You appreciate violence the same as we do, and you swear properly,' he told them that evening. The show immediately led to an offer for Billy of a solo one-hour comedy special on the same cable network. The producer came to see Billy perform in concert in San Francisco and nearly cancelled the whole thing. 'There's too much "farting" material,' he objected.

'Well,' said Billy, for once avoiding the impulse to tell him where to ram his objections, 'why don't you come back tomorrow night? I change it all the time ... so I'll do a whole different show for you.'

'Amazing!' fired the man after the second show. 'I love that bit about you not being white.' Billy had told the audience that, when Scottish people take their clothes off, they're blue and that it takes a whole week of sunbathing to become white. This was an idea that particularly seemed to captivate the race-and-colour-conscious American audiences, and the show was eventually given the title *Pale Blue Scottish Person*.

In that show, Billy talked about dipping in the North Sea when he was a child: 'The fish are saying "There's a fucking pale blue guy coming in." I was standing there with skinny muscles, like knots on a midge's penis. My aunt had hand-knitted my bathing trunks. None of your "Speedo Second Skin". More of your second cardigan. It absorbed water and grew. I've heard that Sumo wrestlers can withdraw their testicles at will. I could do that when I was twelve. One foot in the North Sea, the whole fucking lot disappeared. Just an ugly gaping wound.'

A couple of days after *Pale Blue Scottish Person* went on air, Billy was in a car park on Laurel Canyon when he was recognized by two young African-American women in a convertible.

'Oh look!' they cried. 'It's the blue guy!'

'We'll have no colour prejudice around here, thank you very much!' retorted Billy.

~

It is August 2000 and the heavy green dining-room curtains at Candacraig, our Scottish home, have been drawn to hide the bright evening sunshine of a northern summer night. A few close friends, some of them known to the world as very funny people, have just seated themselves with us around the dinner table. There is a somewhat lengthy pause before the meal begins to arrive. 'Um, Billy ...' frowns Eric Idle, 'will there be any food?'

The conversation gravitates to an uncomfortable discussion of the impetus for comedy, in reply to a question from one of the non-comedians at the table.

'For me,' interjects Billy at one point, 'it's about the desire to win. My audience becomes a crowd of wild animals and I have to be the lion-tamer or be eaten ...'

'Oh, is that so?' Steve Martin challenges him. 'You don't think it's about a little hurt from Daddy?'

~

On 11 February 1988, Florence telephoned to tell Billy that their father had had a second stroke. The following day, she informed Billy that, if he wanted to see William alive again, he'd better get to the hospital right away. He ran like an athlete to Heathrow and caught the shuttle.

12 February
Father looks awful. He has lost control of most of his organs. I stayed for as long as I could. I think he recognized me. I hope he did.

13 February
I had a long talk with Pamela and we came to the conclusion that there was nothing to be gained, especially for him, by my sitting around wishing that death would quietly surround him and take the pain and degradation away. It feels awful that such a thought would cross my mind, to wish for the death of your own father, but it is the way of things. I went to the hospital this morning to make my final goodbye to him, by far the most difficult thing I have ever had to do. I made my farewell and kissed him and walked away. No one will ever know how I felt or how I feel. I thought he might wave to me from the window.

31 March
With Flo and I at his bedside Father passed peacefully away at
three o'clock in the afternoon. Tore my heart out.

After William's death, Billy gathered enough courage to tell Florence
about his 'dark secret' and it absolutely crushed her. Siblings often
illogically feel responsible, or experience a kind of survival guilt, as
though they could have prevented the abuse. Florence was still
working as a teacher, at St Mirin's school in Glasgow. As a result of
Billy's confession, she left St Mirin's and sought a position at a school
for emotionally and behaviourally disturbed children in Glasgow.

'It helped me,' she says now, 'being able to soothe those screeching
children, all in such anguish. I thought of Billy all the time. He had it
for so long ... he must have suffered so much.' Florence blamed
herself for years, but of course none of the responsibility was hers.
Fortunately, as Florence witnessed the change and healing in Billy
over the ensuing years, the pain began to leave her too.

Billy returned from Scotland, back to the family and one 'little
lump person', as he called her. We were expecting Scarlett, who
arrived on 28 July. We called her Scarlett because of her extroverted
high-jinks, even in the womb; she is truly an exuberant person. We
attribute her musical giftedness partly to the Ravi Shankar concert
we attended at George Harrison's house just before she was born. On
hearing his exhilarating evening ragas, she leapt and twirled in her
foetal prison until we were afraid she was going to be born right
there and then among all the incense, beads and flowers at Friar
Park. 'Layla' is the title of one of Eric Clapton's best songs and we
gave it to Scarlett as a great rock 'n' roll middle name.

In August 1988, Billy's entire Scottish tour sold out in three
hours. It was a sensational show, with an unexpected finale: he sang
a Van Morrison song, 'Irish Heartbeat', to a surprise pipe band.
While we were in Scotland during that tour, I acted on a nagging,
intuitive voice and wrote to Mamie to ask if we could all meet her.

She agreed to drive up from Dunoon and I met her alone for a short while first, before introducing her to the children. 'Why?' I asked, pointedly.

'There's a lot more to it. And it was wartime,' she said softly, with a few tears in her eyes. Billy was wary of her. Over recent years, she had communicated with him via the tabloid press, which had hurt him tremendously.

We took a photo of Mamie and the whole family gathered together, but that was all there was to it, really. In the afternoon, we drove to Hughie's house to meet Big Neilly, who was now ninety years old. His wife, Flora, had died ten years earlier and Big Neilly lived alone in the house, stubbornly resisting help from the family. He sat up dead straight in his comfy chair, a veritable cliché of Highland reserve, dressed in a tweed jacket and tie with a full head of beautifully groomed, white hair. 'You'll have had your tea?' he inquired, staring disapprovingly at Billy's messy coiffure.

As if Big Neilly had willed it, Billy's hirsute days were numbered. In October 1989, Billy talked with a film director who wanted to cast him as the manager of a bare-knuckle fighter played by Liam Neeson in *The Big Man*, written by Willie McIlvanney, the Scottish novelist and playwright.

'What do you think?' the man asked Billy.

'Oh, I'd like to do it.'

'The beard will have to come off.'

'The beard' had been a fixture since the days of 'Ho Chi Minh'. A source of self-soothing, Billy had sat brushing it in the mirror before every concert. Like a man heading for the gallows, Billy slow-marched to the bathroom and stared at his raggedy reflection for the last time that whole decade. He had often wondered who lived behind all that fuzz. 'All the things I've lived through ... I wonder what I look like now ...'

He was too fearful to proceed until an encouraging notion occurred: 'Maybe ... maybe I'm actually handsome under there.'

Clinging to that hopeful scenario, he set to work with a Bic. In the meantime, I came home to three unsupervised hide-and-seekers.

'Where's Daddy?' I asked Amy.

'He's in the bathroom,' she informed me, 'scraping off his fur.'

Within fifteen minutes, Billy was confronted by a big Irish potato with a dimple on its chin ... he'd forgotten about that dimple. He was dreadfully disappointed. Covering his lower face, he crouched down and spoke to the smallies through his hands.

'Girls, listen now, I've taken my beard off,' he warned them. 'I look different.'

'But ... are you still Dada?' inquired Daisy.

A man came to take pictures for Monday's newspapers but, in the interim, Billy had the unnerving experience of spending the weekend completely anonymously. 'I know that voice!' people would say on the street. He flew to Glasgow, where not a soul knew him either. It was weird, walking unrecognized through his hometown. A policeman gave him a very old-fashioned look, then looked away. Eventually a picture appeared on the front page of Glasgow newspapers: 'Who's this? Answer ... page ten.' People had no idea.

Billy's new look gave him just the right 'hard man' appearance for *The Big Man*. In one street scene, filmed in the southern Scottish village of Coalburn, Billy was cycling down the street, trying to get used to the old upright bicycle he had been asked to ride. He was wearing a horrible tracksuit with incongruous brown lace-up shoes that looked ridiculous. Liam jogged in front of the bicycle while Billy coached him: 'One, two, one, two ...'

A local man was watching the rehearsal on the other side of the street. 'Hey, Big Yin,' he shouted in the characteristic southern dialect. 'You cannae go a bike wi' thae shin.'

Liam looked completely bewildered until Billy translated. 'You can't ride a bike wearing those shoes!'

In the middle of the shoot, Billy raced to the Albert Hall to perform with George Harrison, Eric Clapton, Ringo Starr, Michael Kamen and others in a concert in aid of a charity I launched called 'Parents For Safe Food'. It was the first time a live audience had seen him on stage without a beard.

'What do you mean, "Who the fuck are you?"' he harangued the audience when he first went on, his short-haired, clean-shaven look seeming incongruous with his multicoloured tie-dyed shirt and red shoes. 'It's ME! Isn't it fucking awful? All these years I looked like I'd swallowed a bear and left the tail hanging out ... THIS was underneath!'

≈

'Billy, don't you get it?' We are in a weird motel in Palm Springs in 1999. Billy has been invited to attend the Film Festival in that desert city, for the opening of his movie *Boondock Saints*.

'Get what?'

'This must be one of those "adult" hotels you hear about in Palm Springs ... that's why that seedy guy just tried to barge in. They have an open-door/clothing-optional policy, which means anyone's welcome for a bit of wife-swapping or "swinging"!'

Silence. 'Wife-swapping, eh? ... I could have swapped you for something useful.'

'Such as what?'

'I dunno ... a mobile home.'

≈

We moved house again. By the end of the eighties, Billy was in the best shape ever, both personally and professionally. He had made serious inroads into North America and we had left the overexposed riverside at Bray for a Victorian house in Winkfield, Berkshire, which gave us more privacy. No more jazz boats interrupting our

245

evening reverie: 'If you look to the starboard side, you'll see the home of none other than Billy Connolly – and, yes it's the man himself in his garden ... offering us a two-finger salute ...'

We renamed the new place 'Gruntfuttock Hall' after a Kenneth Williams character from *Round the Horne*. Almost everything was in place.

'Billy, I've been thinking ...'

'That was your first mistake.'

'I'm serious. I've been thinking it's high time ... I mean, we ought to ...'

'I know. You want us to get married.'

'How did you know?'

'Well, I guess getting me a ring was a big fucking hint.'

∼

When cornered by interviewers on the question of marriage, I had always said I thought we should wait until the children were old enough to enjoy the party. It was not easy to find a comfortable and private setting for our nuptials on 20 December 1989, but we chose a small Fijian island with just a few native cottages, or bures.

It was not a random choice. My maternal grandmother had been a Methodist missionary in Suva. When she lived with our family in Boronia Park, I loved to sit on her bedroom floor, waiting for the magical moment when she raised the lid of her enormous, carved sandalwood chest. Scents of the trade winds would fly out, along with polished conch shells, Fijian rattan fans, lace handkerchiefs and tortoise-shell combs. I had always longed to travel to my mother's birthplace, imagining the colours of Suva to be of the same curious palette as Nana's hand-tinted, Victorian Fijian postcards.

Our wedding invitations were silk sarongs mailed to just twenty people. We were married knee-deep in the turquoise sea by a Fijian minister as part of a traditional island three-day celebration that included spear-fishing by the bride and bridesmaids, Kava Kava ceremonies and a feast of baked sea snake. The children enjoyed some of it, sheltering from the tropical sun beneath leafy parasols made of giant banana fronds.

Palm trees and rainless months became more familiar to them a few months later when we set up temporary residence in California. In the past, Billy had made fun of the place: 'Any town that's got an all-night, drive-in taxidermist has got to be weird,' he would say. Now he's quite used to Los Angeles and enjoys his 'Decaff No-whip mocha' with the best of them.

I had been reluctant to uproot the children, but Billy was invited to be the replacement star of a popular comedy show on NBC network television, and this necessitated his agreeing to a four-year contract. He was to play the immigrant teacher of a group of gifted children in *Head of the Class*.

Initially, Billy was worried about doing something as mainstream as an American sitcom, but he believed it would introduce him to the American public at large and he was right. He was well received and maintained the role until the show came to the end of its natural life when the students grew too old to be believable as youngsters.

Billy's level of comfort in the unlikely situation of this somewhat clean-cut venture was largely due to the efforts of the show's producers, Michael Elias and Rich Eustis. They understood Billy's need for improvisation, so they gave him a weekly studio stand-up spot. Given their mandate to satisfy the corporate sensibility, however, it was hardly surprising that little of that unscripted material stayed in the show. Michael and Rich developed another television series for Billy about a man who marries an American citizen in order to obtain a Green Card. The show, which was titled simply *Billy*, was an uninspiring vehicle for him and not a great success, but it did last for an entire season.

Billy's venture into American TV allowed him to 'achieve

penetration' as managers say, with the American public; he immediately became far better known to them and this in turn influenced people in the film industry to seek him out for movie roles. Los Angeles is really a small industry town in many ways and the word got around that Billy was unique, hilarious, and a 'great guy to work with'.

Our move to California helped to crystallize my realization that I was bored with doing comedy myself, so I embarked on a PhD course in the field of Psychology with a plan to become a psychotherapist. My career switch was ostensibly supported by Billy, his deeper feelings about it emerging only on stage: 'My wife ... who's a very clever person ... considers me a work in progress,' Billy confided furiously to subsequent audiences. 'I was perfectly sane when all this started, but now I'm completely fucked up. I've got abandonment issues! If I say, "No I haven't!" she says, "See, you're in denial!" You just can't win.'

When my studies included the treatment of sexual disorders as a speciality area, Billy seemed more interested. 'I only wish she'd bring her work home!' he complained on every chat show in the world.

~

I called Mamie one day from Los Angeles and found that she had become gravely ill with motor neurone disease. Just a few months later, Florence and Billy attended her funeral in Dunoon. They sat together on the left of the church, while other family members sat on the right. 'I felt no sadness,' remembers Florence, 'only a calm sense of relief.' The two siblings were startled to see a wreath from their half-siblings, Willie Adams and Mamie's children, with a card on it that said 'Ma'. Florence and Billy looked at each other for a moment when 'You Are My Sunshine' was played in church, then stared ahead for the rest of the service. Afterwards, they were introduced to their unknown 'family'.

It had been different for Florence when their father had died. She had been devastated to lose him. In traditional Scottish culture, only men go to the graveyard, help lower the coffin and throw a little earth over it, while the women make sandwiches. Florence and I broke with tradition and went to the graveyard, but she didn't feel entitled to act on her desire to throw earth with the men, so I pushed her forward and she did perform that final ritual. When she watched her mother's body being lowered into the same grave as Willie Adams, Florence felt sad for her father, for she believed he had really loved her. 'She should have been with Father,' she thought.

~

Billy was on an extensive Canadian tour when the film director Adrian Lyne's telephone call reached him in Nova Scotia. 'I want you to play yourself as a charity auctioneer in my movie *Indecent Proposal*.'

'That's nice,' replied Billy, 'but I can't make it. I'm in the middle of a tour.'

'I need you here tomorrow,' insisted Adrian who immediately sent a Lear Jet to transport Billy three thousand miles to the set by 6 a.m. in time for the next day's shoot. Billy hadn't known that Lear Jets lack lavatories, so the pilot had to stop in Indianapolis for him to pee.

'Do you know Bob?' asked Adrian.

Billy shook hands with the star of the movie, Robert Redford.

'I was really glad when I heard it was you,' said the handsome man warmly.

When Billy performed his bit part as the auctioneer, he improvised to keep the audience interested through the many takes. One of the retakes occurred because Redford had failed to leave the scene as early as he should have. 'But it was so funny!' he protested. 'I didn't want to stop listening to Billy!'

Cara went to see the finished movie in a Glasgow cinema, unaware that her father was about to bounce across the screen. The moment he appeared, the entire cinema went: 'Whoooo!!!!'

We had become bi-continentals, living between Gruntfuttock Hall and the Los Angeles house we bought in the Hollywood Hills. The latter is a queer black-painted space that Billy describes as Anthony Perkins' *Psycho* farmhouse. We bought it from a couple of eccentric artists who had even painted the front-yard trees. The neighbourhood turned out to be an enclave of artists, musicians and film-industry people who, like us, had shunned the shiny, palm-decked palaces of Beverly Hills.

One of our new neighbours turned out to be the painter David Hockney, whom Billy adores. 'I've just painted the Grand Canyon.' David sometimes phones us with an invitation to visit him in his studio to view his latest masterpiece. 'The sky's still wet, but I'd like you to see it before it goes to the Pompidou.'

Billy was thrilled to discover that his big hero Frank Zappa lived nearby. He always wanted to knock on the musician's door but he never did. Apparently, Frank had been planning to go into politics. 'Can you imagine that?' Billy would say. 'Frank Zappa ... the President of the United States. In my dreams.'

After Frank died, Billy was walking the dogs past Frank's house when Mrs Zappa came out. 'Are you Billy Connolly?' she asked. 'Frank was your biggest fan.'

'Oh Jesus,' thought Billy, 'I could have been Vice President.'

~

On 4 October 1992, Melvyn Bragg interviewed Billy on the *South Bank Show*, in a special to commemorate Billy's twenty-fifth anniversary year as a performer. Melvyn is unique in always providing a serious platform to Billy's idiosyncratic raison d'être.

Billy certainly deserved to be celebrated, for with twenty-five incredible years of performing behind him, he was more successful than ever. The previous twelve months, for example, had been extraordinary. On top of his American successes, the video of Billy's three-week London Apollo concerts had sold more than half a million copies in the UK. He'd played the Dome Theatre in Brighton, the Apollo in Oxford and the Glasgow Royal Concert Hall.

'Glasgow's a weird town to play in for me,' Billy announced to his Glasgow audience. 'I get nervous here. It's like singing to your aunties.' When I saw him in Glasgow, he had an energy and comic fury that made me think he just might manage to be a prophet in his own land. Billy had been studying Scottish history in great depth. In Glasgow he presented his own unique version of his country's past lives. It was not the same stuff he'd been taught at St Gerard's: 'Bonny Prince Charlie was not the imposing guy you see on the shortbread tins,' he informed his Scottish audience. 'As a matter of fact, he was a gay Italian dwarf.'

Billy's twenty-fifth celebration was overshadowed by news of his Australian friend, Brett Whitely's, death. Brett had been in recovery from his heroin habit but had succumbed to a heart attack. Billy was inconsolable; Brett had been such a kindred spirit of his. Billy had loved Brett's lust for life and his inventive playfulness. This had been illustrated to the whole family when Brett once visited our holiday house in Palm Beach.

'Daisy!' he said, 'did you ever see a man disappear?'

'No,' she replied, whereupon he jumped right over the verandah and landed ten feet below, in the swimming pool.

Brett ate Japanese sushi every single day. He gave Billy a Japanese-style ceramic plate he had made with a little bluebird on it.

'I always thought of him as a bird,' Billy said to Wendy, Brett's widow.

'Yeah,' she said, 'and the little bugger flew away.'

'I love warm wind in the evening,' I remark, 'isn't it lovely?' We are drinking bottled water on our Hollywood deck, tracking the paths of patrolling news helicopters and circling barn owls.

'Warm wind in the evening ...' Billy repeats the phrase, searching for an angle. 'It's my latest medical condition.'

~

Billy's fiftieth birthday party, on 24 November 1992, was celebrated at his friend Phil Coulter's house in Donegal. Billy was on tour in Ireland at the time. My academic studies, as well as the children's schooling, prevented our travelling at that time, so Phil gathered a gang of cronies who, as he put it, 'would have all sung in the same smoky folk clubs and slept in the same sleeping bags above it'.

Ralph McTell, Irish folk singer Christy Moore, songwriter Seamus Healy and others dominated the storytelling while Billy, for once in his life, sat back and savoured each one ... until Phil threw them all out at 4 a.m.

It never bothered Billy to turn fifty, or so he says, but he did seem to be searching for new ways to appear adolescent. When he'd turned forty, he'd complained about his greying pubic hair. 'But it's not all bad,' he informed his audiences at the time. 'In a certain light my willie looks like Stewart Granger.'

Piercing both his ears had been a significant 'fuck you' statement earlier on, but ever since Billy saw a London male traffic warden displaying the exact same symbol of rebellion, the look had lost its appeal.

There is a piercing parlour on Ventura Boulevard run by one Cliff Cadaver. 'So why do you want to have your nipples pierced?' the man inquired on Father's Day, 1994.

'Oh, I've always regarded myself as an alternative,' replied Billy, 'but I feel I'm drifting towards the beige.'

The process of keeping his rebel flag flying turned out to be excruciatingly painful, although it was followed by an endorphin rush 'high' that lasted for weeks.

'You want me to do the other one too?' asked Cliff.

'I think that will do for now,' replied Billy. 'It was fucking agony.'

Cliff swabbed him with antiseptic, then stood back to admire his handiwork.

'Yep.' He looked pleased. 'That's one more of us ... and one less of them.'

Billy was delighted to be an 'us'. Exactly one year later, Cliff was invited to plunge his steel needle into Billy's remaining virgin nipple.

'What possessed you?' I asked when he came home wincing.

'I looked lopsided,' he explained.

As a psychologist, how could I not have been impressed by such grand-scale symbolic gestures of paternal rebellion as these twin-piercings, occurring each Father's Day for two years running? If you're wondering whether I'd ever voice such a thought to Billy, the answer is 'not on your life'. His immediate response would be: 'Quit the psycho-babble.'

Paternal rebellion was an underlying theme of *Down Among the Big Boys*, Billy's next television play, which had been churning around Peter McDougall's mind for years. When it finally materialized, Billy played a Glaswegian gangster called Jo Jo Donnelly, whose daughter planned to marry the son of a police superintendent.

The biggest change in Billy's acting occurred during the making of this film. We were sitting together in the kitchen one day, when Billy awkwardly asked me for acting advice. 'Pamsy, what's "method acting" all about?' He knew I had received formal training and wanted to know everything in a nutshell. I knew I was no Meryl Streep, but I gave him a ten-minute précis of method acting, which included simple tips like how to be quiet in the trailer and think about what had happened previously to his character. 'Right,' said Billy. 'I'll try that.'

In keeping with his extraordinarily laissez-faire style, Billy seemed to think there was nothing more to it ... but he did read some books on acting by the American 'method' master, Sanford Meisner. As soon as he thought he'd got the hang of the method, he was annoyed because acting wasn't as easy for him as before. It was the difference, he decided, between singing 'The Wild Rover' and strumming banjo bluegrass style in accompaniment to singing 'Foggy Mountain Breakdown': much more complicated, yet more joyous because it produced better results.

In *Down Among the Big Boys*, Jo Jo's catch-phrase throughout is: 'tickety-boo'. This became the name of Billy's new management company, after Steve Brown and Billy left John Reid Enterprises to set up on their own. They started a company that continues to be a most successful partnership, spawning a charitable enterprise as well. In October 1999, Billy and Steve launched 'Tickety-Boo Tea' with a party aboard a square-rigger called the *Grand Turk*. Profits of the tea go to charitable causes, particularly neglected and abandoned children worldwide. It's a far cry from bringing a penny 'for the black babies' every Monday at St Peter's. Billy proudly proffers photos of the Indian hostel for abandoned children that is funded by the proceeds.

Billy loves to take photographs himself. Not surprisingly, they are rarely ordinary records of people or places. Instead he focuses on the weird, the angular and the ridiculous aspects of life. In particular he loves to photograph amusing signs. When we first visited the United States together, he recorded 'Don't even THINK about parking here!' on Venice Boulevard. Outside a beach restaurant called Jesse's, he nearly dissolved when he read the sign, 'Parking For Jesse's Only.' In Glaswegian slang, of course, 'big Jessie' is used to describe an effeminate man, or one who is believed to have been coddled by his mother. 'That big fucking Jessie!' Billy will cry. 'He's never had a sore heid in his life!'

The antithesis of a Jessie, Billy's grandfather Big Neilly, died in

October 1998 at the age of ninety-six. Neilly had stubbornly refused adequate care in his old age, continuing to live alone until he was ninety. He had been taken into hospital in 1994 where they discovered he was so malnourished he actually had scurvy, one of the few reported cases since the seventies. Big Neilly had apparently never had any idea what Billy did for a living. Flora had sometimes remarked, 'Oh he's awful funny, isn't he?' but Neilly, who had little social contact because he didn't go to the pub, never mentioned his celebrated grandson. After Flora's death, Neilly relied on Hughie's wife Margaret to care for him.

'Before Flora died,' she says, 'when Grandpa was eighty-two, he was still dressing up and going into town once a week to visit private shop owners he'd known all his life. Flora was worried about this. She asked me one day, "Do you think he has a girlfriend on the side?" "No," I replied, "he's far too stingy."'

Margaret bought Billy's album *The Pick of Billy Connolly* for their son Neil for Christmas. It floored him. He had never met his famous cousin, a fact that had earned him ridicule and at least one beating at school. When Billy and the rock star Midge Ure visited a rival school during the Live Aid campaign, young Neil McLean was lucky to survive. 'If he's your fucking cousin, how come he never came to visit our school?'

Young Neil had known Mamie when he was growing up. She was fun to visit, for she often imparted adult family gossip he was not supposed to hear. 'Does your father know you smoke?' she would inquire slyly, offering him a cigarette. 'Then don't tell him.'

Billy's childhood visits to the Kelvingrove Art Gallery bore fruit when he was inspired to present *The Bigger Picture*, a six-part television series on Scottish art. The plan was to find Scottish art wherever it resided in the world, show it and tell its story. Since a great deal of Scottish art ended up in Rome during the Enlightenment, especially in the eighteenth century, Billy and his crew travelled to Italy, where they were given access to the entire art collection in the Vatican museum. He discovered that Bonny Prince Charlie was buried in the crypt in St Peter's and learned why Scottish art had flowered in Italy during the Prince's later years. 'Having your own king in town was a social plus,' Billy explained.

He loved the endless Vatican rooms jam-packed with 'heathen' art, and he especially admired one huge sarcophagus sculpted from marble the colour of plain chocolate with satyrs bursting out of its sides. Billy had imagined that his Catholic roots and education might have prepared him to feel comfortable in the Vatican, but its opulence was so over-the-top, it felt just as foreign as might a mosque. Billy felt sad about that. He preferred tiny French churches, plain and dark, with a meditative atmosphere. 'It's a shame about St Peter's,' he mourned his shattered illusion. 'It's the Harrods of religion.'

~

In keeping with Billy's love of rambling, he likes to take walks when he is on location or tour and staying in a hotel. In each location, he embarks on a route that will establish a pattern for all future walks in that place, for he seeks consistency. It will take him from, say, the coffee shop to the postcard shop, to the post office and back to the sanctuary of his room. In Vancouver in 2001, during the filming of a cameo role in *Prince Charming*, Billy had a week off, during which he took his regular walk. He first stopped at Starbucks and then at a newsagent, where he liked to purchase a particular journal with a very good crossword puzzle.

A homeless man always sat with his wine bottle outside Starbucks, so Billy gave him a little cash every day for three days in a row. On the fourth day, the man spoke to him with more than a little irritation in his voice. 'You don't need to give me money every time, you know.'

'I know that!' Billy snapped back.

They ignored each other on the fifth day but, on the sixth, the man again challenged him disdainfully. 'Don't you got any friends, man?'

'Yeah,' frowned Billy. 'I just like being alone.'

∾

In 1995, Billy spent a week on Ellesmere Island off the coast of Greenland for the BBC documentary *A Scot in the Arctic*. The plan was to create a television programme where viewers would be able to see, through Billy's own video diary and the interviews and observations of a daytime crew, how he survived on the freezing glacier.

The town of Gris Fjord is the furthest northern human habitation on earth, consisting of merely a village and a cooperatively run hotel with all the comforts of a grade-B youth hostel. When Billy arrived, it was almost spring. He spent a couple of nights in the hotel while local Inuit women made him some special clothing: a sealskin suit and elk socks. The latter were boots with the furry part on the inside, which were supposed to be worn with bare feet. Billy was apprehensive about doing so at first, thinking his feet would not be warm enough, but a short trial proved immediately that the Inuit footwear style was far warmer than five pairs of socks with regular boots.

A dog-sled team transported Billy and the crew for miles and miles through the frozen landscape until eventually they found a campsite close to some icebergs, where Billy set up a tiny one-tent camp. He was supposed to build an igloo but halfway through the task, he sat down on the top and demolished it.

An SAS soldier watched over him from miles afar, in case he was stalked by something huge and hairy. In fact, the threat of polar bears attacking him from the sea was a considerable one. Fortunately, the soldier, an outdoor terrain expert, helped Billy to brush up his rifle-shooting until he was competent again: he had become rusty since his days in the Territorial Army.

It was a glorious feeling, being left alone on the iceberg. He was completely isolated for twenty hours every day, until the film crew arrived in the morning to do some filming and check the self-operated camera that Billy used to create a video diary. Then the crew would disappear again at midday, leaving Billy to his own devices.

At first, Billy would be longing for them to return but, after a couple of days, his enforced solitude began to have a profound effect on him: he began to dislike the crew and resented their daily intrusion. He could hear them for miles, ploughing towards him on their snowmobiles, spoiling the lovely silence. After they left, the snow around Billy would be all messed up, its virgin whiteness all slushy like a city pavement, and littered with their cigarette butts. Billy became the protective housewife of his pure, white home, obsessively cleaning it and hoping they wouldn't turn up the next day to ruin it again. He learned there is no connection between being alone and lonely.

Arctic spring has no darkness at all, so Billy had to remember to sleep. At first he would wake up with a start in the sunlit night thinking a bear had come, because the iceberg was very noisy. Icebergs are freshwater giants floating on seawater and, as they are raised and lowered by the tide, they growl. 'It's like sharing a room with an old guy,' thought Billy. He would wake in a panic and grab his rifle but there was never anything threatening outside his tent. He gradually came to recognize the iceberg's language.

Although the temperature was thirty degrees below freezing, the locals complained to Billy about the heat. He loved the local Inuit people and was fascinated by their culture. He learned that Inuit names are not gender-specific. When a child is born, a name is not given until they recognize who from the past has been reincarnated. Once the traits of a particular ancestor are perceived, the child is named after that person, whoever it is. So a boy, for example, might be given his grandmother's name; as a term of endearment his own mother might call him 'mum' and he in return would call her 'daughter'.

The Inuit visited Billy every now and again to give him ice from the iceberg for his tea. They have a spiritual connection to the iceberg, so they first talked to it, to explain what Billy was up to, dwelling in its vicinity. They believe the spirits of their ancestors come to see them every year in the icebergs then disappear until the next spring. By the end of his time, Billy could see little groups of people inside the iceberg, groups of four and five huddled together, all with their hoods up talking. Billy would tease his daytime visitors. 'Gosh, your ancestors were a bit noisy last night.'

He watched the Aurora Borealis completely on his own, as if he were the only man in the world. It was such a privilege. Sometimes it was so quiet in that place, he could hear his own heart beating. 'I can even hear liquid stuff sloshing around inside me,' he marvelled.

～

'Where has Daddy gone?' asked Daisy, studying her picture book about parrots.

'To Mozambique,' I replied. 'To help some hungry people there and make a film.'

She looked at me curiously. 'He's helping some people in Nose and Beak?'

Billy's trip to Mozambique later that year was a mind-and-body-shocking contrast to his Arctic experience. I was opposed to Comic Relief's idea of sending him to the famine-stricken war zone. 'They're shooting down passenger planes over there,' I protested to the organizers. 'And if he survives that, I'm afraid he'll drink putrid water by mistake and end up with cholera or something.'

I lost the battle and Billy set off for Africa carrying a pint of his own rare blood (A Rh (D) Negative), a pack of sterile needles, water purifiers, malaria tablets and diarrhoea pills. He expected to experience a people hungry through famine, but there was plenty of food in the fields for anyone brave enough to try to harvest it. It was because members of the Renamo group were waiting to dismember field workers that the people were starving. Everything he learned and witnessed there was profoundly shocking to Billy. There was barely enough water. Village chiefs would invite him and the crew to their home for a bowl of mealie, the white porridge staple of Mozambique, while villagers stood watching them through the window. Billy thought it tasted awful so he mixed it with salad dressing to create 'mealie vinaigrette'.

He tried to create some comedy in that harsh place. He improvised silly walks to make the children laugh and invented a new way to groom his hair, sticking his head down low enough for hundreds of tiny brown fingers to run through his hair to the accompaniment of infectious giggling.

Comic Relief helped to reunite families who had been separated by the war and the most moving part of the TV programme is a moment when a father finds his lost son. Billy is seen to be deeply affected by the reunion, but unsure how to behave. He tentatively paws the man on the shoulder, but his own lack of family bonding prepared him badly for such a moment.

Billy went back a year later to report on developments in the area, and this time it was mercifully a more hopeful picture. Artificial limbs were being provided for those who needed them and the people could go into the fields with impunity. Schools had been built and the little boy who had no legs but managed to crawl a mile to his classroom touched Billy's heart. That second television special was given the title suggested by Daisy's confusion, *Return to Nose and Beak*.

Daisy had no conceptual difficulty when Billy's voice was featured in the Disney animated children's film *Pocahontas*. When he was asked to meet the director, Billy was mystified that animated film should even have a director. 'How do you direct Pinocchio or Donald Duck?' he wondered. 'They're not even there.'

Billy did a test playing Ben the sailor, first with a gruff cockney voice and then with a smooth one. 'Try it in your own accent,' suggested the director. It worked.

Early in the project, the animators gave Billy a tiny taste of the finished product: the opening scene of the film. Billy was still only a pencil drawing, leaning over the gunwale of a sailing ship, welcoming John Smith aboard. Billy nearly fell on the floor. 'There is nothing to equal the weirdness of seeing a drawing speaking in your own voice,' he says.

In the same vein, Billy also appeared as Billy Bones, the pirate in the new Muppet movie version of *Treasure Island*, and maintains the record of being the only man ever to die in a Muppet movie. Billy never had more fun on a film set, although he found one of the actresses rather difficult: Miss Piggy stayed in her dressing room and refused to grant him an audience on the grounds that 'he wasn't big enough'. He couldn't decide if she was just a bitch or a very private person; the wardrobe people told him they'd never even seen her naked, for she dressed behind a screen.

Difficult divas aside, Billy absolutely loved working with all the other characters, seeing the puppeteers working from underneath the floor. In between takes, he would look around the room. A massive reindeer head on the wall once winked at him unexpectedly, while a dog that lay sleeping on the landing and a group of chickens all nodded at him when he glanced their way. Billy's scenes were mainly with Gonzo and the little rat called Rizzo. He'd always loved Gonzo, ever since he'd seen him doing his own version of the song 'Macho Man' in a satin shirt and oversized medallion. It was always fun when things went wrong in the middle of a scene. One of the characters would suddenly say: 'The pupil just fell out of your eye!'

As a result of *Pocahontas* and *Muppets' Treasure Island*, Billy has become a firm favourite of six-year-olds all over the world. 'It's Billy Bones!' they cry in shopping malls and ice-cream parlours.

'Never wave,' their mothers fuss, 'at weird men with tattoos.'

~

Billy's 1994 Scottish tour provided the footage for his celebrated six-part *World Tour of Scotland*, which was broadcast in the summer then released on video. He hadn't intended to create such an interesting travel film – it just turned out that way. Billy had decided to play little Scottish towns for a change. In recent years, he had only played the major cities, but he missed the unique atmosphere in places like Dumfries, Orkney and Wick.

He began to present such a quintessentially personal flavour of Scotland that it became a whole series, a pot-pourri of his favourite haunts, landscapes, people and monuments of the north. Some of the inconveniences and realities of life there became the basis of the most engaging episodes. When the ferry to Arran was cancelled, Billy and his crew had to try another crossing at Gourock and they filmed the whole thing, including a piece to camera, sailing on the Clyde, in which Billy spoke of his affection for the river and its meaning in his life.

Old friends from Billy's early folk-scene days played music with him. George McGovern turned up ... and so did the usual evangelist demonstrators outside the hall in Ayr. In the Shetland Isles, the Garrison Theatre had been modernized. Billy thought this was a shame because, years ago, he would go to the hall keeper's house to get the key to the hall. 'We'd like to hire some ushers,' he used to say. 'Could you give us some names? How much should we pay them?'

'Och, they'll get in free and they'll be delighted,' was always the answer. Billy's sound technician, Malcolm, was always tickled by that kind of quaint behaviour. He had spent twelve years on the road with the rock band Status Quo and loved the contrast with the kickbacks and ticket-touting in the great stadia of the world.

In Dundee, the snow and poor visibility made panoramic filming impossible, so Billy took the opportunity to recite an entire epic poem: McGonagall's *The Tay Bridge Disaster*, in the middle of a furious blizzard. In Shetland, he had to cram in two shows per night to cope with the numbers, which amounted to five hours on stage every night.

Orkney is a magical Viking place with its own peculiar atmosphere that intrigues Billy. That's where he invented the bare-bum dance. He did it because he didn't know what to do with the standing stones. 'At the end of the day, they're just standing stones,' he complained. 'You can eulogize all you like about astronomy and pre-Christian religions, but no one knows what the fuck they are.'

Billy strongly recommends that the notice boards in historical sites such as that do a rethink. Instead of guessing the purpose of the stones, he would prefer something rather more frank: '*We have no idea what this is. Try and leave it the way you found it.*' His own solution to addressing the mystery of the ancient stones was to resist stating the obvious and simply dance around them naked, like an old Celt.

The *World Tour of Scotland* was a huge success. It was all the more appealing because Billy had not shown all the usual tourist sites, but had introduced his audience to the Scottish places he had liked over his many years of touring, from the treacherous seaside stairs near Wick to the haunted underground city of Edinburgh, and from the bleak tundra of snowy Sutherland to a graveyard in the middle of Glasgow.

When the show was broadcast, Billy wanted to go into hiding. 'Fuck, they're going to think I'm trying to be some kind of amateur Alan Whicker,' he moaned, but he was wrong. His deep and genuine love of the Scottish landscape, as well as the people, was perfectly apparent.

16

NIPPLE RINGS AND FART MACHINES

It is mid-afternoon in a California school, 2001. Earthquake reminders are posted on the board: 'Drop, Cover and Hold!' Scarlett's twelve-year-old classmates, an ethnically diverse bunch of denim-and-T-shirt wearers, are enthralled by her hairy father who has turned up to play the didgeridoo for their Humanities Class's Australian studies unit. The teacher sits at the back of the classroom with a bemused expression on her face.

'I saw people playing this when I was on Bathurst Island,' Billy informs them. 'I was making a film there, talking to an Aboriginal woman who gave me a big worm to eat.'

'Eeeuuggghhh!' the class moans.

'It wasn't a wriggly worm,' he continues, 'it lies quite still inside the mangrove tree until someone wants to eat it and hacks it out – tasted like an oyster. The funny thing was, when we'd finished filming the Aboriginal women all took off their clothes.'

'Oooohhh!' they all squeal. The teacher is thinking about intervening.

'They hate wearing clothes. As the crew were loading the camera into the boat, someone saw a shark just off the beach.'

'Aaaggghhh!' they yelp.

'What happened then perfectly illustrated the cultural differences between the Aboriginal people and us ... the Caucasians all ran out

264

of the water, while the Aborigines all ran in, shouting, "Where? Where? ... DINNER!!!"'

≈

During Billy's 1995 Australian tour, he made an enchanting television series, *Billy Connolly's World Tour of Australia*, where the viewing audience was treated to an experience of the Australian continent that essentially comprised all of Billy's favourite parts and more, from the wilderness of Kakadu to the hairy-nosed wombat.

He travelled around the countryside on a beautiful Harley Davidson trike, a purple three-wheeler he rode in the 'bad-boy' reclining position. 'It's not a "peep-peep-excuse-me" bike but more a "go-fuck-yourself" one,' he said. 'I zoom past people in beige Nissans and they tell their children off for staring. "Don't look at him, Dorothy! Next thing you know, you'll be pregnant. Pregnant and taking drugs. He's a madman! I saw him on the telly. His tits are pierced ... he's probably got a big tattoo on his willie."'

Billy loves most things about Australia, but is particularly engaged by its dangerous and challenging aspects. 'I heard about a saltwater crocodile that attacks and eats sharks and can run on land at thirty-five miles per hour,' he enthused over the phone. 'Fuck! That would be like being chased by a hungry train!'

He sorely missed Brett. There were posters all over Sydney for his retrospective exhibition, cloth banners hung from every lamppost; Brett was around everywhere except in the flesh. Billy wondered where his sculpture of the big matchsticks had gone, the one that used to stand in the grounds of the Gallery of New South Wales. It turned out it was still there, no longer viewable from the road to Woolloomooloo because it was now hidden by the new motorway they built for the Olympics. Billy loved those matchsticks and still wears a tiny replica brooch on his lapel. They represent something in himself that was part of his deep connection to Brett: two sticks side by side, a healthy one and a burnt-out one. Billy never discussed it with Brett, but he always thought of them as two sides of the same person.

Billy is always interested in playing characters that have those two opposing sides to them: both light and darkness. Deacon Brodie was one of those. In March 1996, Billy starred in the BBC costume drama *The Life and Crimes of Deacon Brodie*, about the eighteenth-century councillor who was hanged on the gallows of his own making for robbing banks to fund his womanizing.

The deeply anarchic sensibility of this historical figure, as well as Brodie's loathing of middle-class Edinburgh society in his time, also appealed to Billy. His curiosity about death and dying were engaged during the shoot, for he had to simulate being hanged and fall through the trap door from some gallows. It felt very odd, being on the edge of danger and safety. 'I did it with my eyes closed but wish I had done it with them open,' he confessed enigmatically to the director, Phillip Saville.

In May that same year, Billy was honoured by the BBC by being allowed to schedule an evening of all his favourite programmes. It was an eclectic collection, from videotaped performances by the Incredible String Band to Stanley Baxter's funniest flourishes. *Billy Connolly's World Tour of Australia* was shown in October on BBC1, attracting over nine million viewers.

Satisfying though that was, Billy was still pining to get back to acting. He took a call from Douglas Rae. 'If it's with Judi Dench, I'd be very interested in doing the movie, but if not, I don't know.' That was Billy's reply to Douglas's invitation to play John Brown in a project in which his relationship with Queen Victoria was to be explored in a dramatic format.

'If it's Billy Connolly, then I'm interested.' Dame Judi's reply echoed Billy's.

'Do me a favour, though,' added Billy to Douglas, 'tell Judi she wasn't the first choice for the movie ... and if she squeezes it out of you, tell her the first choice was Bob Hoskins.'

The first time Billy had met Bob, Bob had been playing Queen Victoria in a Ken Campbell show in Edinburgh. He had apparently nipped into a public toilet dressed as the queen and had whacked somebody who passed a disparaging remark. Billy thought Bob was the living image of her. 'You put a hanky on his head and he *is* Queen Victoria,' he claims.

Mrs Brown was the best and fastest film shoot Billy's ever done: only twenty-eight days long. It was a brilliant cast all around, but with him and Judi, it was love at first sight. He thought she was a riot. She liked to gamble with him, betting on everything from what time they'd stop for the day to what time dinner and lunch would be – and she never lost. Billy would have to pay up on demand so in return she'd buy him cigars and fishing flies. Her husband, the late Michael Williams, wanted reports from the set of things Billy had said and done every night. 'He's humorous and delightful,' she would say. 'It's like someone picking at a fish. He starts with one subject and picks away at it until just the bones are left.'

Billy had had to temporarily remove his nipple rings for a scene in *The Life and Crimes of Deacon Brodie*; however, with some difficulty, he squeezed them back in. By the time Billy filmed *Mrs Brown*, he had moved up to thicker rings, having increased their width every year for the past five years. When he did the naked swimming scene in *Mrs Brown*, Billy had to take them out before plunging into the November water of the English Channel. When he came out, he couldn't get them back in. 'I think my nipple-ring days are over,' he decided and got a banjo tattooed on his hand instead.

When *Mrs Brown* was released in cinemas in 1997, Billy was genuinely surprised to be welcomed into the ranks of admirable contemporary, serious actors. 'Talent is talent,' says Billy's acting hero, Dustin Hoffman. 'I saw *Mrs Brown* and I thought that his performance was the most exciting male performance I'd seen that year and I called him and told him. It was just a very real, depthful, subtle piece of work.'

'He must have been pissed when he said that,' returns Billy.

Billy's next couple of film roles hardly followed suit. Stanley Tucci cast him as a gay, Scottish tennis player called Sparks in his 1920s-style movie, *The Imposters*. It was a broad type of comedy role in which Billy had to act falling in love with a fellow train passenger, played by Oliver Platt.

The slapstick behaviour in that film was not confined to the screen. Allison Janney turned up one day with a fart machine made from a tumbler with special putty inside; when she rammed her fingers in, it made a most realistic noise of breaking wind. Everyone rushed to procure more of these and there were many more on set the following day. It was absolute mayhem, with Steve Buscemi doing the splits in mid-air to a loud farting noise.

Stanley Tucci encouraged improvised inventiveness so, during one of the scenes, Billy sneaked in a favourite greeting he'd received from a passing drag act when he had appeared with his banjo and earrings on the breakfast show *Good Morning Massachusetts* in the early seventies. In a lovers' tiff between the two gay characters in *The Imposters*, Oliver had to slap Billy in the face. 'Savage gypsy lover!' Billy returned, to off-camera howls, followed by: 'Don't you like the taut roundness that exercise brings to the buttocks?'

Billy was most reluctant to audition for his next role. 'I'm telling you, I don't want to go to the interview.' Billy's emphatic tone, on a long-distance call to his long-suffering manager Steve Brown, echoes throughout the house.

'What's the story?' I ask when it's all over and Billy is sulkily smoking a cigar outside on the deck.

'I don't fucking want to read for the part of a dog. Can you imagine if they turned me down? I'd never survive being rejected as the voice of some wee mongrel. I'd rather be burgled!'

To Steve's great relief, it didn't come to that; in fact Billy rather enjoyed the project. The Australian film *Paws* was released later that year, and had Billy playing the charismatic voice of a dog called PC, whose owner wires him to a computer so he has a voice – a Scottish one of course. Lip-synching an animal with no lips proved to be quite a challenge, especially when Billy was required to say words containing the letters 'f' and 'p'. He had to improvise all the way and he became very interested in the technical aspects of that type of work, inventing ingenious ways to simulate doggy breathing and swallowing. At least Billy wasn't asked to be a cat: 'I've never trusted cats,' he says. 'They're a sneaky bunch. Any animal that stays when you move house is a little bastard.'

Danny Kyle died in 1996 at the age of fifty-nine, and his passing rocked Billy to the core. The two had been so close for so long, it was terribly hard to say goodbye. Danny had always supported Billy, been so proud of him. With his fat, cheeky face framed with a short monk's fringe and ponytail, his shabby ensemble straining over a pudding-like rotundity, he had been ever the perfect Sancho Panza to Billy's errant, Quixotic anti-Knight. 'The fact that you loved him,' Ralph tried to console him, 'always made Danny a few inches taller.'

∼

Even the children have become quiet, touched by the grandeur of purple-clad granite against teal skies and the surprise of a stag or two leaping off the tarmac into rock-bound safety. Travelling around the north-east of Scotland in a camper van has not been an ideal 1996 summer-holiday choice for our family of young children, but Billy is determined to show us everything. 'See, Pamsy,' he says proudly, 'isn't it just the most amazing, awesome place?'

I wholeheartedly agree. It is not the land of my childhood, but is breathtaking all the same. We turn a corner, chancing upon a shepherd ahead of us on the road with a large flock of sheep. Billy hits the brakes and we crawl at the sheep's pace while the man tries to herd his animals off into the field.

'Such a peaceful way of life,' continues Billy. 'Now, that man, for instance, he's living out here, miles from anywhere ... got no need for television, newspapers, modern living. He wouldn't have a clue who I am or what the hell's going on in show business, lucky bugger, and he wouldn't care less ...' The shepherd finishes his task and stands watching us on the driver's side of the road as we pass.

Billy winds down the window. 'Thanks, man,' he nods.

'You're welcome, Mr Connolly.'

∾

Since an Aberdeen holiday in Torry with his school, Billy has had a special place in his heart for the north-east of Scotland. During his 1988 tour of Scotland, Billy wrote in his diary:

13 October
All in all a good gig and a jolly good time in Aberdeen. God bless the North East!

Billy is constantly drawn back to Scotland. It's as though he would fade into depression without a regular 'fix' of his fishing and folk pals from all over the country, 'the fierce crack' of Glasgow folk, as well as the reassurance of hearing his own accent reflected back to him. For years, Billy and I had toyed with the idea of owning a place in the Scottish countryside where he could fish and walk and ruminate by himself. We bought our Highland home, Candacraig, partly because we loved its location in Aberdeenshire and partly because Billy fancied being able to rise from his bed and go fishing in his slippers. Over the years Billy has come to dislike going on holiday to hotels and all that entails, because that's like going to work without the concert in the evening. 'It's a bit like paying for the aspect of my work that's as much fun as being burned,' he explains.

So, for many years, we often talked about having our holidays in some place where we could invite friends we don't see too often. In 1997, we bought a wonderfully peaceful property that provides necessary rest and quietness for us all ... as well as a little partying now and again. Billy has even taken to wearing a kilt at home, both because it seems right to do so in that setting and because I bully him into it. We whirl around dancing the 'Gay Gordons' and 'Dashing White Sergeant', him in his kilt, hose and velvet jacket and me in a dress and plaid.

'You're becoming more Scottish by the minute!' he shakes his head at me as I gaily 'Strip the Willow', and I have to say that he's right. I absolutely love it all: the people, the countryside and the extraordinary culture. Some of the nicest times we've ever had have been at Candacraig.

One Saturday during one of our summer stays in the Highlands, Billy had a hankering to drive to Glasgow to play the banjo in a pub with some of his friends, so he carefully devised a lovely day for himself. He knew that a football match between Rangers and Kilmarnock would be broadcast on the radio, so he planned to leave Candacraig early, drive to Aberdeen to buy coffee and a good cigar, then head for the motorway. By the time he reached the motorway, with his take-away coffee in its little holder and his cigar lit, he should be cruising nicely south and could hear the entire game on the radio. 'Bliss!' thought he.

Once in Aberdeen, Billy parked his car across the street from the cigar shop on a double-yellow line next to a bank treasury truck. As soon as he parked, he was besieged by Aberdeen supporters en route to the local game. Billy dutifully sat in his car and signed autographs, some on bank notes, which were passed to him for signing. As he passed them back, he thought, as he always does when people ask him to sign money: 'I wonder what these people are going to do with them? Frame them, I suppose.' People were passing five-, ten-

and twenty-pound notes through his window and he was signing them and passing them back: eventually, the crowd dispersed, so Billy was able to nip across the road to purchase his cigar.

Billy returned to his car, relieved he hadn't been booked for waiting on a double-yellow line. He signed a few more autographs, then headed south for the motorway. He hadn't even reached the outskirts of Aberdeen when there was the wailing and flashing of a police vehicle behind him and he was requested through a loud-hailer to pull into the next side street. 'Fuck,' thought Billy. 'That's the last time I stop on a double-yellow. I'm going to miss the match.'

He stopped his car and got out, whereupon he was met by a policeman who took hold of the cuff of his jacket and led him to the police car. Billy was quite taken aback. 'What's this?' he asked. 'I wasn't speeding ... and I don't drink any more ...'

'It's all right, Mr Connolly. If you'll just get into the back of the car, everything will be explained.'

Billy was completely mystified. The officer sat him in the back seat, with police officers beside him, and got on the radio to headquarters. He proceeded to speak to a voice at the other end. 'Well, Sir, we found the driver of the red Range Rover ... yes we apprehended him ... and, believe it or not, it's Billy Connolly.'

There was a sharp intake of breath at the other end of the radio and then a pause. Then the voice said quietly: '*The* Billy Connolly?'

'Aye, the comedian.'

'Put him on ... Mr Connolly, were you parked in Market Street today?'

'I don't know. I was parked next to a toy shop in town on a double-yellow next to a security van opposite the cigar store.'

'Yes, that's Market Street.'

'Then I was parked there.'

Billy was puzzled. He thought they'd gone to incredible lengths to apprehend a man who'd parked on a double-yellow, unless someone had robbed the security van in the meantime.

'What were you doing there?'

'Buying a cigar.'

'We were watching you on CCTV while you were speaking to a crowd of people.'

'Oh yes – I was signing autographs. Mostly for Aberdeen supporters on their way to the game.'

There was a silence for a minute or so. Then: 'On what were you signing these autographs?'

'Money mostly, fives, tens, twenties ... and some little bits of paper, but mostly money.'

He could hear laughing on the other end. The policeman in the car was nodding sagely.

'What exactly is going on?' Billy was getting fed up.

'Mr Connolly, we were watching your car,' explained the voice, 'and we saw a great deal of money changing hands. We couldn't see the driver, but we were concerned because two of the people were the most notorious drug dealers in Aberdeen.'

'I can assure you I'm clean,' protested Billy, 'and have been for a long, long time. You can search my car if you like.' They declined to do so.

'I would appreciate it if you wouldn't tell anyone about this,' the voice appealed to Billy as he left the car.

'Are you kidding?' Billy snorted. 'I'm a comedian for God's sake, this is manna from heaven.'

Billy's brush with the law extended to his creative life that same year, when he played two outlaws of a very different nature. He firstly played the hard man Dryden in *The Debt Collector*, directed by Anthony Neilson in 1998, a role which elicited praise from his hero, Sean Connery. 'He's a terrific actor,' says Sean. 'He did a very good job in that movie.' 'That's better than what he usually says,' remarked Billy, imitating his friend's vocal style: 'Billy, my boy, you're a shite for shore eyes!'

The Debt Collector was followed by his portrayal of an intensely violent assassin in *The Boondock Saints*, which was filmed in Canada. For Billy it was a dream come true to wear six nine-millimetre guns inside his vest in the latter film. He'd always fantasized about being in that kind of movie.

It's scary to imagine what my husband might have done with all that furious energy if he hadn't become a comedian, but he's not alone. Hardly a week goes by when he doesn't meet some fellow latent homicidal maniac who raves about the movie. 'You're in *Boondock Saints?*' they approach him in American shopping malls. 'That's my favourite ... I've seen it nine times!'

～

At the BAFTA ceremony in 1999, Billy was asked to present Sean Connery with the Life Achievement Award. Unable to be physically present due to his filming commitments, Billy filmed a piece in Los Angeles that was shown on a giant screen on the awards night. Sean and his wife, Micheline, watched the screen with anticipatory grins across their faces.

'You've done awfully well for a man with a speech defect, don't you think?' Billy inquired to howls from the live audience. He then announced that he had not one, but two speeches, a long one and a short. The longer, praise-filled piece followed a one-sentence first one: 'Congratulations, Baldy. I wish I had your money!'

Two years earlier, Billy had hosted the BAFTA tribute to Dustin Hoffman in Los Angeles. Throughout the show, Billy referred to him as 'Daniel Hoffnong' and to Jon as 'Bobby' Voight, while Dustin's wife, Lisa, was 'the lovely Maureen'. Billy never let up the entire evening. At one point he looked down and thought Dustin had left. The actor had actually laughed so hard he'd slipped way down in his chair. The next day, a lovely orchid arrived at the house with a note: 'from Daniel and Maureen'.

'He destroyed the formality of the evening,' observed Dustin.

'Some people were extraordinarily offended, which made him realize he was on the right track.'

Dustin returned the favour by appearing in the BBC's 1998 *Erect for 30 years* – a celebration of Billy's career spanning three decades. The programme also included interviews with Robin Williams, Dame Judi Dench and Whoopi Goldberg. What Billy's heroes say about Billy publicly, matches what they say about him in private.

'It has been through hanging out with him that his genius has been slowly revealed to me,' says comedian Steve Martin about Billy. 'And also his kindness – I didn't expect that. He's not meanly competitive about anyone else in the field. That is so unusual.'

'The way he allows you into his brain ...' says Eric Idle, 'whether he's musing over dinner or on stage ... it's just the same, give or take a couple of thousand other people being there.'

'He's human marijuana,' says the anarchic American comic Bobcat Goldthwait. 'If they put him in the water we'd all be a lot happier.'

When I took my teenage Australian nieces, Sally and Holly, to the Hollywood premiere of *Still Crazy*, I didn't know they would witness their uncle as a volatile seventies rock-band roadie, clowning around with a couple of penises on his head like horns and having oral sex with a groupie.

'Uncle Billy was beaut in that,' they said afterwards, quite thrilled by the whole outrageousness of the occasion.

'Don't tell your mother about it,' I replied.

Every bit as outrageous was the 1999 Barry Levinson movie *An Everlasting Piece*, about two barbers attempting to bring toupées to Northern Ireland in the eighties. Billy turned in a cameo as the crazy 'Scalper', a hairpiece manufacturer in Belfast who had taken to scalping people for their hair. Barry used to be an improvisation comedian and gave Billy a very free hand to be inventive, which Billy always regards as a real luxury.

'Where are you off to now?' asked Barry at the end of the shoot.

'I'm doing five weeks at the London Apollo,' replied Billy. 'My manager regards my movie career as an expensive hobby.'

In recent years, Billy's live work has taken on new dimensions. 'It's really become performance art,' remarks Ralph McTell. 'He thinks of his audiences as malleable and he pulls them magnetically, knits them together, touches them in a vulnerable spot. It's incredible what he does now ... and he still has that deep anger: his edge hasn't diminished one bit.'

Billy's live performing has been liberated by the radio microphone. He resisted it at first, clinging to his old stand and hand-held mike, but now he can move more freely over the whole stage, and use both hands. He strides back and forth, crossing the audience from side to side, almost forcibly yanking people into the world he's exploring and drawing them together as he explores the depth and width of the space as well. 'Yeah,' he'll say after the show, 'I was pushing them tonight.'

For Billy, there is a price to pay for knowing he's excelled himself on a particular night. 'I heard that Tony Hancock became inconsolable just after he had done his brilliant "blood donor" sketch,' he told me once. 'He was in his dressing room with his head in his hands moaning "How am I going to follow that?" I completely understand that. When I do really well, I go to bed and say, "Oh God, I've got to do it again tomorrow night!"'

Apparently, Hancock used alcohol to reduce his post-performance excess adrenaline. Fortunately, Billy has developed a capacity for non-destructive self-soothing over the years. As Ralph puts it, 'We all need something more than a Polo mint and a cup of tea.' Billy's method involves taking people hostage in his dressing room after the show and carrying on for an extra couple of hours, while they clutch their stomachs and check their watches at the same time.

When Billy tells a story on stage, we may be roaring, but we unconsciously sense his underlying rage and it speaks to our core. It connects with our own existential fury, for all of us have, at some level, a fundamental need to gain mastery over something: our powerlessness, our frailty, our vulnerability. Billy is the living embodiment of the truism that states that aggression is a vital feature of all great art. As Robert Stoller so aptly put it, 'Kitsch is the corpse that's left when art has lost its anger.'

~

'So, Billy, who are your ultimate fantasy women of all time?'

'Wouldn't you like to know!'

'Absolutely, I would ... and I promise I won't hold it against you.'

'Well, when I was a boy, I liked Betty Grable and Veronica Lake with the peekaboo hair ... after them I liked Sophia Loren ... and then I had a lot of disappointments – I was crazy about Dusty Springfield but she turned out to be a lesbian. Now I think Sandra Bullock is sexy ... and Paul Newman's wife, Joanne Woodward. That wee Australian soap opera star that looks like you, Kimberly something ... and Sharon Stone of course, but I've already been to bed with her ...'

~

Billy must have been in Ms Stone's bad books when they filmed their bedroom scene in *Beautiful Joe*. Being a very huge diva indeed, she had enough clout with the director to redirect the scene so that the entire crew saw her naked upper-half while Billy faced the other way and saw nothing. Not that he's a voyeur or anything but, like any other red-blooded heterosexual man he was looking forward to a sexy little clandestine moment. He could already picture his fellow transatlantic, male airline passengers glancing at him approvingly when the scene flashed across their in-seat personal video screens.

Billy played a character who, discovering he only has a few months to live, embarks on a soul-searching journey where he meets Hush, a white-trash character played by Stone. Billy still doesn't know where everything went wrong. He lost count of the troubles that afflicted the project before it bypassed cinema release altogether and went straight to the well-shuffled shelves of Blockbuster Video Stores.

He returned to Candacraig that summer a broken man, but was soon cheered up by the arrival of a number of jolly pals to stay with us for an annual event called 'The Lonach'. Two hundred kilted men carrying pikes march up our drive accompanied by a pipe band, a centuries-old ritual. Billy makes a speech, everyone has a wee dram and then it's off to the Highland Games in Bellabeg where he presents the cup for best bagpiper.

In Billy's construction of the universe, everyone gets his due rewards except him. 'I wanna prize too!' He is apt to wail that ad nauseam on any given day of his life. Being nominated for a Golden Globe award, for *Mrs Brown*, receiving several BAFTA awards and umpteen other gongs have never been enough. The 'People's Award for Outstanding Contribution to the Arts' in 2000 was a nice tribute too, but Billy has a real bee in his bonnet about Oscars, Grammys and, probably, Best in Show. In truth, he's probably due the honour for 'Most Macabre Filming Experience':

'What's it like filming in a real mortuary?' I called Billy in Toronto when the summer was over. He'd already completed filming *Gentleman's Relish*, in which he swanned around as an Edwardian artist, and was now playing a contemporary coroner who sold dead people's identities to baddies, played by Richard Dreyfuss and Christian Slater, in the movie *Cletis Tout*.

'The worst thing is the smell,' he replied. 'Corpses have a very peculiar stench and sometimes you have difficulty with your lunch.'

'You don't eat in there, do you?'

'No, but it's weird. Dead people keep coming in and being stashed away before our very eyes!'

'Ugh.'

'But it's like being at a funeral ... it gives you a great lust for life when you look at someone who was alive a few hours ago. Especially the suicide, who should still be alive – I mean, the guy had a choice ...'

Perhaps all would-be suicides ought to visit a mortuary before they make the final decision. It certainly was a serendipitous opportunity for Billy to satisfy his own death-curiosity. His lifelong flirtation with the romantic aspect of self-expiration seems to have been quelled once and for all by that graphically real, cold confrontation there in the mortuary. It was as if he had at last fully grasped the finality aspect of dying.

After a day's filming, he wandered the streets of Toronto, searching for some light relief. In a craft shop he found a little tartan beanie hat that was a bit like the Jewish skullcap, a yarmulke, so he bought it for Richard Dreyfuss. The star immediately donned it and insisted on being called 'Hamish' from that moment on.

Richard was not the only one to assume an alter ego that month. 'I've gone prematurely blond,' announced Billy, returning home after his hairdresser had dyed his locks for his role of the Archangel Gabriel in *Gabriel and Me*. 'Blonde hair is a delight when it's on a blonde woman ... and so scary when it's on top of a face like mine,' he added, peering at his reflection in the hall mirror. 'As my father used to tell me in the sixties, I look like a tramp staring out of a hayloft.'

Before Billy's portrayal in *Gabriel and Me*, not many people in the world knew that the Archangel Gabriel was a gold-toenailed Glaswegian with a penchant for Issey Miyake clothing. Nor are people yet generally aware that God colludes with insurance companies, the premise of Billy's first film of the year 2001, *The Man Who Sued God*, co-starring Judy Davis, who plays Billy's romantic partner.

For a man who thinks he's not particularly appealing to women, Billy has been paired with some of the world's most beautiful and famous actresses. 'Not bad, eh Pamsy?' He looked so pleased with himself after his first day on the film *White Oleander*. 'I met Michelle Pfeiffer today ... *and* Renée Zellweger, who gave me a wee cuddle. Lovely women! It's a shame I get bumped off by Michelle on page twenty-six.'

As I observe him settling down to study his script for the next day's shoot, I notice my own feelings, a mixture of envy, admiration and incredulity. The process of writing about him has connected me more than ever before to the unlikelihood of his extraordinary life story. Billy's old fear remained when a friend once said: 'Look at you ... You're a welder who got away with it!' He even repeats it on occasion, as though the truth of his life could be encapsulated that simply ... for there's a part of Billy that believes he's still just scraping through, by the hair on his chinny-chin-chin.

The friend, however, missed the point completely. A highly combustible mixture has been bubbling away inside Billy his whole life. A huge dose of abandonment pain, a dollop of existential fury, a giant scoop of performing talent plus a massive portion of hell-bent-on-vengefulness has whirled around inside him since infancy, catapulting him from tenement to 'tinsel town' in five extraordinary decades. It is the kind of volatile compound that could have exploded at any time, and it is the containment and alchemy of those elements that constitutes his most admirable work.

~

It is a proud moment for a father: at a post-graduation party on the lawn of Glasgow University, Cara wafts around in a mortarboard while her sisters and I pore admiringly over her certificate of achievement.

'I believe we have a friend in common ...' A man interrupts Billy as he is trying to eat a strawberry tart.

'... My aunt taught you at St Peter's School ...'

'Really?' Billy turns to him, face full of crumbs. 'Who?'

'Rosie McDonald.' The man is beaming nostalgically. 'I believe you kids called her "Big Rosie".'

Billy turns ashen. I am wishing the man would take his smiling family and disappear before the inevitable explosion.

'Oh yeah?' Billy goes all quiet and dangerous. 'She was a sadist.'

'Aye, aye,' titters the man, 'she was a bit eccentric ...'

'No, no, see – that just doesn't cover it.' Billy puts down his plate. I freeze. 'She was sadistic and cruel ... as a matter of fact, she was a fucking bitch!'

He has raised his voice to a pitch that causes people around us to abandon their china cups and take notice. Billy doesn't care; his fury escalates: 'Did you know she called kids who wore glasses "four-eyes"? Did you?!!! Is that "eccentric", do you think, or FUCKING PSYCHOPATHIC?!!!'

The man smirks in embarrassment and shuffles away, stuttering over his shoulder: 'Well anyway ... she died in 'ninety-one ...'

Billy stares after the man and takes a long, deep breath.

~

With all his childhood abusers now dead and gone, he is thankfully a somewhat calmer man. *The Lake Isle of Innisfree* continues to elude him but, some clear summer evenings, he can be spotted fishing happily alone in the twilight; hearing loch waters lapping with low sounds by the shore.

EPILOGUE

LIFE, DEATH AND THE TEACUP THEORY

LIFE

Today, Billy's stated life's ambitions include the following:

To be a tramp.

To be on Eric Clapton's fridge door.

To wake up one morning and discover he's become Keith Richard.

To grow old without ever growing up.

To learn to sail a boat.

To change his mind as often as he fucking well pleases.

Billy's main ambition in life was always to be a tramp. When he was a boy, he had a book about a tramp, with an illustration of a pleasant-looking man with a beard and a big coat, with rope holding up his trousers.

Once upon a time there was a jolly tramp. He was a tall man with a bushy beard. The tramp had been walking all day, so he was hungry. He saw a pretty little cottage with a white fence and a rose garden. He trudged up the garden path and knocked at the green door.

'Anyone home?' he called.

A woman popped her head out of the kitchen window.

'Can I help you?' she asked.

BILLY

'I'm hungry,' said the tramp. 'Please may I have something to eat?'

The kind woman came out and gave him a jam sandwich. The tramp thanked her and went merrily on his way.

Billy thought that would be a great life, in fact he was sick with envy. His aunts used to give him marmalade sandwiches and he couldn't bear marmalade. He discerned from the coloured illustration that the tramp got the red stuff, the delicious raspberry jam. It was obvious what Billy had to do. 'It's a tramp's life for me,' he decided then and there.

As Billy grew older, probably from about his tenth year when he discovered Hank Williams, he began to aspire to being a more exotic version of the tramp. 'The Rambling Man', as he now appeared in Billy's fantasy, was a confident drifter in jeans and cowboy boots with a leather bag slung over his shoulder. The ideal rambler had long hair, played a string instrument and was very attractive to women who always gave him quite a bit more than a jam sandwich.

Billy has certainly achieved something of that style, but to his chagrin he has essentially been thwarted in his hobo ambition by monumental success. 'In my dreams,' mourns Billy, 'I'm a happy, rambling, hobo man playing the banjo ... In reality, I'm a successful man trying to find a room in any one of my houses to ramble in because I make such a din on the banjo.'

A rambling man would never own a tuxedo but, in 1988, Billy was attired in one of his many evening outfits when he spoke at a dinner to celebrate Eric Clapton's twenty-fifth year in rock 'n' roll. He followed Bobby Ball, of the comedy duo Cannon and Ball, who announced he had just bought a new, boxed set of Eric's early recordings. 'Some of us don't need to buy it,' Billy scoffed. 'We've already got all that stuff.'

Billy was seething with envy because he'd seen a signed photo of Bobby Ball on Eric's fridge door. Eric had a great fridge door. There was a picture of Bob Marley on which Marley had written '*I shot the*

EPILOGUE

Sheriff', with the 'I' underlined. Both men had recorded the song, but Marley was the one who had actually written it.

Rock 'n' roll is clearly still a major driving force in Billy's life. Keith Richard turned up backstage to see Billy after his show at The Bottom Line in New York in the seventies. 'Champagne, Keith?' someone offered. 'I never mix the grape and the grain,' replied the man.

Billy thinks he has been carved in granite: a talking sculpture. To wake up one morning and discover he'd become Keith Richard would guarantee our divorce but Billy would apparently abandon all in favour of metamorphosing into the coolest rocker on earth, or, at the very least, to be the lead guitarist in a world-famous rock band.

This wish seems to be consistent with Billy's fourth ambition: to grow old without ever growing up. I think we can all safely assume Billy will never be a card-carrying 'grown-up'. He resists the process with all his might, believing that most of the social wars are between the people who've grown up and the people who haven't. 'The people who've grown up think it's natural to do so, but it isn't,' he explains. 'Rock 'n' roll starts to hurt your ears, bright colours hurt your eyes and you start talking about common sense as if there was such a fucking thing ... It's the "beige-ing down"'.

Heaven forbid any one of us should gravitate towards the beige. Far better to don our Docksiders and shorts and set sail with the tide. Billy's plan to control a life-sized version of his father's first gift to him is a lofty plan for a man who turns green and vomits the second he sets foot on any sea-going vessel. Seasickness aside, he'd love to sail round the world single-handed: a mariner version of his hobo fantasy. Could he trim a sail and play the banjo at the same time, I wonder? Perhaps he'll change his mind about that one, for, as he says, he loves to turn his back on any previous idea. 'I do love changing my mind,' he insists. 'It's been held against me, but I haven't stopped doing it. If someone else's theory seems more true, I change.'

That's why I worry when he listens to American talk-radio. If he doesn't watch out, we could soon see a switch of allegiance few of us could stomach: a blazer-wearing William Connolly, founder of 'Beige Apparel Inc.', a company that manufactures neutral-coloured leisure wear for the discerning older gent. He'll have a set of golf clubs, a crewcut and a savage aversion to rock 'n' roll, bright colours or anyone with facial hair. It could happen.

DEATH

Billy is glumly pushing a dim sum around his bowl with his chopsticks.

'What's the matter?' I pour him some more jasmine tea.

It is late in an April evening, 2001, after a visit to Cara and our new grandson in Glasgow. The waiters are dying to go home.

'Looking at Walter ...' Billy speaks hesitantly ... 'has caused me to think about the whole cycle of life ... I can't help thinking I'm in a David Attenborough film ...'

He adopts a bad university-derived English accent.

'And now ... the older chimpanzee is returning to the outer circle ...'

≈

When Billy read that the painter Salvador Dali agreed with his muse Gala that whoever died first should eat the other as a sign of never-ending love, he thought it was a great idea. 'I'll probably die first,' he announced to me, 'so will you promise to eat me?'

When Gala died, Dali decided not to eat her after all, which disappointed Billy terribly. He emphasized his wish that he'd die first to save him the embarrassment of possibly reneging on his vow to eat me. 'Maybe,' he says, sounding unintentionally horribly macabre, 'if you were close to death we could cut a bit off and I could fry it with my egg in the morning.'

Some people are horrified that he plans to leave his tattoos to his daughter Cara. 'It's a hilarious plan,' she says, 'although the idea was really spawned during my now defunct Heavy Metal period.' When Billy's body dies, he wants a huge parade. Six black, high-plumed horses should draw a see-through carriage bearing his daisy-covered coffin to a magnificent tent in George Square, Glasgow, full of folks telling great stories about him. He would like a gravestone on an island in Loch Lomond – any one would do, such as the one that's closest to Balmaha. 'The stone should be horizontal like a table,' he says, 'so you can have a cup of tea on it.'

At his funeral, he hopes aeroplanes will zoom overhead writing '*Fuck the Begrudgers!*' in the sky. This saying came from Phil Coulter and has always been a consoling mantra for him. Every time he has a great concert but is wailed at in the papers, he repeats it to remind himself to shrug the feelings off.

Billy has made me promise to put '*Jesus Christ, is that the time already?*' on his gravestone. 'I'm not going to be there anyway,' he says. 'I want to be scattered all over Loch Lomond.' The only other gravestone inscription he'd settle for is tiny writing in the middle of a huge stone. The writing should be so small that people would have to get up really close to read: '*You're standing on my balls.*'

THE TEACUP THEORY

In the planetarium in Los Feliz, 1999, the snoring of a bearded man is punctuating the sky-show presentation. As the features of the Californian night sky are illuminated on the wide, domed ceiling,

Daisy, Amy and Scarlett glance at each other uneasily. They've already experienced the hopeless task of attempting to wake their father once he's settled in for a comfy snooze.

'Dad! Wake up! It's embarrassing ...'

Billy opens one eye, surveys his surroundings, then immediately returns to his lovely theta-zone. The girls try once more to shake him into consciousness, then tiptoe out into the foyer for a soda, leaving him to the wrath of the ushers.

'That was boring,' he explains later. 'I was losing the will to live.'

'Why?' asks Scarlett.

'Well, it's like fly-fishing. If nothing bites it's not the fault of the fly, it's the presentation. You see, the map of the sky you just saw has been very badly drawn by Galileo and others who weren't very good at joining the dots. The Great Bear is nothing like a bear, the Southern Cross is bugger all like a cross ... and that goes for all the other cosmic things. I'd like to redraw it.'

Not surprisingly, the children are staring at him in wide-eyed bewilderment.

'Because ... I've seen things up there – "The Great Elvis" would make a pleasant change, don't you think? Or "The Wee Willie Winkie". People wouldn't take the whole thing so seriously if they could find Noddy ...'

'... or Tinky-Winky?' suggests Daisy.

'Quite right, plus relatives, like your Uncle Ian ... or the triplets ...'

'But Dad ...' Amy is forming a splendid counter-argument, but it's no use for her father's in full flight.

'... If you find a constellation shaped like a car, why not call it the Morris Minor? There are as many shapes up there as people, so we could each have our own view of the sky. Then it would belong to us and not to some long-dead Italian.'

~

EPILOGUE

When Billy looks at a picture of the solar system it reminds him of the basic atomic structure with a nucleus surrounded by protons and electrons in orbit. 'It's amazingly like our solar system,' he says. 'Maybe we're just a proton in a huge structure, the size of which we can't comprehend ... But if we are part of an atom that's part of something huge, then what exactly is that giant thing?'

Billy prefers to conceptualize physical and spiritual infinity as a cosy, familiar model. 'Maybe it's actually a chair, or my favourite, a cup of tea,' he wonders hopefully. Billy would much prefer to think we were part of a huge cosmic cup of tea, but he acknowledges there might still be pitfalls to such a theory. 'If I'm right and this philosophy is taken up by others in the future,' he speculates, 'people will eventually be going around with little gold cups of tea around their necks. The only problem then is that they'll probably start worshipping lumps of sugar and you're back to square one. It's time we started worshipping each other.'

Billy calls the Internet 'The Great Anorak in the Sky'. 'You know why those people are on the Internet?' he asks. 'Because you wouldn't speak to them in the pub, that's why!' Billy has sent one email in his whole life, to Eric Idle. He knows there's a reply for him somewhere out there in the electronic cosmos, but he's buggered if he can remember how to retrieve it.

It's no secret that Billy disagrees with the way things are generally run. For example, he'd like to see the House of Lords emptied out completely. They could still call themselves 'Lords', if they liked, for all eternity but, instead of their sitting in the House, he'd like to see it populated by the ordinary people of Britain: engineers, nurses, teachers, welders could all take a turn, like jury duty.

'I think you'd get a much better picture if you took it out of the hands of professional politicians,' says Billy. 'Besides, the desire to become a politician should bar you for life from ever becoming one.'

BILLY'S DESIDERATA

Griping aside, Billy has a few suggestions for us all on how to lead a proud and happy life. Imagine syrupy music playing in the background while reading the following out loud with the deepest voice you can muster:

Tread gently on anyone who looks at you sideways. Have lots of long lie-ins. Wear sturdy socks, learn to grow out of medium underwear and, if you must lie about your age, do it in the other direction: tell people you're ninety-seven and they'll think you look fucking great. Try to catch a trout and experience the glorious feeling of letting it go and seeing it swimming away. Never eat food that comes in a bucket. If you don't know how to meditate at least try to spend some time every day just sitting. Boo joggers. Don't work out, work in. Play the banjo. Sleep with somebody you like. Eat plenty of Liquorice Allsorts. Try to live in a place you like. Marry somebody you like. Try to do a job you like. Never turn down an opportunity to shout, 'Fuck them all!' at the top of your voice. Avoid bigots of all descriptions. Let your own bed become to you what the Pole Star was to sailors of old ... look forward to it. Don't wear tight underwear on aeroplanes. Before you judge a man, walk a mile in his shoes. After that, who cares? ... He's a mile away and you've got his shoes. Clean your teeth and keep the company of people who will tell you when there's spinach on them. Avoid people who say they know the answer. Keep the company of people who are trying to understand the question. Don't pat animals with sneaky eyes. If you haven't heard a good rumour by 11 a.m., start one. Learn to feel sorry for music because, although it is the international language, it has no swearwords (if you don't count Wagner, which in my opinion is one long one and should be avoided at all cost). If you write a book, be sure it has exactly seventy-six 'fuck's in it. Send Hieronymus Bosch prints to elderly relatives for Christmas. Avoid